*Jack Drescher, MD*
*Ann D'Ercole, PhD*
*Erica Schoenberg, PhD*
*Editors*

# Psychotherapy with Gay Men and Lesbians
## Contemporary Dynamic Approaches

*Pre-publication*
*REVIEW . . .*

"It is a postmodern truism that psychoanalysts inevitably become part of the disease they set out to cure. Nowhere is this more evident than in the hotly debated, anxiety-laden arena of gender and sex. In this superb volume of articles, clinical presentations, and discussions, these issues are engaged with sophistication, frankness, and, dare one say, rare humility. The contributors represent a wide spectrum of approaches, both toward the etiology of sex and gender problems, and toward current debates in the field about the therapist's use of her or his own experience.

In no way doctrinaire, or presuming simple solutions for these very obdurate issues, this book will certainly be of great interest and value to anyone, lay or professional, concerned with issues of sex and gender. Moreover, its sophisticated grappling with the clinical complexities of the uses of countertransference and analyst participation goes far beyond its applicability to a limited class of patients and will be illuminating for all clinicians."

**Dr. Edgar Levenson**
Fellow Emeritus and Training and Supervisory Analyst, William Alanson White Institute; Author, *Fallacy of Understanding*, *The Ambiguity of Change*, and *The Purloined Self*

# Psychotherapy
# with Gay Men and Lesbians
## *Contemporary Dynamic Approaches*

# Psychotherapy
# with Gay Men and Lesbians
## *Contemporary Dynamic Approaches*

Jack Drescher, MD
Ann D'Ercole, PhD
Erica Schoenberg, PhD
Editors

**HPP**

Harrington Park Press®
An Imprint of The Haworth Press, Inc.
New York • London • Oxford

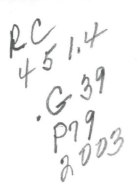
Published by

Harrington Park Press®, an imprint of The Haworth Press, Inc., 10 Alice Street, Binghamton, NY
13904-1580.

PUBLISHER'S NOTE
Identities and circumstances of individuals discussed in this book have been changed to protect
confidentiality.

Cover design by Jennifer M. Gaska.

**Library of Congress Cataloging-in-Publication Data**

Psychotherapy with gay men and lesbians : contemporary dynamic approaches / Jack Drescher,
Ann D'Ercole, Erica Schoenberg, editors.
    p. cm.
    Includes bibliographical references and index.
    ISBN 1-56023-397-4 (hard)—ISBN 1-56023-398-2 (soft)
    1. Gays—Mental health. 2 Lesbians—Mental health. 3. Psychotherapy. 4. Homosexuality—
Psychological aspects. I. Drescher, Jack, 1951- II. D'Ercole, Ann. III. Schoenberg, Erica.

RC451.4.G39 P79 2003
616.89'008'664—dc21

                                                                    2002068776

# CONTENTS

# ABOUT THE EDITORS

**Jack Drescher, MD,** is Training and Supervising Analyst at the William Alanson White Psychoanalytic Institute; Clinical Assistant Professor of Psychiatry at the State University of New York at Brooklyn; and in private practice in New York City. Dr. Drescher chairs both the Committee on Gay, Lesbian, and Bisexual Issues of the American Psychiatric Association and the Committee on Human Sexuality of the Group for Advancement of Psychiatry. He is Past President of the APA's New York County District Branch.

A noted scholar and clinician with specialized academic and clinical experience in psychotherapy with gay and lesbian patients, Dr. Drescher has received awards recognizing his unique contributions from the Association of Gay & Lesbian Psychiatrists, as well as from the psychoanalytic community. He has also provided a professional voice representing the mental health concerns of the lesbian and gay community in a variety of popular forums, including "The O'Reilly Factor," PBS's "In The Life," The Village Voice, and "Fox Network News," as well as *OUT* and *Genre Magazine.*

Dr. Drescher has been a teacher and supervisor of psychoanalytic candidates, psychiatric residents, medical students, and graduate students in psychology and social work. He has lectured extensively on issues of gender and sexuality both in the United States and Europe. The author of *Psychoanalytic Therapy & the Gay Man,* Dr. Drescher has published numerous papers in books, peer-reviewed journals, and professional newsletters in the United States and abroad. He is on the editorial boards of *Studies in Gender & Sexuality* and the *Journal of Homosexuality.*

**Ann D'Ercole, PhD,** is on the faculty and supervises at the New York University Postdoctoral Program in Psychotherapy and Psychoanalysis. She is editor, with Jack Drescher, MD, of the forthcoming book *Unconventional Couples/Uncoupling Conventions: Reappraisals in Psychoanalysis and Same Gendered Couples* and is co-editor of the

*Journal of Gay & Lesbian Psychotherapy.* She has published numerous papers on the issues of gender and sexuality.

**Erica Schoenberg, PhD,** is co-editor, with Ronnie C. Lesser, of *That Obscure Subject of Desire: Freud's Female Homosexual Revisited.* She is a book review editor for the *Journal of Gay & Lesbian Psychotherapy* and has written and presented numerous papers on psychoanalysis and sexuality.

# CONTRIBUTORS

**Gilbert W. Cole, CSW, PhD,** is a member of the editorial board of the *Journal of Gay and Lesbian Psychotherapy;* an instructor at the Institute for Contemporary Psychotherapy; and author of *Infecting the Treatment: Being an HIV-Positive Analyst* (The Analytic Press, 2002). He maintains a private practice in New York City.

**Martin Stephen Frommer, PhD,** is a member of the editorial board of the *Journal of Gay and Lesbian Psychotherapy;* a faculty member and supervisor at the Institute for Contemporary Psychotherapy; and maintains a private practice in psychotherapy and psychoanalysis in New York City.

**Adrienne Harris, PhD,** is a member of the editorial board of the *Journal of Gay and Lesbian Psychotherapy.* She is affiliated with the Postdoctoral Program in Psychotherapy and Psychoanalysis at New York University and maintains a private practice in New York City.

**Ubaldo Leli, MD,** is a member of the editorial board of the *Journal of Gay and Lesbian Psychotherapy;* Clinical Associate in Psychiatry, Weill Medical College of Cornell University; Lecturer in Psychiatry, Columbia College of Physicians and Surgeons; and a faculty member of the Columbia Center for Psychoanalytic Training and Research.

**Ronnie C. Lesser, PhD,** is a member of the editorial board of the *Journal of Gay and Lesbian Psychotherapy.* She is co-editor of *Disorienting Sexuality: Psychoanalytic Reappraisals of Sexual Identities* (Routledge, 1995) and *That Obscure Subject of Desire: Freud's Female Homosexual Revisited* (Routledge, 1999). She maintains a private practice in New York City and Westchester County, New York.

**Petros Levounis, MD,** is Clinical Assistant Professor of Psychiatry, New York University School of Medicine; Associate Director for Training, Division of Alcoholism and Drug Abuse, New York University School of Medicine; and Director, Dual Diagnosis Training Unit, Bellevue Hospital Center, New York City.

**Kenneth Lewes, PhD,** is a member of the editorial board of the *Journal of Gay and Lesbian Psychotherapy* and author of *Psychoanalysis and Male Homosexuality* (Jason Aronson, 1995). He maintains a private practice in New York City.

**Karen J. Maroda, PhD,** is Assistant Professor of Psychiatry, Medical College of Wisconsin; a faculty member of the Minnesota Institute for Contemporary Psychoanalysis; and author of *Seduction, Surrender, and Transformation: Emotional Engagement in the Analytic Process* (The Analytic Press, 1999).

**Joyce McDougall, EdD,** is Membre titulaire, Societé Psychoanalytique de Paris; an honorary member of the Association for Psychoanalytic Medicine of New York; and a member of the New York Freudian Society.

**Linda I. Meyers, PsyD,** is Training and Supervising Analyst, a faculty member, and a member of the Board of Directors at the Institute for Psychoanalysis and Psychotherapy of New Jersey. She maintains a private practice in Princeton, New Jersey.

**Florence Rosiello, PhD,** is a faculty member and supervisor at the Institute for Contemporary Psychotherapy, the Psychoanalytic Psychotherapy Study Center, and the New York Institute for Psychoanalytic Self Psychology. She is author of *Deepening Intimacy in Psychotherapy: Using the Erotic Transference and Countertransference* (Jason Aronson, 2000).

**Bertram Schaffner, MD,** is a member of the editorial board of the *Journal of Gay and Lesbian Psychotherapy* and Supervising Psychoanalyst and Medical Director of the HIV Service at the William Alanson White Psychoanalytic Institute. He maintains a private practice in New York City.

**Adria E. Schwartz, PhD,** is a member of the editorial board of the *Journal of Gay and Lesbian Psychotherapy;* is affiliated with the Postdoctoral Program in Psychotherapy and Psychoanalysis at New York University; and is the author of *Sexual Subjects: Lesbians, Gender, and Psychoanalysis* (Routledge, 1998). She maintains a private practice in New York City.

**Barbara Tholfsen, CSW,** maintains a private practice in Westchester County, New York.

**Robert S. Weinstein, PhD,** is Founding Director, Training Analyst, and a faculty member at the Object Relations Institute for Psychotherapy and Psychoanalysis. He maintains a private practice in psychoanalysis, group psychotherapy, and supervision.

# Queering the Therapeutic Dyad: Introduction to Psychotherapy with Gay Men and Lesbians

Jack Drescher
Ann D'Ercole
Erica Schoenberg

This book brings together a series of clinical papers and discussions that have been previously published in the *Journal of Gay and Lesbian Psychotherapy*. The JGLP's ongoing objective in publishing such papers is to provide a forum for addressing some of the new paradigm shifts in psychotherapy and psychoanalysis, particularly as they relate to the treatment of gay, lesbian, and bisexual patients. This project takes place during a time of enormous change, both clinical and theoretical, particularly in the ways in which therapists are coming to think about gender and sexuality. Current revisions have grown out of old disputes about femaleness and maleness, femininity and masculinity, and heterosexuality and homosexuality (Young-Bruehl, 1996).

Rather than totally replacing old paradigms with new ones, new ways of thinking coexist with the old—they include both essentialist and constructionist paradigms and variations along that continuum. Essentialists assume, for example, that sexuality is a natural phenomenon existing outside of culture and society and that it is made up of fixed and inherent drives that organize sexual identities. Constructivists, on the other hand, assume that sexuality has no inherent essential quality but that it represents a system of cultural meanings which are themselves created within matrices of social power relations (Harding, 1998).

Since Freud first provided his account of human subjectivity, the therapeutic field has seen a proliferation of new perspectives on human behavior. Interpersonal, intersubjective, and relational models more inclusively address the complexities of social and psychological life. The contributions of academic feminism and its offspring, queer theory, provide a constant leitmotif for revisionist attitudes in all psychotherapeutic projects. Embedded within each of these perspectives lies a postmodernism sensibility whose aim is to break the "crust of convention" (Flax, 1990). At the same time, a therapist approaches clinical work with an essentialist hope that some objective facts can be known. As clinicians, we may find ourselves lodged in a space between essentialist and postmodern perspectives. Nevertheless, we can no longer take refuge in psychodynamic theories that exclude social concerns, cultures, and conflicts. Today, personal values, opinions, and attitudes, along with the models in which a therapist is trained, are all acknowledged as part of the therapeutic process. Furthermore, clinicians acknowledge that all therapists do not think alike. In fact, these differences are welcomed as each offers a piece of experience that has potential meaning and value.

In the first section of this book, Petros Levounis generously shares an account of his work with a patient in "Gay Patient–Gay Therapist: A Case Report of Stephen." Case reports are an important testimony to very careful and thoughtful therapeutic work. A lasting scientific value is inherent in such reports, revealing as they do the complex issues involved in human discourse. Levounis's sensitive account of his work with Stephen provides an opportunity to reflect on the myriad interweavings and complications involved in clinical work. The discussants of the case—Adria E. Schwartz, Kenneth Lewes, Ronnie C. Lesser, Martin Stephen Frommer, and Jack Drescher—are positioned in different places along the essentialist/social constructionist theoretical continuum. The discussants were asked to make their personal theoretical perspectives overt within their discussions. In doing so, they contributed to our understanding of the various ways the therapeutic process can be viewed and understood, elaborating on the meanings of gender and sexuality in the background and foreground of the therapeutic process (D'Ercole, 1996, 1999).

Each of these discussions provides ways to examine the dynamics of the therapeutic situation, our own ideas about gender and sexuality, and their places in our lives and our work. Although there is much difference in the ways each clinician approaches the therapeutic process, there is also a fascinating convergence of thought that does not take for granted established meanings, values, and power relations. In fact, each discussant challenges traditional notions of gender and sexuality while shedding light on the complexity of transference and countertransference.

From a relational psychotherapeutic position, Adria E. Schwartz, draws our attention to the set of cultural assumptions embedded in the discourse between this patient and therapist. She makes clear how terms such as "gay," "lesbian," "homosexual," "bisexual," "transgendered," etc., are signifiers that represent different subsets of cultural assumptions, each subset organized around spurious gender categories and a conflation of gender and desire, identity, and object choice. Her analysis goes beyond the academic discussion of these concepts into the heart of the clinical work. She takes up the term "recognition" (Benjamin, 1992) to understand what Stephen wants, indeed needs from Levounis, and shows us how Levounis is implicated in this formulation of "recognition." In her discussion, culture, once considered background, becomes foreground. She hungers for more information, more dreams, and more ways to know both Levounis and Stephen.

Kenneth Lewes also wishes to know more about Stephen and the course of his treatment. In his discussion, Stephen's culture also comes to the foreground. Lewes sees Stephen as keeping a low profile, avoiding a profound sadness and a sense of helplessness. He focuses on how Stephen is passive rather than active in his life. He draws our attention to the kinds of bargains Stephen has made to appease his guilt, including his denunciation of sex. Here is a therapist who takes a traditional developmental position (Lewes, 1988).

From a very different vantage point, Ronnie C. Lesser, using a social constructivist position (Domenici and Lesser, 1995; Lesser and Schoenberg, 1999), asks what is missing from sight in this case. She brings our focus to the hidden feelings at work in this treatment. Drawing upon the film *Life is Beautiful,* she enters the material from her own associations concerning holding on to hope in the face of despair. She provides a clear example of the difference between essentialist versus social constructionist models of psychoanalysis, and of psychotherapy as well. Here the lines are plainly drawn between essentialist-minded and social constructionist-minded positions. The former seeks to uncover innate truths which are hidden in the patient while the latter examines and understands subjective factors unique to each dyad. Lesser also reminds us how every aspect of the therapeutic process varies with each therapist and each patient.

Martin Stephen Frommer grounds his comments in the language of a two-person psychology which focuses on the relational life of the therapist and patient. He acknowledges the recent, and increasingly not so rare, event of an openly gay therapeutic dyad within the consultation room and the larger therapeutic community. With that as the background, he draws attention to how Levounis's story about a gay male dyad is one in which the therapist does not disclose his sexual orientation to his patient. This asymmetry, Frommer argues, may have influenced the intersubjectivity between Stephen and Levounis, particularly since the narrative focuses on the emergence of the patient's erotic desire. Frommer challenges us to think about issues of self-disclosure and how they can have an impact on treatments. He also asks us to explore the dangerousness of sexual feelings in a same-sex therapeutic dyad and how those feelings have not yet received our due attention. In fact, Frommer argues that left unexplored, shame and guilt may dominate the transference and countertransference, presenting a gridlock in the emotional engagement between patient and therapist.

Finally, Jack Drescher (1996, 1998) takes an interpersonal position and focuses attention on Stephen's detached and intellectualizing character. Drawing on Sullivan's (1956) concept of "selective inattention," he illustrates how Stephen functions in the world. Culture again moves to the foreground as Drescher brings our attention to Stephen's religious beliefs and their relationship to the meaning he ascribes to being gay. Drescher asks us to listen to both the voices of Stephen's family and the voices of Levounis's colleagues. He suggests that both Stephen and his therapist are engaged in parallel projects to integrate their gay identities into the rest of their lives.

The second section features several papers which explore the therapist's participation in enacting sex and gender issues in treatment. While recognizing their inevitable contribution to the interactions that shape the therapeutic dialogue, these papers also question the complex, over-determined variety of motives that position therapists in an emotional fray as they attempt to disentangle their own issues and needs from those of their patients.

As psychotherapists explore the realm of sexuality, the following questions are important to consider: When and how much should we disclose about our own erotic experiences of and reactions to our patients? How can we evaluate and distinguish when such disclosures are seductive and when they are responsive and clarifying? What are the possible ramifications of not articulating these countertransferential feelings? To what extent and for how long should we engage in sexually charged interactions?

There are also questions to consider in the realm of gender: How should we proceed when patients want to know our actual attitudes toward their gendered presences, their masculinity and femininity? What if patients believe that "real" men and women think, desire, and behave in certain specifiable ways while we see sexuality and gender as multifaceted and independent from each other? Do we see gender and sexuality as fundamentally fluid or stable? How do we manifest our own attitudes in the room and how does this affect the therapy?

Florence Rosiello, Barbara Tholfsen, and Linda I. Meyers offer piercingly honest observations of their own clinical work, and each reflects with great thoughtfulness about their own impact on their patients. All struggle with the enormity of their own influence in shaping the treatment, and thus the future course of the patient's life. Karen J. Maroda (1999) then discusses these three clinical papers. She agrees that these clinical disclosures are necessary and enormously significant, but she also, at times, takes strong exception to the manner and the extent to which these disclosures are made. Rosiello then responds to Maroda's discussion. The open discussion of clinical and theoretical differences provides the reader with an opportunity to sharpen his or her own thinking on the matter, a crucial contribution in these times of post-therapeutic neutrality. Readers interested in further exploring issues related to the contemporary understanding of the uses and meanings of countertransference should see Aron (1996), Bollas (1994), Bromberg (1991), Davies (1994), Domenici and Lesser (1995), Drescher (1996), Frommer (1995), Gabbard (1991), Greenberg (1991) Hirsch (1994), Lesser (1995), Levenson (1995), Lionells et al.

(1995), Maroda (1994), Mitchell (1988), Orange (1995), Racker (1968), Stern (1997), Winnicott (1947), and Wrye and Welles (1994).

The third section, Joyce McDougall's "Gender Identity and Creativity," was the first in an ongoing series of contributions from senior psychoanalytic writers who have been rethinking their earlier, and usually unflattering, theories about the meanings of homosexuality. The impetus for publishing this paper originated at a psychoanalytic meeting where McDougall said she was incorrectly perceived by some authors as having antigay beliefs; and that those erroneous impressions were based on some early papers she had published about female homosexuality. One of us (Drescher) asked her, "Where have you published the fact that you changed your mind?" With the model of Roy Schafer's (1995) pioneering paper, "The Evolution of My Views on Nonnormative Sexual Practice" in mind, the JGLP was delighted to offer her a forum in which she could clarify her changed views on homosexuality for a contemporary audience.

For those unfamiliar with her work, McDougall is a sought after speaker and influential writer in the worlds of both French and English psychoanalysis. The sensitivity and liveliness of her clinical work clearly comes across in her many books (1980, 1985, 1989, 1995) and is quite evident here. In fact, "Gender Identity and Creativity" is a clinical paper whose publication fulfilled another primary goal of the JGLP: to show the reading audience of psychotherapy practitioners, through the use of clinical material and process notes, the ways in which experienced clinicians actually work with lesbian and gay patients.

The fourth section of papers offers a glimpse at two different kinds of psychotherapeutic treatment with gay male patients who have AIDS. These two distinct case histories make the point that patients with diverse personalities and in differing circumstances will inevitably require different kinds of treatment. The first paper by Ubaldo Leli describes a classical psychoanalytic treatment of an asymptomatic, HIV-positive gay man. Leli felt

> This patient presented a formidable challenge to psychoanalytic treatment, independently of his serological status. The patient's history of alcoholism, suicide attempts, depression requiring

pharmacological maintenance, and his general proclivity to acting out, coupled with the restricted nature of his object relations,
made the decision of whether to treat him with psychoanalysis
versus psychoanalytic psychotherapy a very difficult one.

Leli, in the end decided, "that only the intensity and depth of classic
psychoanalysis had a chance of producing mutative change in this patient." Whether he made the right choice is up to the reader to decide,
as the results of that treatment are presented herein.

Leli's paper is written from the perspectives of both a candidate
and a recent graduate from psychoanalytic training. In contrast, Robert S. Weinstein presents a psychotherapy case from the perspective
of a seasoned clinician who nevertheless found himself unprepared
for the intensity of emotions he would experience when his patient
with AIDS was hospitalized. In sorting out the boundaries of the traditional psychoanalytic frame, Weinstein argues that "therapists need
a sensitive and caring flexibility with their patients if they are to promote the health and integration of body and spirit, establishing the
kind of contact with ill patients which enable them to connect to life
and to hope." Again, readers can decide for themselves.

Discussing these two clinical papers are three very different clinicians. Gilbert W. Cole writes from the perspective of "a therapist who
has become interested in discussing his own HIV positive status publicly." He sees Leli's and Weinstein's contributions as important "because they demonstrate, in very different ways, how questions of mortality that have been so inextricably bound up with HIV/AIDS figure
into the therapist's daily work." Cole also notes that "As the world enters the 'protease era,' the meanings associated with HIV/ AIDS can be
considered in a different context; that of life continuing rather than impending death."

The next discussant, Adrienne Harris, has been a thoughtful spokes-
person for a postmodern feminist perspectives in psychoanalytic theory (1991, 1996, 1997) and a prominent figure in the relational school
of psychoanalysis (Greenberg and Mitchell, 1983; Aron and Harris,
1993; Mitchell and Aron, 1999). It is from a relational perspective
that Harris sees Leli's and Weinstein's papers as "demonstrating the
difficulties of our current situation in which psychoanalytic para-

digms are changing but clearly are also still in transition." She also offers some thoughtful comments about the "problems and pressures and values of working outside the psychotherapeutic frame."

The final discussant, Bertram Schaffner, is a pioneering clinician in providing and advocating for adequate psychotherapy services for Persons with AIDS (PWAs) and HIV-positive individuals (1985, 1986a,b, 1987a,b, 1990, 1994, 1996). Among the issues that Schaffner discusses are those of how one determines the frequency of psychotherapy visits, the use of the couch in psychoanalysis, what degree of self-disclosure should be allowed to therapists in response to personal questions, and a therapist's willingness to step outside a traditional therapeutic "frame." In contrast to Cole's optimism about living in the protease era, Schaffner raises his concerns that although HIV-positive patients may be maintaining their health quite well, their therapists can be misled by excessive hopefulness, and in the process overlook the patients' continuing underlying terror.

## REFERENCES

Aron, L., Ed. (1996), *A Meeting of Minds: Mutuality in Psychoanalysis.* Hillsdale, NJ: The Analytic Press.

Aron, L. and Harris, A., Eds. (1993), *The Legacy of Sandor Ferenczi.* Hillsdale, NJ: The Analytic Press.

Benjamin, J. (1992), Recognition and destruction: An outline of intersubjectivity. In *Relational Concepts in Psychoanalysis,* N. Skolnick and S. Warshaw (Eds.). Cambridge, MA: Harvard University Press, pp. 43-60.

Bollas, C. (1994), Aspects of the erotic transference. *Psychoanalytic Inquiry,* 14:572-590.

Bromberg, P. (1991), On knowing one's patient inside out: The aesthetics of unconscious communication. *Psychoanalytic Dialogues,* 1:399-422.

Davies, J. M. (1994), Love in the afternoon: A relational reconsideration of desire and dread in the countertransference. *Psychoanalytic Dialogues,* 4:153-170.

D'Ercole, A. (1996), Postmodern ideas about gender and sexuality: The lesbian woman redundancy. *Psychoanalysis and Psychotherapy,* 13(2):142-152.

D'Ercole, A. (1999), Designing the lesbian subject: Looking backwards, looking forwards. In *That Obscure Subject of Desire: Freud's Female Homosexual Revisited,* R. C. Lesser and E. Schoenberg (Eds.). New York: Routledge, pp. 115-129.

Domenici, T. and Lesser, R. C., Eds. (1995), *Disorienting Sexuality: Psychoanalytic Reappraisals of Sexual Identities.* New York: Routledge.

Drescher, J. (1996), Across the great divide: Gender panic in the psychoanalytic dyad. *Psychoanalysis and Psychotherapy,* 13(2):174-186.

Drescher, J. (1998), *Psychoanalytic Therapy and the Gay Man.* Hillsdale, NJ: The Analytic Press.

Flax, J. (1990), Postmodernism and gender relations in feminist theory. In *Feminism/Postmodernism,* L. Nicholson (Ed). New York and London: Routledge, pp. 39-62.

Frommer, M. S. (1995), Countertransference obscurity in the treatment of homosexual patients. In *Disorienting Sexualities,* T. Domenici and R. C. Lesser (Eds.). New York: Routledge, pp. 65-82.

Gabbard, G. (1991), Psychodynamics of sexual boundary violations. *Psychiatric Annals,* 21:651-655.

Greenberg, J. (1991), Countertransference and reality. *Psychoanalytic Dialogues,* 1:52-73.

Greenberg, J. and Mitchell, S. (1983), *Object Relations in Psychoanalytic Theory.* Cambridge, MA: Harvard University Press.

Harding, J. (1998), *Sex Acts: Practices of Femininity and Masculinity.* Thousand Oaks, CA: Sage Publications.

Harris, A. (1991), Gender as contradiction. *Psychoanalytic Dialogues,* 1(1):197-224. Reprinted in *That Obscure Subject of Desire: Freud's Female Homosexual Revisited,* R. C. Lesser and E. Schoenberg (Eds.). New York: Routledge, 1999, pp. 156-179.

Harris, A. (1996), Animated conversation: Embodying and gendering. *Gender and Pyschoanalysis,* 1(3):361-383.

Harris, A. (1997), Aggression, envy and ambition: Circulating tensions in women's psychic life. *Gender and Pyschoanalysis,* 2(3):291-325.

Hirsch, I. (1994), Countertransference love and theoretical model. *Psychoanalytic Dialogues,* 4:171-192.

Lesser, R. C. (1995), Objectivity as masquerade. In *Disorienting Sexualities,* T. Domenici and R. C Lesser (Eds.). New York: Routledge, pp. 83-96.

Lesser, R. C. and Schoenberg, E. (1999), *That Obscure Subject of Desire: Freud's Female Homosexual Revisited.* New York: Routledge.

Levenson, E. (1995), A monopedal presentation of Interpersonal psychoanalysis. *Review of Interpersonal Psychoanalysis,* 1:1-4.

Lewes, K. (1988), *The Psychoanalytic Theory of Male Homosexuality.* New York: Simon and Schuster. Reissued as *Psychoanalysis and Male Homosexuality.* Northvale, NJ: Aronson, 1995.

Lionells, M., Fiscalini, J., Mann, C. and Stern, D., Eds. (1995), *Handbook of Interpersonal Psychoanalysis.* Hillsdale, NJ: The Analytic Press.

Maroda, K. (1994), *The Power of Countertransference: Innovations in Analytic Technique.* Northvale, NJ: Aronson.

Maroda, K. (1999), *Seduction, Surrender and Transformation: Emotional Engagement in the Analytic Process.* Hillsdale, NJ: The Analytic Press.

McDougall, J. (1980), *Plea for a Measure of Abnormality.* New York: International Universities Press.

McDougall, J. (1985), *Theaters of the Mind: Illusion and Truth on the Psychoanalytic Stage.* New York: Basic Books.

McDougall, J. (1989), *Theaters of the Body: A Psychoanalytic Approach to Psychosomatic Illness.* New York: Basic Books.

McDougall, J. (1995), *The Many Faces of Eros: A Psychoanalytic Exploration of Human Sexuality.* New York and London: W. W. Norton and Company.

Mitchell, S. A. (1988), *Relational Concepts in Psychoanalysis: An Integration.* Cambridge, MA: Harvard University Press.

Mitchell, S. A. and Aron, L., Eds. (1999), *Relational Psychoanalysis: The Emergence of a Tradition.* Hillsdale, NJ: The Analytic Press.

Orange, D. (1995), *Emotional Understanding: Studies in Psychoanalytic Epistemology.* New York: Guilford.

Racker, H. (1968), *Transference and Countertransference.* Madison, CT: International Universities Press.

Schafer, R. (1995), The evolution of my views on nonnormative sexual practice. In *Disorienting Sexualities,* T. Domenici and R. C. Lesser (Eds.). New York: Routledge, pp. 187-202.

Schaffner, B. (1985), Emotional reactions of medical personnel and intimates of persons with AIDS. *Forum of American Academy of Psychoanalysis,* 29(2):10-13.

Schaffner, B. (1986a), Psychological impact of AIDS upon the social environment, health care providers, families and friends and methods of modification. In *Proceedings of the Second International Conference on AIDS,* Paris, pp. 295-298.

Schaffner, B. (1986b), Reactions of medical personnel and intimates to persons with AIDS. In *Psychotherapy and the Memorable Patient,* M. Stern (Ed.). Binghamton, NY: The Haworth Press, pp. 67-80. Reprinted in *Behavioral Aspects of AIDS,* D. G. Ostrow (Ed.). New York: Plenum Medical Books, 1990, pp. 341-354.

Schaffner, B. (1987a), Some thoughts about AIDS. *Journal of Substance Abuse,* 4:141-142.

Schaffner, B. (1987b), Review of *The AIDS Movie. Hospital and Community Psychiatry,* 38(6):567-568.

Schaffner, B. (1990), Psychotherapy with HIV-infected persons. *New Directions for Mental Health Services,* 48:5-20.

Schaffner, B. (1994), The crucial and difficult role of the psychotherapist in the treatment of the HIV-positive patient. *Journal of the American Academy of Psychoanalysis,* 22(3):505-518.

Schaffner, B. (1996), Modifying psychoanalytic methods when treating HIV-positive patients. *Journal of the American Academy of Psychoanalysis,* 25(1):123-141. Reprinted in *Hope and Mortality: Psychodynamic Approaches to AIDS and HIV,* M. Blechner (Ed.). Hillsdale, NJ: The Analytic Press, 1997, pp. 63-79.

Stern, D. B. (1997), *Unformulated Experience: From Dissociation to Imagination in Psychoanalysis.* Hillsdale, NJ: The Analytic Press.

Sullivan, H. S. (1956), *Clinical Studies in Psychiatry*. New York: W. W. Norton and Company.

Winnicott, D. W. (1947), Hate in the Countertransference. In *Through Pediatrics to Psycho-Analysis*, Author. New York: Basic Books, 1975, pp. 194-203.

Wrye, H. K. and Welles, J. K. (1994), *The Narration of Desire: Erotic Transferences and Countertransferences*. Hillsdale, NJ and London: The Analytic Press.

Young-Bruehl, E. (1996), Gender and psychoanalysis: An introductory essay. *Gender and Psychoanalysis*, 1(1):7-18.

# SECTION I:
# GAY PATIENT–GAY THERAPIST

Chapter 1

# Gay Patient–Gay Therapist: A Case Report of Stephen

Petros Levounis

## *Identification*

Stephen is a twenty-seven-year-old man, single, gay, of Northern European descent, who now lives by himself in a large Northeastern city. He is a PhD candidate in the humanities at a prestigious university and supports himself by a university fellowship which is supplemented by occasional small parental contributions. His primary social support group consists of fellow graduate students, mostly gay men and straight women, in their twenties.

Stephen is a handsome man, six feet tall, slim, with dark hair and lighter facial features. He is fairly well-groomed, although he occasionally gives the appearance of having just gotten out of bed. He wears casual clothes, in the uniform of an intellectual: black jeans and soft fabrics with earth tones. He dresses in multiple layers and accessorizes with scarves, books, and a briefcase, all of which often take more than a minute to take off and put back on at the end of our sessions. He often starts the session talking about the difficulties he had "preparing material for discussion," as he says. Then, during the first half of the session, he talks almost nonstop with little affect and many well-articulated sentences giving the impression of a college professor at work. The second half of the session is usually more interactive, characterized by the patient's stereotypical nervous laughter when the material becomes more emotionally charged. He is often a few minutes late but has missed only a handful of appointments during the almost one and a half years of treatment.

### Presentation

Stephen was referred to the long-term psychotherapy clinic by the university student counseling and psychological services in the fall of 1996. The patient self-presented to the student health center on his twenty-sixth birthday and asked for a long-term psychotherapy referral and additional support to assist him with adjustment difficulties as he was reentering the PhD program after a year-long medical leave of absence. Stephen was diagnosed with a life-threatening illness in the fall of 1995 and had to return to his mother's home in a different part of the country for treatment. Multiple HIV tests turned out negative, and Stephen remains HIV negative to this day. The illness was complicated by a bowel infection that necessitated two major abdominal surgeries and the experience of a temporary colostomy. Stephen came close to losing his life several times during that year. By the time he returned to the university in the fall of 1996, his chances for complete remission were good, and, since then, his medical doctor has been consistently optimistic about Stephen's prognosis since his blood counts have remained within normal limits.

When Stephen presented to the student health center, he complained of overall malaise, low energy, an impulse to withdraw from school, loneliness, disappointment with friends, and a sense of alienation. The psychologist at student health noted the following: "The patient admitted to being overwhelmed with existential level questions about goals and sexual identity, as well as long-standing feelings of depression, social anxiety, low self-esteem, and ambivalence about sexual orientation." A history of vague suicidal thoughts without action or plan was also noted: "The patient expressed a desire to evaporate or retreat into the world of books." Two weeks after the initial presentation, the patient's chemotherapy maintenance regimen changed. The new regimen included semimonthly intravenous treatments at the same hospital ward where he was sick before. The patient became tearful upon seeing "the ashen faces and no hair" of the patients at the hospital ward, but the experience acted as a motivating agent for him. He expressed a renewed desire to seek help and enjoy life. Stephen saw a psychiatrist at the student health service who started fluoxetine 20 mg a day with good results and no noticeable side effects. His mood improved, and he started "feeling like [himself]—not in the paralyzed crisis stage" he used to be in.

### Developmental History

Stephen grew up in a military family with his mother, father, and three-year-older sister. They had to move every two to three years until Stephen was ten years old, when his parents divorced. He describes his family in his own words as "a classical Freudian constellation with an overbearing mother and an absent father." He recalls the divorce as an unemotional, matter-of-fact event, that he had to simply "announce to friends and neighbors, something like the family getting a new car." Stephen went on to live with his mother, visiting his father for about two weeks every year. Both parents have remarried since then.

Stephen's father is a retired military professional, and Stephen describes him as distant, cold, and controlling, preoccupied with physical fitness, bowel movements, and fear of constipation. He gave lectures to Stephen on a variety of topics of hygiene, ranging from exercise and the correct way to ride a bicycle, to masturbation and defecation. When Stephen was fifteen years old, his father gave him a lecture on how to go to the bathroom and ordered Stephen, "Show me how you wipe!" Stephen showed him how, with his clothes on, but felt very humiliated. His father had plastic surgery on his tongue to improve enunciation and persuaded Stephen's mother to have a nose job. Stephen remembers that during his childhood his father would order his mother to step on the scale and then tell her, "No sex for you; you are too fat." Stephen says, "My father has a fetish for foreign women. He thinks that they are superior to American women, who are disastrous, have difficulties in dressing, and are clearly more masculine than foreign women." Stephen came out to his father as a gay man when he was twenty years old in a letter from overseas where he was studying at the time. Stephen's father wrote back, "That's not what I would want. I have gay friends in the service, but it's different when it's your son. But that doesn't change the way I feel about you." He enclosed a hundred dollar bill in the letter which Stephen only used after a considerable amount of time. He felt that he was being "bought off," and the gesture was motivated by "guilt for the paternal estrangement."

Stephen's mother came from a higher social class, studied art in college, and always wanted "to rise social-wise." Stephen describes her as "a failed artist, who values languages, traveling, and a college education." Stephen recalls her saying to him throughout his childhood: "I really expect you to do exceptional things. When you were born, I knew you were meant for greatness." On one hand, Stephen feels that his mother was always on his side, protecting him from paternal wrath and unjust punishments. On the other hand, he resents his mother's projected elitism that pressured Stephen to always try to live "a life that *she* would have liked to have lived." He came out to his mother when he was eighteen years old and expected a sympathetic response. Instead, she experienced a "nervous breakdown," locked herself in her room for days, and eventually sought professional help from "a psychologist who worked with hypnosis." She asked Stephen to simultaneously see the same therapist for individual psychotherapy in an attempt for them to address together the fallout of his coming out. Stephen complied, only to find out, two months later, that his mother had quit therapy shortly after the initial visit: now, the only patient was Stephen, and, in his mother's words, he was "the one with the problem." "The whole thing felt like a setup," he recalls; he felt "bamboozled" by his mother and left the weekly treatment after two and a half months. This was Stephen's only prior experience with psychotherapy.

Stephen used to be very close to his sister and shared with her his frustration with the paternal control. Stephen's sister became a born-again Baptist in her early twenties and then got married and moved with her husband to Europe "to get away from the family," as Stephen says. She was divorced shortly thereafter, and, upon return to the maternal home, she became a Catholic, disapproving of her brother's homosexuality and relentlessly preaching and praying for her brother's conversion to heterosexuality.

Throughout grammar school, junior high, and high school, Stephen was always the best student in the class. He "reliably got great grades, except penmanship," and was in the gifted student program. Throughout high school, he always had "a best friend" but did not consider himself popular or sought after. He was not good in sports, in particular, team sports. "I was among the last to be chosen for teams," he recalls. He often fantasized about trading his academic achievements for success in sports. "I envied other children who were better looking and more athletic, and had social success which I didn't have." Interestingly, Stephen has not talked about his earlier sexual fantasies and experiences.

Stephen went on to a prestigious state college where he majored in the humanities. When he was a junior in college, he studied overseas for a year and that's where he met his first boyfriend, Victor. It was a humiliating experience for Stephen, as Victor was officially engaged to a woman and only occasionally slept with Stephen. Stephen remembers that during their only weekend trip, with friends to the country, he had to pretend that he and Victor were just friends, as Victor and his fiancée were having loud sex to everybody else's amusement.

### Course of Treatment

During the eighteen months of Stephen's treatment, we addressed several issues, including his ambivalence about his career path as a university language professor, his relationship with his parents and his sister, his connection with his friends, his religious anxieties, his struggle with his illness, and his difficulties adjusting to a predominantly heterosexual world as a gay person. For the purpose of this paper, however, I would like to present aspects of the development of Stephen's transference, especially its erotic component as it manifests in his dreams, and some of the transference/countertransference issues that have emerged in the course of treatment from our encounters out of session.

At the time I first met Stephen in early December 1996, eight weeks after presenting to the student health center, he had lost all his hair from the new chemotherapy regimen, looked tired and ill, and was noticeably psychomotorly retarded from being sick. However, he was no longer depressed and told me that his primary interest in psychotherapy was to "fully engage in life, get over inhibitions, and have a greater appreciation for life." He added, "Before I got ill, I often got the feeling that I would get sick or paralyzed. When I *did* get ill, I said, 'Oh, oh, this illness will help me address issues in my life.' " In discussing these issues, Stephen said that he had often felt different from other people, "superior intellectually and inferior socially/sexually," but expressed no ambivalence about his sexual orientation. I was impressed with Stephen's motivation for psychotherapy, but, at the same time, I was struck by the absence of affect in recounting near-death experiences. I also felt that *I* could have been absent from the room without any significant change in the process.

During the first few sessions of the treatment, Stephen talked about his experience with his illness. What he found as the most pivotal event in the experience was a full-blown manic episode with psychotic features that he had as he was being tapered down from a dexamethasone (steroid) treatment.

> My brain was going at double speed. I thought I finally had become what I always wanted to be. I was playing the piano. I determined I was going to do Greek and I actually went out and bought lots of Greek books. I thought I had published a novel about my illness, had completed my master's thesis, and there was a black tie party in my honor. Then I thought I had a dialogue with God; the voice told me all these fantastic things. I asked all these questions and I got all the answers: The illness wouldn't come back. Everything was exactly what I wanted to hear. Then, Friday night, I became unmanageable. I thought I had a great insight into the Pythagorean nature of the Universe. I had to renounce the sin that I was gay through a cleansing ritual by eating leaves off a bush; and I tried to have everybody in my family eat them too. I was convinced I had a taste of hell and that I would never be able to sleep again. My mother kept keeping me away from knifes, and my father kept giving me huge amounts of temazepam. Finally, I became indifferent and concluded that turning away from God was the only sin; I decided to embrace life and creation and went to sleep.

Stephen tried for a long time to "make sense" out of this event, but in the end he felt two things: (1) "really confused," and (2) "much less sure about the existence of God." For me, two themes seemed potentially important at this early stage of the treatment: (1) the patient's dichotomous understanding of the world, good versus evil, heaven versus hell, and (2) the central role that transference and countertransference could play in our work. In a most concrete way, I felt that since I am both Greek and gay, I could symbolize both sides in the patient's central conflict. My fantasy was that I could help him understand, metabolize, and eventually bridge, his split world.

At the end of our third session, right before he went on a month-long trip home over the Christmas break, Stephen described his first dream. He said:

> The night after the first time that I came here I had a dream. I was lost with my sister. Then we saw a zoo. And then it was a hospital resembling this hospital. And we had to get through it . . . up and down . . . up and down . . . there were a lot of staircases and elevators in the context of general danger. It was almost like a World War II Nazi-run institution . . . and I was reading Sylvia Plath before going to bed that night.

Stephen told me that he always associated his father with the Nazis and that his first feelings of being in therapy with me were vaguely related to such themes. He agreed that he might have been concerned that his new doctor at the hospital where I practiced could turn out to be as sadistic as his father or a Nazi interrogator, but essentially dismissed my interpretation, pointing out that he did not find this to be a scary dream. I thought that strong feelings and transference projections were present and in full swing in the session, but they seemed to be largely inaccessible to Stephen.

The next time I saw Stephen was a month later, out of session, at the university gym where he was doing sit-ups. I did not recognize him at first, not only because his hair had started to grow back, but also because deep down I knew that running into patients outside the office was troublesome, at least at this stage of my training. Thinking that he was someone else, I said, "Hey, what's up?" and slapped him lightly on the shoulder as I passed by without stopping. He replied something like, "I'm doing well," or "I'm fine," at which point I realized who he was. I smiled, acknowledging his reply, and walked away. I felt bad for not recognizing my patient, and I felt bad for touching him. I thought Stephen could have interpreted my gesture as sexually provocative, and that the treatment could be in danger. It brought back memories of my first long-term therapy patient who quit therapy days after she saw me at a café in the university neighborhood, believing that I was pursuing her. I braced myself for working through the fallout of the gym incident.

A few days later, Stephen came on time for his scheduled session, the first one after the Christmas break. He opened the session by saying:

> I had this very bizarre dream last night. The setting was out of *Who's Afraid of Virginia Woolf?* I went to visit my uncle and aunt; Richard Burton was my uncle and Elizabeth Taylor was my aunt, and they had a plot to poison me. All three of us were in the bathroom and they had an eyedropper with a green-and-white label. They measured the poison, and they gave it to me. Then Richard Burton put a stamp with green ink on my back for processing at the hospital. One of the options on the stamp was seropositive. I had twenty-four hours before the poison would take effect. Then, my family and Richard Burton and Elizabeth Taylor and I had a picnic, but I got anxious, and my sister had to take me to the hospital. And we drove and drove and drove, in a little white car, in a street lined up with walls, like a sled, like a roller coaster. We arrived at the hospital, and I woke up, and I was disappointed. It was not a nightmare, I was not anxious, and I was not horrified. There was a general lack of concern. Richard Burton and Elizabeth Taylor were joking about things. The whole thing came as a matter of course.

Stephen talked about the obvious association of the dream with his illness and the chemotherapy, the feeling of being "processed as part of a greater plan while everybody is saying 'it's for your own good.'" He also noted that although he repeatedly tested HIV negative, "there was always a doubt about HIV; it was a mark that would always be there." I asked him about his relationship with his medical doctors, and Stephen said, "My MD back home is someone whom I really trust, but my new MD is not quite the same; I haven't known him long enough. . . . It is an issue of intimacy and trust." I found out that over the break Stephen had decided to go back to his original chemotherapy regimen given by his doctor "back home." This regimen included only oral medications, no intravenous treatments, and no hair loss, but Stephen felt guilty that the less aggressive treatment may be less effective, despite medical evidence that the two regimens have comparable efficacies. Later in the session, when I asked him about what he felt seeing his therapist at the gym, he said, "It was strange. The gym is a leisure activity," implying perhaps that therapy is not. Stephen did not elaborate on the incident, and I did not pursue it further. At that moment, I felt that I was probably shying away from exploring the sexually charged and uncomfortable topic of the gym encounter. I also felt that Stephen had just presented to me a dream about emotional numbness, loss of control, humiliation, passivity, and learned helplessness in the face of a sadistic father and a life-threatening illness with horrifying treatments. Imposing yet another treatment through further interrogation of a difficult subject, again "for his own good," was probably not the best idea, at least this early in our relationship.

As I was debating with my supervisor and my fellow colleagues how cautious I should be in pursuing difficult topics in treatment, I saw Stephen again at the gym, only this time in the showers. We were both naked, and he had just finished showering when I walked in. We recognized each other right away, and we said, "Hi." To me, running into your patient in the gym shower or in the sauna had always been one of those dreaded possibilities that, after they happened, generations of residents would talk about. And it was happening to me! Armed with the conviction that much more terrible things can happen to a patient than seeing his therapist naked, I presented the incident to my colleagues. The responses ranged from elation (one fellow resident exclaimed, "Excellent! More grist for the mill!") to gloom and doom (another resident announced, "This is definitely the end of the treatment, Petros. Now you have to find your patient a new therapist.") My supervisor, an openly gay psychiatrist, advised me to continue working with my patient, listening very closely to the material, and interpreting the erotic transference judiciously. At the beginning of the next session, Stephen told me that the first encounter at the gym was fine, the second one was a little different, but, altogether not of great concern to him. "It was inevitable," he said. Then, he said, "Now, I would like to talk about my two major issues: I am held back by fear and hesitation in my creative work and in my intimacy with friends."

In the next session, he voiced for the first time "vague dissatisfaction with therapy," as he said. He then went on to describe a dream: "I dreamt that I got athlete's foot from the gym, but it wasn't ordinary athlete's foot; it was more like leprosy. There were horrible, crusty wounds covering my feet." I asked if he had already seen me at the gym showers when he had the dream, and he answered:

> Yes. The gym is a place with sexuality. Even more so for a gay person, seeing other men in various stages of undress. It is an erotically charged place and a pickup place, but it's not the type of interaction that interests me. I am not interested in one-night stands. I find the idea morally uncomfortable, but the fantasy is very attractive. I can imagine meeting someone for anonymous sex, and having very limited emotional engagement, but this is not my favorite fantasy.

"What is?" I asked. "The student-teacher relationship," he replied. "All my friends are teaching young undergraduates. How nice to have a little group of boys and not necessarily have to be in physical contact. The roles are implied there." Then, Stephen told me that he had not had sex or masturbated since he got sick (long before he started taking fluoxetine), and that he did not have as many fantasies, nor as much libido. He said, "I feel hesitant and removed from myself as a sexual being. I have this disease. And I have these scars," pointing to his abdomen and possibly implying that now his therapist, too, who saw him naked, had proof that he could no longer be a sexual being.

During the next session, Stephen recalled a very long and complicated dream unfolding in a restaurant where the menus were all screwed up and his sister kept preaching in the background, much to Stephen's embarrassment. In the end, Stephen did not eat anything and got out to the parking lot. He said:

> There was my car. A huge white car. The lights were on, and I realized that I had left my lights on. They were still shining a little bit. I tried to start the car, but I couldn't. I started looking around for a jump start. But everybody around was in small VW Bugs, and they did not have enough power to start my car. Then

a man on foot that looked like you came by, and I asked, "Can you help me?" The man said, "Sure," and he successfully jump-started my car. But then I thought to myself, "Great! Now I have to drive for two hours," and it had not been my intention to take such a long trip.

After listening to this dream, I felt that the success of the treatment would most likely rely not as much on whether Stephen felt that I could deliver a successful jump start, but, more important, on whether he felt that I could be trusted to take a long trip with him. I thought that the erotic transference, at this stage, reflected less the one-night stand fantasy and more the student-teacher fantasy.

For the next few months, Stephen kept having many dreams that shared a common theme. Stephen would be found in a convoluted, vaguely familiar, and somewhat dangerous place with the task to escape. Somewhere in the maze, he would encounter a helping person, such as a neighbor with directions or a customs officer with a passport. But, in other dreams, he would encounter a scolding authority figure, such as the medical school professor who pointed out that Stephen was the only one in the autopsy room without gloves. Stephen kept going back and forth between positive and negative transference, and I felt that my interpretations started sounding a little less hollow to him as the treatment went on.

After recounting a dream that took place in St. Petersburg, Stephen told me that men fall into three categories according to their sex appeal. He said:

> Type Ones are the ones with the good genetic material, like the French and the Dutch. Type Twos are the failures like the Canadians, the Austrians, and most of the rest of the world. And Type Threes are somewhere in between. They are average, but with stunning exceptions among them, like the Russians, the Spaniards, and the Americans.

I asked, "Where do the Greeks fall in this scheme?" Stephen got flustered and answered, "I just can't say." At that time, I realized that we had never talked about my being Greek despite my accent, my name, and Stephen's numerous references to the ancient Greeks. I also realized how much easier it was to talk with Stephen through his dreams.

In the summer of 1997, Stephen had his first date in two years. He started dating regularly, and his affect in session brightened. His dreams no longer had this emotionally vacant quality. While dangerous and horrifying images continued to dominate his dreams, his affect in describing these scenes became more congruent.

In the fall, the treatment was interrupted by my month-long vacation in November and then later by Stephen's month-long Christmas trip home. Although we had started talking about my June graduation, the end of his treatment, and issues of intimacy and separation before my vacation, it was not until Stephen came back in January that such themes became central in the patient's erotic transference and dreaming.

In one of Stephen's more recent dreams, two months ago, he finds himself again at a big family picnic, similar to the Richard Burton and Elizabeth Taylor dream picnic, a little more than a year ago. He said:

> We were somewhere where there were a lot of people that I knew. It was a big family picnic. I went and got some food, and I sat down at a table, and you were there, and we were talking. We were talking like we were going to have a session, but there were all these people around, and I said, "This is impossible!" But you couldn't see that. Then you took me into this tent. We were separate from the crowd. You looked relaxed and Mediterranean. Only, in the tent I realized how good-looking you are. It was a vacation session. We didn't have much time left, but I had to go to the bathroom, and I thought, "Why should I have to wait to the end?" I went on a quest for a bathroom. I went into this huge hotel. It was a building with different levels and rooms. It was a very confusing and complicated maze, until I finally found a bathroom. After that, I was going to go back to you, but I took a different route back. The route was long and complicated, but I was not lost. I was thinking to myself, "Why did I take this long walk while he is waiting for me?" And the answer was: "Because this is a difficult but very beautiful hike."

This dream opened up the erotic transference for Stephen, to the point that he could now start really feeling the possibility of being intimate with someone in a nonabusive relationship. I feel that over the past two months, and as we are approaching termination in June, Stephen has started becoming aware of me in the room. The process in sessions has slowed down since then, and Stephen lectures less frequently. He often starts the session saying, "I was thinking about what we talked about last time," with the curiosity to find out if I remember the last session as well as he does. He now asks me to repeat phrases that he does not understand, and changing notebooks no longer goes unnoticed.

Last month, I also found out more about Stephen's chief complaint: "Feeling intellectually superior and socially/sexually inferior." Now, more than a year after our first meeting, Stephen is starting to talk about his initial fantasies about his therapist. He said:

> When the clinic director told me that she thought we would work well together, I thought that you had to be either an intellectual or gay. I would like you to be gay, and you could be; you seem to know the culture, but you could also be an intellectual and you have studied well.

Last year, the two identities—the intellectual man and the gay man—seemed to be mutually exclusive. A year later, as Stephen has started the process of identifying and accepting his own feelings, I believe that he will experience a more flexible and integrated internal world and will go on that beautiful but difficult hike of which he dreamed.

Chapter 2

# A Place of Recognition:
# Commentary on a Case Report
# (Gay Patient–Gay Therapist)

Adria E. Schwartz

I have been asked to discuss this case from my own clinical/theo-
retical perspective. It was further suggested that I locate my position
on the essentialist–social constructionist continuum. An apparently
reasonable task, yet I find myself in trouble.

I read this case identifying primarily as a relational psychoanalyst,
informed by feminist/gender/queer theory, and hear the melody of this
narrative from that perspective. The "Gay Patient–Gay Therapist"
frame tells me what is salient in this dyad for the therapist, but does not
adequately define my experience in working with this case post hoc.

As a relational analyst I am somewhat befuddled by the concept of
a gay or lesbian psychotherapy, as it may be distinguished from a heterosexual or "straight" psychotherapy; and, as a practicing clinician,
I am unclear at times what the categories gay and lesbian (and I would
include bisexual and transgendered as well ) really mean in a collec-
tive cultural consciousness that is experiencing such a sea change in
the epistemology of mind/body/self states.

Gay, lesbian, homosexual, bisexual, transgendered—each is a sig-
nifier. Each represents a different subset of assumptions in a psycho-
social culture which is organized around spurious gender categories
and where there is a conflation of gender and desire, identity and object choice (Schwartz, 1998).

Being gay or lesbian infers a reification of a discrete identity that I
do not think actually meets with the vagaries of human sexuality as

I understand them. "Being" gay, in this case, is a cultural ascription, which does adhere, and can be internalized, but does not describe what is more accurately apprehended as a performative aspect of sexuality. The term "homosexuality" implies a binary sexuality which I reject, and comes embedded in a moral/medical model of health and psychology. Same-sex sexuality, a cumbersome phrase at best, emphasizes the performative over the interior, but eschews the cultural environment that surrounds that sexuality, as it is represented internally and lived in society.

In plainer language: I may not know generically what being gay or lesbian is as a fixed self-state in the consulting room, but I do know that I sometimes jeopardize my safety by holding another woman's hand as I walk down the street.

However, I leave this conundrum for another arena in order to address the ways in which I was engaged in this case report.

Like Dr. Levounis, I am interested in the vagaries of the transference. However, I prefer to think about "transference fields," which to my mind, include the feelings, projections, unconscious communications, constructions, and enactments which unfold within and between the therapist and the "therapized."

As I read the case, I am also mindful of differences in training between the therapist and myself (medicine/psychiatry versus clinical psychology/psychoanalysis) and am aware that these differences may lead to different ideas, not only about therapeutic action, but also about the very data from which foundational conceptions are formulated.

So for me, throughout the case as presented, certain information is missing. For instance, the frame of the treatment was not clear. How were the residents assigned patients? How many times per week was the patient seen? Session schedules seemed to follow the academic calendar. Did the patient know that his therapist was in training? Had he requested a gay therapist? Was the therapist looking for a gay patient?

Of greater importance, I hungered for more detailed associations to the rich dreams that the therapist generously provided. There were so many gaps between what the patient actually said and what the therapist infers or omits that I often found myself frustrated, wanting to know much more about how the patient structured his internal world, so that I could think clearly about the therapist's formulations.

Recognizing the structural limitations of a case presentation, one that was originally oral at that, and acknowledging that the field encompasses different ways of listening and different modes of inquiry, I will now proceed to comment within the frame of those differences.

When I read the case, I was initially struck by how the therapist identified his patient. I wondered about the therapist's transference: the shape, texture, and unconscious resonances of his feelings for the patient.

The patient is identified as a "handsome man, six feet tall, slim, with dark hair and lighter facial features. He is fairly well-groomed, although he occasionally gives the appearance of having just gotten out of bed . . ." We are given a fairly elaborate description of his clothing, including the feel of the fabrics, and even told how he "accessorizes." Was the therapist attracted to his patient? If so, how might this have played out in the therapy? There appears to have been an unacknowledged sexual air in the room from the start.

In general, I found the report a bit androcentric. The patient's sister is loudly present in his dreams, but virtually absent in the treatment. His mother, too, remains more or less locked in the room to which she retreated at Stephen's "coming out." "Straight" women are noted early on as part of Stephen's support network, but are never mentioned afterward. I found his network, consisting of gay men and straight women, quite interesting and wondered if there were some parallel there to the way in which Stephen unconsciously coded his parents' sexuality. However, I was most engaged by the issue of recognition in the treatment, and it is here that I want to focus the bulk of the discussion.

I use the term recognition in the relational sense, as it refers to the apprehension of one's own or an "other's" subjectivity. According to Benjamin (1992), the subjectivity of the "other" must be fully recognized in order for the self to fully experience his or her own subjectivity in the other's presence. Benjamin critiques much of psychoanalysis (and its derivatives in psychodynamic psychotherapy, I would assume) as being infantocentric, viewing the mother or caretaking other solely as an object of the child's need, and failing to see the child's recognition of the mother's subjectivity as a developmental achievement.

Benjamin superimposes Winnicott's idea of object usage onto an Hegelian formulation of recognition. The survival of the object against the onslaught of omnipotent fantasies of aggression/negation ensures the survival of the object in the real external world and allows its usage. In the Hegelian model, there is a constant tension between recognizing the other and asserting the self.

I suggest that optimally, just as the mother's recognition of her child's nascent subjectivity forms the basis for the baby's "sense of agency," so should psychoanalysis/psychotherapy balance attention to the intrapsychic and the intersubjective, whether it is for a session or a term of treatment. The relational approach, as I theorize and practice it, requires consistent effort to explore and recognize the patient's subjectivity and to create a safe holding environment in which the therapist's subjectivity can be ignored or addressed in accordance with the patient's need.

How does this apply to the case at hand?

The patient first came to the student health center complaining of "overall malaise, low energy, an impulse to withdraw from school, loneliness, disappointment with friends, and a sense of alienation." He was recovering from a life-threatening illness, and was "overwhelmed with existential level questions about goals and sexual identity . . ." Medication helped him through a debilitating depression so that upon entering longer term psychotherapy he started "feeling like [himself]—not in the paralyzed crisis stage."

But the patient's concerns upon entering treatment remained: his loneliness, and alienation, his tendency to withdraw into a world of books and split in his self-representation between his "social" and "intellectual" selves.

As I frame the task in treatment, Stephen seeks recognition from his therapist so that he might recognize himself.

Coming out as a gay man, as the patient did as a young adult, is a more direct quest for recognition of one's sexual subjectivity.

According to the case material, the patient came out to his mother at eighteen. Expecting a compassionate response, he was met instead by a "nervous breakdown." The patient's mother locked herself in her room for four days, and then allegedly sought professional help to deal with the "fallout." It was further disconcerting to him when she used this collapse to try to manipulate him into treatment instead of seeking it for herself.

Stephen's father, harsher and more estranged, seemed to offer the more sympathetic response. Yet it was unsatisfactory in Stephen's eyes. He felt "bought off" rather than recognized and respected.

It is unclear from the case material whether the patient had particular issues concerning what the referring psychologist termed "sexual identity" when he sought long-term psychotherapy. We do know that Stephen felt alienated and didn't quite recognize himself as a sexual being. "I feel hesitant and removed from myself as a sexual being."

Recognition is also central to the therapist, who tells us about his early experience with his patient: "I could have been absent from the room without any significant change in the process." This is in marked distinction to the therapist's fantasy, in which he acts as a transformational object (Bollas, 1979) for his patient: "My fantasy was that I could help him understand, metabolize, and eventually bridge his split world." He believed he would be able to do this by virtue of being both Greek and gay, yet it is unclear what the therapeutic action would be: identification, incorporation, transmuting internalization? Each of these would entail recognition of the therapist as a desirable, intellectual gay man, a kind of man whom the patient might have or might be.

In fantasy, the therapist wants to be recognized. In reality, he demonstrates greater ambivalence. He appears to be interested in paternal transferences to him in dream or session material, and in the patient's erotic transferences, as they may arise from extra-therapeutic encounters in the gym; but the therapist seems much less interested in countertransferences, either as they arise in this treatment or as a natural course of being in a therapeutic dyad.

The therapist does not appear to recognize the possibility of his own transferences, erotic or otherwise, nor does he appear to recognize himself in the patient's dreams/associations, notably the "new MD at the roller coaster hospital whom he hasn't known very long . . ." and with whom there is an "issue of intimacy and trust." The therapist keeps his patient at bay. In his first encounter at the gym, he doesn't recognize his patient.

"I did not recognize him at first, not only because his hair had started to grow back, but also because deep down I knew that running into patients outside the office was troublesome, at least at this stage of my training." He was "thinking he was someone else." Who, we might ask? What were the therapist's feelings about that person? Why him? Might his feelings have some transferential bearing on his feelings for his patient?

We do not have that information. What we do know is: "I felt bad for not recognizing my patient, and I felt bad for touching him. I thought Stephen might have interpreted my gesture as sexually provocative, and that the treatment could be in danger."

I was struck with the use of the word "bad" in place of "badly." It is a common grammatical error, true enough. Yet, is there some way in which this therapist felt that he was bad in the etymological sense of immoral or base? The therapist associates to his first long-term therapy patient, who quit therapy after she saw him at café and thought he was pursuing her. What were the therapist's feelings about this patient? Are we to infer that he could not feel attraction for her because he was gay?

The therapist chooses not to pursue an inquiry into the patient's feelings after the first gym encounter. He acknowledges that "I was probably shying away from exploring the sexually charged and uncomfortable topic of the gym encounter," but likened further inquiry to an "interrogation" where he would become the "sadistic Nazi interrogator."

In the service of protecting his patient, the therapist misses an important communication from Stephen about intimacy and trust, "My MD back home is someone whom I really trust, but my new MD is not quite the same; I haven't known him long enough. . . . It is an issue of intimacy and trust."

By not discussing either meeting, I suggest that both the patient and his therapist were engaged in some form of collusion. According to Frankel (1993):

> collusion involves an unconscious deal—a mutual denial, by patient and analyst, of some aspect of their relationship that frightens them both. Each party acts to insure that both remain unaware of the collusion. (p. 228)

Frankel proposes that intimacy is the opposite of collusion. He defines intimacy as

> what is innermost in oneself and to an interpersonal relationship in which one can make this known to another . . . intimacy implies the desire to know, and the capacity to accept, all one may find in oneself and in the other. It therefore also implies the acceptance of the other as an "other": a separate person not in one's grandiose orbit. . . . (p. 229)

In this case report, the therapist fails to recognize the patient as an interpreting subject who constructs his object world, and in doing so, negates himself as another interpreting subject in the dyad. There is a failure of recognition of subjectivities and within that subjectivity, perhaps, the recognition of the possibility of desire or its absence: "Stephen did not elaborate on the incident, and I did not pursue it further."

The therapist's transferences remain veiled.

Another opportunity arose, however, when therapist and patient again meet in the gym, this time in the showers! "We were both naked, and he had just finished showering when I walked in. We recognized each other right away, and we said 'Hi.' "

What does that mean, we recognized each other right away?

How did they recognize each other? As persons? As gay men? What about each other's subjectivity was recognized and unspoken? What about each other's bodies, and the way in which they were constructed?

Stephen appears to dismiss the significance of the incident in lieu of his two "major issues . . . fear and hesitation in my creative work and in my intimacy with friends."

The therapist consults with his "openly gay psychiatrist" supervisor and is told to listen for erotic transference material closely. The therapist's possible transferences are not discussed. We may only suppose that he finds none and then moves on to other material.

We don't really hear much about the therapist's feelings other than his understandable fears that he will lose the patient, and that treatment will end. Again, the therapist's transferences remain veiled.

In the next session, the patient voices "vague dissatisfaction" with the therapy and reports a dream where he contracts a leprosy-like encrustation covering his feet at the gym. His associations run to his encounter with his therapist, and one-night stands: anonymous sex with "little emotional engagement." Not his favorite fantasy!

The therapist doesn't seem to hear the transference implications here; he doesn't associate these sexual encounters and their limited emotional engagement with the patient's possible experience of the therapy. Nor does the therapist consider that in voicing his favorite erotic fantasy (that of a student-teacher relationship where the roles imply no physical contact), the patient may be conveying a wish for firmer boundaries in the therapeutic relationship.

Within the context of a gay-affirmative treatment, the therapist eschews some of the more classical formulations about same-sex sexuality and desire, its etiology and/or pathology. Nonetheless, he operates within the domain of a one-person psychology. Shifts in the patient are understood as reflective of shifts in the transference, not as reflective of shifts in the patient-therapist dyad. The patient is expected to somehow incorporate the therapist as a role model and metabolize his interpretations—the processes that allow for therapeutic change.

Concomitantly, when the therapist tells of changes in his experience of the patient, his reports are largely devoid of a relational context. In the final dream, the patient "takes a hike," perhaps in reaction to the forced termination of his treatment by his therapist. The therapist does not interpret the dream that way, interpersonally, but rather as a foreshadowing of the path Stephen wishes to take in the next phase of his life.

Dr. Levounis ends with his hope that he has accomplished his goal of helping his patient to integrate a split between his sexuality and his intellect. We can infer that Stephen's willingness to share his initial fantasies about his therapist indicate that he has moved along in that direction.

Dr. Levounis is clearly pleased to feel more recognized. Stephen notices his behavior and seems more curious about him in the room. He writes, ". . . as we are approaching termination in June, Stephen has started becoming aware of me in the room."

We have less data about the patient's experience of recognition, and can only infer that his increased ability to recognize the other within the context of a relationship indicates that he is feeling less vulnerable about the possible annihilation of self.

What is most clear to me is that it is unfortunate that this treatment had to end precipitously. The therapist and his patient have obviously taken some very important steps together. We can only wonder what might have been accomplished if they had been able to take that long hike together, extending and deepening their work, and perhaps seeing each other more frequently.

Some of us are incurable in our analytic dreams.

## REFERENCES

Benjamin, J. (1992), Recognition and destruction: An outline of intersubjectivity. In *Relational Concepts in Psychoanalysis,* N. Skolnick and S. Warshaw (Eds.). Cambridge, MA: Harvard University Press, pp. 43-60.

Bollas, C. (1979), The transformational object. *International Journal of Psychoanalysis,* 60:97-100. Reprinted in *The British School of Psychoanalysis: The Independent Tradition,* G. Kohon (Ed.). New Haven, CT: Yale University Press (1998), pp. 83-100.

Frankel, J. (1993), Collusion and intimacy in the analytic relationship: Ferenczi's legacy. In *The Legacy of Sandor Ferenczi,* L. Aron and A. Harris (Eds.). Hillsdale, NJ: The Analytic Press, pp. 227-247.

Schwartz, A. (1998), *Sexual Subjects: Lesbians, Gender and Psychoanalysis.* New York: Routledge.

# Chapter 3

# Unspoken Questions:
# Unsayable Answers

## Kenneth Lewes

Some morning from the boulder broken beach
He would cry out on life, that what it wants
Is not its own love back in copy speech.
But counter-love, original response.

Robert Frost, "The Myth of It"

I should like to thank Dr. Levounis for sharing with us an account of this interesting and moving young man, and also to compliment him on his sensitive portrayal of his patient and his tactful and gentle treatment. My major dissatisfaction stems from my wish to know more about Stephen and the course of his treatment and to have an account that is at least five times as long as the present one. Quite apart from issues of curiosity, several large issues seem to require greater elaboration and explanation. Dr. Levounis is, I think, quite correct in suggesting that this particular therapy, more than most cases, operated largely by unconscious transference feelings, and its apparent beneficial results came about through the transmutative effect of a benevolent transference relationship as much as, if not more than, through any particular set of interpretations or reconstructions. It is all the more important, therefore, that we have some notion of what Dr. Levounis means to his patient.

As in all such accounts of genuine therapies, the reader feels much like a visitor to an archeological museum, where one particularly suggestive artifact has to summon up an entire complex set of experiences and structures. There are many such moments in Dr. Levounis's account. The richest are, of course, Stephen's dreams. But it is an equally frustrating experience to attempt to summon up a feeling for their therapeutic interactions, informed as they are by what is said, anticipated, fantasized, hoped for, projected, or received with fear and gratitude. Another rich set of moments occurs, of course, in the gym (or "the naked place," as its etymology reminds us), which, despite Dr. Levounis's trepidation, provided the occasion, I think, for a deep exchange and thereby figured in Stephen's larger quest to find permission to have a life as an active, productive, and loving man.

To more fully appreciate the depth and complexity of Stephen's thoughts and feelings we need to know more, of course, about his associations to dreams. So literary a type would necessarily have complex associations to Sylvia Plath's masochistic fantasies of Nazi concentration camps, and his wish to "do Greek" would, one supposes, have both linguistic and sexual meanings for him. In addition, dreams occurring in St. Petersburg (the city of Petros) relate in complex ways to other spaces presided over by the feared and yearned for therapist: the hospital, the zoo, the concentration camp, the family picnic. Similarly, the image of athlete's foot would seem to relate to leprosy, AIDS, and sexually transmitted diseases, as well as to phallic activity and the fate of that swollen-footed Greek hero, Oedipus.

Part of the pleasure of reading case presentations is indulging rather irresponsibly in one's own associations to the material presented. But Stephen, like everyone else, is constantly associating, not just to Greek etymologies, but to such implied ideas (again the present writer's association) as "the run-around" and to his feelings about Richard Burton. Dr. Levounis is unable to provide us with an account of this, given the limitations of length, but this omission is especially regrettable in light of how "literary" his patient is and how, even before therapist met patient, the ground was being prepared for what Dr. Levounis would come to mean to Stephen: his being "Greek," being Petros, being a physician, being gay. What does Dr. Levounis look like, how does he dress, what jokes does he make? These are all terribly important impressions, especially when Dr. Levounis enters his patient's dreams, and they serve both to inform the therapeutic relationship and to provide a ground against which so explosive and so promising an event as the naked meeting in the shower takes place.

I am not suggesting that presenters should attempt the impossible by trying to give us an account of the myriad details and impressions that help constitute the therapeutic relationship, but rather wish to call attention to the huge gap that separates even the fullest account of a therapy from the actual experience of that therapy. An intimacy develops between therapist and patient in large part through the shared process of associating to material, whether dreams, events, or memories. The therapist demonstrates his attentiveness, caring, and memory not really by showing whether he "remember[s] the last session," but by the liveliness of his responses to symbolic and semiotically rich events. In this regard, I consider it entirely appropriate for the therapist to reveal his own associations, provided he does so discreetly and modestly, as it is a way of establishing the dialogue of unconsciousness that provides the basis for real therapeutic relationships. In addition, with such a patient as Stephen, whom Dr. Levounis correctly senses as being somewhat fragile and vulnerable to humiliation and shame, this exchange of associations can serve some of the function that interpreting and challenging might provide in a more robust patient.

Quite apart from this general hunger for more details, one wishes to know more about certain aspects of this particular patient's background, especially his family. First of all, despite their apparent high economic and educational level, there are signs of rather gross disturbances in all members. The father's near-abusive curiosity and intrusiveness in sexual, especially anal, matters is striking, as is the mother's "nervous breakdown" and amazing avoidant and devious behavior following Stephen's self-disclosure. Finally, the sister's religious conversions and bizarre judgmentalness regarding her brother's sexual orientation suggest a borderline level of psychopathology at best. Some adequate sense of the family members' level of psychological functioning is important for several reasons. First, we need to establish some understanding of Stephen's own psychotic episode. Was it the result of a change of medication, some genetic predisposition, or a crisis in a rather brittle and unstable mental structure? In particular, one wonders what Stephen himself presently thinks of his psychotic episode. Does he recognize it as being as bizarre as it was, or does he think of it as some quirky event in the past? We are partly interested in this question because it relates to a more general characteristic of Stephen, which we shall discuss later: his apparent inability to distinguish between love and abuse, sanity and craziness in those around him.

Finally, one wishes for more information about his past and present relations with others: his friendships, relations with authority figures, his ability to work, his interest and distastes. In particular, does he have any real friendships with men, especially heterosexuals? One also wonders about his sex life, his attractions, crushes, and fantasies, and, most important of all, his claim to have relinquished all sexual activity, including masturbation. These details are especially important since they not only provide information about the patient's background and character, but also allow us to see, in parallel fashion, how the transference unfurls and is transformed in time, as it is affected by and in turn affects current experiences and relationships.

Leaving aside these general considerations for the moment and turning to the material at hand, I should like to begin by thinking about Stephen as he presents himself at the beginning of treatment. We are interested here not so much in a formal diagnosis as in Stephen's sense of himself and his place in the world. What seems so striking about him, and here Dr. Levounis must be complimented on so successfully conveying this quality, is not really his depression as, and this is an important distinction, a deep and inescapable sadness, a sense of being caught in a helpless and bleak isolation from the interests and joys of real life. His appearance, as Dr. Levounis describes it, is not so much that "of an intellectual" as of an epicene, a sexual neuter. Homosexual, but neither butch nor swish, he has simply withdrawn from the arena of sexual activity and relinquished any claims he might make on phallic pleasure or achievements.

This keeping a low profile and trying to duck the exchanges of life must, of course, relate to his recent illness, which, though I presume it is not AIDS, has had a profound negative effect on Stephen's sense of being entitled to the perquisites of a human being and a man. Though not sexual in nature, his illness has for him many of the characteristics of a sexually transmitted disease. It is infectious (he is rebuked in his dream for not wearing rubber gloves), it results in ghastly skin eruptions, it wastes the body so that its sufferers resemble advanced AIDS patients, and it requires as part of its treatment a humiliating castration in the form of a colostomy. He cannot convince himself, despite blood tests, that he is not HIV positive. He has nearly died from it "several times," but his reaction is not outrage or self-pity, but a passive acquiescence. Significantly, he has given up sex entirely since his illness and, by his own account, no longer even masturbates.

It is as if he had struck a bargain with God. If he will be spared, he will renounce sex and the sense of himself as a sexual, phallic being. The unconscious logic of such a bargain sees the divine rebuke and punishment as directed at the offending action and the reprieve as requiring the repudiation of that offense. Stephen will be allowed to live if he renounces sex. This is an elaborate way of saying that Stephen has always felt guilty about his sexuality and that when catastrophe descended on him, he already knew that he deserved it. And if he pursues an active gay life, he knows that he will certainly contract AIDS. This is, after all, what his sister believes and insists on reminding him of. Thus, we see how another condition of Stephen's transference had been laid down even before he met Dr. Levounis. As much as Stephen vaguely yearns for a free, rich life, he dreads reneging on his bargain. And as his therapist, a young gay man himself, whom he sees naked in the gym, begins to suggest subtly that he too might have a real life, both Stephen's transference and his resistances to experiencing it begin to become charged.

In other words, Stephen's profound sense of guilt about his sexuality preceded his illness, gave it a meaning when it struck him, and stemmed from early experiences in his family. Stephen himself intuits this, although it assumes the form of an unconscious projection. When Stephen's father responds to his son's disclosure of his sexual orientation by enclosing a $100 bill, Stephen interprets it as a bribe motivated by "guilt," an attempt to buy him off. There is much to say about Stephen's response to this parental offering, but we may note his reluctance to use it. Instead, he keeps it, not fully accepting it, unwilling to let his father off the hook.

When we look at some of the details of Stephen's memory of his childhood, we see that much of his remorse results from his feeling that he has betrayed his own masculinity and sided with his mother in the long parental battle that led up to divorce when he was ten. In general, he has accepted his mother's goals for him, pursuing a career in an artsy, literary field, but he constantly feels guilty and inadequate because he has not fulfilled his father's hopes by being outgoing and athletic. This is a common enough scenario, and one frequently hears similar accounts from male homosexual patients of staying up in their room listening to opera while the neighborhood boys were outside throwing footballs at each other. What is so striking about Stephen's family, even from the few details offered here, is how highly ambivalent both parents were about their own sets of values and how they projected their ambivalence onto their son in the form of contradictory responses to his developing sexuality. Although one can understand a mother's disappointment in hearing of her son's homosexuality, this one's "nervous breakdown" and bizarre and sadistic machinations seem quite extraordinary, especially in light of her extremely inappropriate previously expressed wishes for vicarious triumph through her son. Similarly, while the father behaves rather decently when his son informs him of his sexual orientation, there seems to be a pattern of intrusiveness regarding his son's sexuality, especially concerning anal matters. One wonders if the father's plastic surgery on his tongue was undertaken to correct a lisp and therefore points to a larger anxiety over his own masculinity.

These details from Stephen's history are in themselves not all that remarkable, but arising as they do out of an embattled marriage that was to end in divorce, they make one wonder what the issues were that separated and embittered the two parents, and in what ways the children were pressured into choosing sides and then rewarded and made to feel guilty for having done so. Needless to say, Stephen, with his characteristic inability consciously to experience any emotional reaction to their warfare, will tell us little. We do know that as a result of the divorce, Stephen was left, just as puberty was beginning for him, alone with his mother and sister, an abandonment to the world of women that was to be repeated when he was forced to return to his mother's home when he fell ill.

We find Stephen at the beginning of treatment having barely and equivocally survived the catastrophe of his illness, but trapped in an intolerable situation. He is wildly guilty, not only about his sexual orientation, but about his general claims on life. His life has been purchased at the price of forswearing any real pleasure, achievement, or intimacy. The few relationships that he permits himself seem to be abusive and demeaning: a lover who humiliates and taunts him, a sister who insists on discussing her conviction that he is damned to hell, and a mother whose life seems to have been ruined by events that happened to the patient. There is no better phrase for these communications than mind-fucks. They are done in the name of love, and Stephen seems unable to defend himself against them, either by severing such toxic relationships or by psychologically distancing himself by becoming angry at people who abuse him while claiming to be acting lovingly and in his own best interest. His difficulty in acknowledging any negative reaction on his part is the affective correlative to his general inability to lay claim to the common good of life, to stand up for his own self-interest or to distinguish friend from foe, those who wish him well from those who derive pleasure from torturing him. It is in these terms that I understand the recurrent plot of Stephen's dreams: he must go somewhere, do something, but he does not know how to get there from here, does not possess the tools or vehicles he needs. He is always being given the runaround, and his only salvation, he dimly intuits, is a genuine benevolent man who will help him.

He cherishes another hope, which informs his recurrent dreams of family picnics and gatherings, that his mother and father will be reunited and that he will not have to choose between them, or, even worse, renounce ties to both of them. He bleakly symbolizes this possibility in his evocation of *Who's Afraid of Virginia Woolf?* where the hate-filled violent couple is held together only by the fantasy of a dead child. One wonders if this is the central highly ambivalent fantasy that governs Stephen's life. Since he cannot be dead, he will at least be dying, but this alternative fills him with horror and sadness. He is quite right about his motivation in beginning treatment: having finally attained, with the crisis of his illness, the only way of reuniting his parents, he is horrified, but unable to save himself.

This is the way that I, for one, make sense of the information presented by Dr. Levounis. It is, I recognize, constituted of too much of my own associations, values, and sense of propriety, but given the nature of these kinds of discussions, it is my view of Stephen, and it informs what I imagine the shape and content of his therapy have been, especially in regard to the transference. The major issues that I expect will surface repeatedly, both as discussions of values and feelings as well as derivatives, all revolve around the issue of guilt. Now, Stephen is a sophisticated literary type at a "prestigious university" and can be expected to be acquainted with the latest in queer theory as well as to have reaped some of the benefits of the new social cachet being gay has assumed in these circles. One would expect, then, that Stephen would be relatively free of the crushing effects of social and internalized homophobia that plagued generations of gay men before him. It has, however, been my experience that, without exception, no gay person, even the most militant of political activists or the most sophisticated Foucaultian deconstructivist, is ever free of a huge burden of guilt about his sexual orientation. There are several reasons for this. First and most obvious, years of secrecy in a homophobic family and society during latency and puberty necessarily leave a thick residue of guilt and shame attached to sexual fantasy for people who are homosexual. Second, the normative amount of guilt and castration fear that attends heterosexual development is not absent from homosexual developments, but instead coalesces around social prejudice, where it finds its alibi. Last, there is a special furtiveness intrinsic to homosexual oedipal dynamics, where the father, who in heterosexual boyhoods serves as the prohibitor of sexual striving, is eroticized and himself made the object of libidinal desire. Thus, it is not at all surprising that guilt and shame should figure prominently in Stephen's dynamics.

Much work must be done in making conscious Stephen's rather primitive religious beliefs. We do not know anything about his parents' religious convictions, but the sister's double conversion to fundamentalist belief and her readiness to repudiate any bonds of loyalty and affection with her brother suggests a vast reservoir of infantile, primitive, and superstitious thinking, which, in a family of such educational accomplishment, necessarily suggests psychological disturbance, probably of a paranoid nature. This is confirmed by Stephen's own psychotic episode, which, though it may have been occasioned by a change in steroid medication, reveals similar primitive religious beliefs involving sin and atonement. The "taste of hell" that Stephen attempts to purge from his mouth may mean anything, and we need Stephen's associations to make sense of the episode, but one wonders if it relates in some way to a wish, memory, or fantasy of fellatio.

It is quite clear that Stephen, whatever his stated opinions are, regards his homosexuality as a kind of psychic damage. He assumes that the hundred dollars his father sent him in response to his coming out is a bribe, and he hesitates to accept the offer. In addition, he has adopted with approval the Bieberian etiology for homosexuality, "an overbearing mother and an absent father." Unlike other kinds of damage, Stephen's homosexuality is a totalizing corruption of his very faculty of desire, and of every occasion of seeing an attractive man, of any possibility of surrendering himself to anger, pleasure, or sleep. It is no wonder that Stephen, PhD candidate in the humanities though he is, cannot tell his sister that she is a ridiculous bigot and that she should shut up. In fact, we may consider Stephen's inability to become angry in his own self-interest as a primary characteristic of his condition. Without the power of justified anger, he is unable to separate himself from those who abuse him in the name of love: his mother, his sister, his lover Victor.

The inability or refusal to feel anger is part of a larger stifling of Stephen's personality. He constricts affects of all sorts. He is unable to feel anger at those who abuse him, to feel sexual excitement for those who attract him, or to experience fear when his life is threatened. Dr. Levounis's presentation is remarkable for documenting Stephen's minimal affective response to the events of his life, whether they are horrific nightmares or the exciting sight of his therapist's penis in the shower. This internal constriction is the affective correlative of a larger relinquishment of active powers. Developmentally, the male child's assertion of individuality as he rises up out of the maternal matrix is achieved through the exercise of various of his faculties, all of which in complex ways are the correlatives of the others: his physical mastery of the world and his own body, his intellectual probing and comprehension of the physical and interpersonal world, his sexual pride in his genitals, and his sense of the propriety and validity of his affective response to his experience. In Stephen's case, there is an almost global stifling of these active phallic powers. The only area he can excel in, the artistic and intellectual, belong, of course, to the world of mother, and whatever rewards it brings must at least partly be experienced with guilt and shame.

I think we can therefore regard this therapy as addressed to lifting massive phallic inhibition. Stephen's beginning to feel entitled to lay claims to some real achievement in his life, both academic and interpersonal, will occur along with an evaporation of deep, not quite conscious homophobic attitudes and judgments. His sexual and interpersonal relationships will improve and increase, his affect should brighten and become more varied and responsive to the flow of experience, and his depression should lift. Dr. Levounis has not told us very much about his specific probings, interpretations, and reconstructions or about Stephen's reactions to them, but he is quite right, I think, in claiming that it was the transference itself that maintained and nourished the therapy as a whole.

It is important to note Stephen's yearning for a transference figure, an older man who will lead him out of his mental imprisonment and enslavement. His treatment of his father's $100 gift/bribe dramatizes Stephen's highly charged oscillation between anger at his abandoning father and yearning for his return. He does not entirely accept the father's offering by spending it, and refuses to absolve him of his paternal failures, but neither does he return the money or rip it up. Instead, he keeps it, both hoarding and cherishing the token of connectedness to his father and keeping its reality in abeyance, suspended *in potentia*. Enter Dr. Levounis, who is young and gay himself and, by virtue of his very position, seems to have resolved some of the contradictions of phallic assertiveness that have baffled Stephen. Yet he is also an authority figure, a doctor, one who by virtue of his position, has the power to grant Stephen the right to make his own claims on the world.

The first meeting in the gym, which I assume occurred toward the beginning of treatment, confirms Dr. Levounis in Stephen's imagination as the benevolent figure who can lead him out of his thralldom. Dr. Levounis fears he has made a dreadful error in greeting and touching his patient. Although such contacts are generally to be avoided, this particular encounter has had, I think, a peculiarly beneficial effect on the therapy. The very spontaneity and unselfconsciousness of the gesture has, I think, communicated the therapist's benevolence. He affectionately greets him in a place that is fraught with issues of sexuality, health, narcissism, and desire. Such a moment could very well prove to be the first signal to Stephen that he has a life and possesses basic rights to achieve some of its pleasures and satisfactions. He is beginning to protest that he does not want to die or to be dying in order to hold his family together or to preserve the sanity of any of its members. It is finally for him, not for others, to decide what is best for him. This last assertion is, I think, the goal that this segment of the therapy might arrive at: the permission granted him to lead his own life.

Stephen's transference relation to Dr. Levounis is, of course, sexual in nature, but the transference seems not to have itself been sexualized. That is to say, Dr. Levounis functions in Stephen's transference fantasies not so much as a libidinal object but as a figure Stephen can internalize and identify with. We do not know what his specific fantasies of incorporation are, most likely they are oral and not anal in nature, but we see evidence for an identification beginning to form. It takes, oddly enough, the form of the patient beginning to mimic his own father's somewhat prissy sexual judgments. Where once the father indulged in opinions regarding the sexuality of various national types, now Stephen himself begins to formulate his own epicurean hierarchy of sex appeal. My own sense is that the most delicate and crucial moment of the therapy occurred at this point. Stephen is both trying out the role of gay man on the hunt and passive aggressively indulging in some rather provocative bitchy behavior. Like all moments in a productive therapy, this one represents both progress as Stephen begins to embrace an active phallic role and resistance as he provocatively invites judgment and punishment. Here, the veil of silence falls over the treatment room as therapist and patient negotiate again the complex and treacherous maturational process that was so badly mishandled the first time with the father.

In conclusion, we must observe that Stephen's treatment can be considered really only the beginning of a larger therapy. Dr. Levounis, with his tact and genuine goodwill, seems to have nudged Stephen back on the proper developmental path, but much more remains to be done. Quite apart from the rather disturbing issue of Stephen's primitive superstitious thinking, which points, I think, to a basic disturbance in his early relation to his mother, there is the general area of Stephen's phallic competence and the question of whether he will embrace an active, achieving role or a passive, masochistic one. The terms of such an outcome are not which sexual role Stephen will adopt socially or in bed, but whether he will undertake to brave the dangers, physical and moral, of an active engagement in the world of ideas, people, and events, or fall back into a passive acceptance of what other people may do to him, with all the attendant compensatory gratifications of self-pity, blame, and martyrdom. Stephen seems to have had the good fortune of encountering Dr. Levounis at a crucial moment of decision in his life and has profited deeply from the meeting. At similar crucial moments in his future development, he will be able to draw on the continuing beneficent presence of one who presides over and blesses Stephen's claims to manhood and life.

# Chapter 4

# Discussion of Gay Patient–Gay Therapist: A Case Report of Stephen

Ronnie C. Lesser

I'd like to begin by asking you to ponder with me the difficulty I've had writing this discussion. Each weekend, I'd sit down at the computer, only to jump up after writing a sentence or two. I'd then return the following weekend and repeat the same process. Since I don't have several years to finish writing this, I'm going to shorten what has felt like an interminable process by analyzing my resistance. I believe my reactions illuminate the central issues of both the case and the essentialist versus social constructivist debate I've been asked to write about.

Consider my thinking prior to turning my computer off: I'd try to focus on Dr. Levounis's account of the erotic transference, only to find myself mesmerized by the negative feelings in the relationship. I'd feel some of what I thought was Stephen's terror of Levounis, wonder what that was about, and then find myself thinking that the erotic feelings were really disguised negative feelings. After all, I thought, the bulk of the evidence Levounis used to hypothesize an erotic transference rested on shaky essentialist ground: his touching Stephen in the gym and their seeing each other naked during their next gym encounter. As a social constructivist, I find myself uncomfortable with assuming that these events would necessarily create desire.

I'd mull all this over for a while, and, at some point, turn off my computer and get busy thinking about something else. After several weeks of not getting anywhere, I began to think about my view that the erotic was a transform of hatred. I reflected that my own binary thinking was a way of simplifying complexity. What gives, I thought? Do I find Manichean thinking preferable to bearing the tension of a paradox? What psychological reasons underlie this preference? Different possibilities occurred to me: I found the erotic transference too hot to handle; Stephen's fear of being destroyed by Levounis was too frightening to stay with; there was something too difficult about keeping love and hatred in mind at the same time. Since I find the latter explanation the most compelling (although not necessarily the only one that is true), it is the one I will develop here.

What makes it so difficult to consider discordant emotions or ideas simultaneously? One of the reasons I'm interested in this question is that it makes more ubiquitous some quality that psychoanalysts used to see as afflicting only very disturbed patients. Levounis rightly points out in his narrative that Stephen has a "split" object world, but I ask you to consider that this is a problem plaguing not only Stephen and myself, but psychoanalytic theorists and clinicians (who become polarized in different camps), those who engage in essentialist versus social constructivist debates, politicians, etc.

Since I'm writing this discussion a short time after tuning in to the House of Representatives' Impeachment Hearings, I will use these to illustrate the ubiquity of polarized thinking (called partisanship in this context). Consider that never, in the course of all the speeches I listened to, did I hear anyone of either party take the other side's point of view seriously. What happened instead was that each side demonized the other, while painting a rosey, one-dimensional portrait of its own perspectives and motivations.

My recent experience seeing the movie *Life Is Beautiful* is also illustrative. As I sat in the theater buoyed by the protagonist's optimism and humor, it became almost impossible to keep in mind the fact that I was watching a movie about a concentration camp where people were being brutally murdered. I became aware of my dissociation only when I noticed that while I was laughing at the main character's comic antics, my shoulders were incredibly tense. Apparently, my body could remember what my mind (and the movie?) needed to forget. Being hopeful in the face of despair does not come easily.

I believe that binary thinking also afflicts the two sides of the essentialist versus social constructivist debate. While on the one hand I applaud the *Journal of Gay and Lesbian Psychotherapy* (JGLP) for wanting to highlight the important clinical and political consequences of each perspective, on the other hand, I think that polarizing them is fraught with difficulty. Consider Elizabeth Grosz's (1994) work on embodiment. Grosz discusses the way that both essentialist concepts of a prediscursive body and social constructivist ideas of a body that may only be viewed through cultural perspectives create an artificial dysfunction between these two categories. Both views avoid the fact that we can never really know where biology stops and culture begins. Perhaps polarization is a way of avoiding their inextricability.

I return now to my own problem with binary thinking in relation to the erotic feelings and hatred in this case. I believe that my reaction is closely related both Stephen's experience of being in therapy and to what went on between him and Levounis. On the one hand, Stephen felt endangered and terrified of Levounis: in his dream after their first session Levounis is depicted as a Nazi interrogator in a Nazi-run hospital. Many of Stephen's subsequent dreams take place in an atmosphere of extreme danger and terror. On the other hand, Stephen comes to sessions and manages to be open and hopeful that Levounis will help him. He deals with having these discordant images of Levounis by disconnecting himself from negative feelings. He is, after all, a master at disconnection. Consider that as a child he was neutral about his parents' divorce, and that now he is able to forget his fear of being annihilated by Levounis by telling himself that he is not afraid. (I wonder what his shoulders looked like. Did they hold his fear and tension?) His terror is submerged into a kind of neutral stance where he can maintain the hope that Levounis will help him.

From the extract of the case study being presented here, it seems that Levounis also had difficulty keeping both erotic feelings and hatred in mind. Did he feel more comfortable with the part of Stephen that was open to him (erotically and emotionally) and want to forget the part of him that was terrified? Was it difficult for him to find himself in Stephen's portrayal of him as a sadist and to ponder what he was doing that made Stephen see him this way?

I have the impression from what I've read that Levounis viewed Stephen's negative transference in an essentialist (i.e., classical) way; as something that existed inside Stephen rather than as something that was constructed between them. By looking at Stephen's fear solely as something inside of him, I think Levounis made it difficult for himself to become more engaged with this part of Stephen. I have the feeling that Stephen felt this way too. Consider this quotation from Stephen's narrative of his dream:

> We were talking like we were going to have a session, but there were all these people around. And I said: "This is impossible!" But you couldn't see that. . . .

This quotation captures the differences between essentialist versus social constructivist models of psychoanalysis. I read it as Stephen telling Levounis that because he adheres to an essentialist or one-person model of treatment, he can only see part of what is going on in the room. I consider Levounis to be an essentialist because he appears to define his role as helping Stephen uncover essential truths which lie hidden within him. By letting himself be used as a blank screen (or in this case, a naked blank screen), he "allows the transference to develop." Transference, sometimes negative, sometimes positive, is understood as projections from within the patient which attach themselves to the therapist. The classical view of transference is another type of binary thinking that diminishes the ambiguity that arises if one considers both the analyst and patient's contributions. Yet Stephen wants Levounis to know that there are other people in the room whom he has to see. Look at what's going on between us, he seems to be pleading.

At the beginning of treatment Stephen has a dream which reveals something about who these other people are. As previously noted, in this dream Levounis is depicted as a Nazi interrogator. Although the therapist sees this as an expression of "negative transference," i.e., projections, Stephen wants him to understand that Levounis has become his sadistic, sexually provocative father and that they are enacting a sado-masochistic scenario that must be recognized. Because I don't think of transference as something projected onto a blank screen, but rather as something that occurs between a therapist and patient (based on subjective factors unique to each of them), I don't see anything out of the ordinary about this happening. Rather, I view it as inevitable and helpful if it can be analyzed. I imagine that if I had a patient who was as detached as Stephen, who communicated mostly through powerful dreams whose affective coloration he then denied, that I might feel compelled to break through to him in ways that might be sadistic, or to withdraw and be inaccessible myself. Yet, because Levounis appears to adhere to an essentialist model of psychotherapy, he doesn't think to stop to look at his own contribution to Stephen's negative transference and nightmares.

Consider what I am calling Levounis's essentialist view in the context of what happened when the two of them met in the gym and Levounis didn't recognize Stephen. This odd interaction may be interpreted as an enactment rich with significance. If it had been worked with in this manner, it could have opened the treatment up so that Stephen's terror and dissociation could be discussed. Consider the multiple meanings that Levounis's not recognizing Stephen might have had. On the one hand, it repeats what went on in Stephen's family: no one recognized him as a separate person. In addition, it underlines how I imagine Levounis felt being with Stephen in sessions: not recognized. It also repeats a dynamic in Stephen: his long-term inability to recognize his feelings. Both in dreams and in waking life Stephen drains life, himself, and Levounis of any affective significance. This draining of life, of course, has added meaning since Stephen has literally come back from the dead.

Levounis recounts that he was uncomfortable bringing up the gym incident because the patient came to the next session reporting a nightmare in which Elizabeth Taylor and Richard Burton poison him. They all go on a picnic together. But Stephen gets anxious, and gets his sister to take him to the hospital. He wakes up. "And I was disappointed. It was not a nightmare, I was not anxious, and I was not horrified. There was a general lack of concern. Richard Burton and Elizabeth Taylor were joking about things. The whole thing came as a matter of course."

I read this dream partly as a vivid depiction of Stephen's dissociation. After being poisoned he goes on a picnic, as though everything is all right, i.e., a "matter of course." He then allows himself to engage with the experience by being anxious and asking his sister to take him to the hospital, only to lose the anxiety when he wakes up. Does going to the hospital signify that he wants Levounis to help him hold on to his terror, explore it, and not push it away? It is as though Stephen is trying to hold on to his two experiences of Levounis: as a dangerous killer and as a source of help.

Interestingly, Stephen is disappointed when he wakes up from the dream. What does this signify? Is he talking about his distress with his own numbing and neutrality, his effort to make everything a "matter of course?" Is he warning Levounis not to treat the dream and their gym encounter lightly? How is this dream related to Stephen's encounter with Levounis at the gym? Was it Levounis's not recognizing him that made him feel poisoned? Or was it the experience of being touched by him in an intimate way that felt so dangerous? The reference to *Who's Afraid of Virginia Woolf?* might be read as signifying that for Stephen the experience of love and hatred are very close to each other, as they are to the characters in this play. It's hard to know where one stops and the other starts off. Is Stephen saying that he was poisoned by his parents' inability to separate love from hatred in their sadistic treatment of each other? Because the incident at the gym and the dream provide a space to discuss all of these issues, I found myself disappointed that Levounis didn't take it further. Sensing how frightened Stephen was, Levounis decided not to push him to talk about their meeting at the gym. While this decision showed sensitivity, I do not feel it was therapeutically justified. Had Levounis related the dream to the meeting at the gym and encouraged Stephen to talk about it, he might have communicated that the difficult feelings between them didn't have to be flattened out into "a matter of course." I believe that avoiding this topic communicated to Stephen that Levounis was afraid to recognize the hateful and hating aspects of their relationship, the ways that they were enacting *Who's Afraid of Virginia Woolf?*

Because Levounis didn't pay sufficient attention to the negative transference, he was unable to see how it colored the erotic transference. Consider the patient's reference to Sylvia Plath after his first dream about Levounis as a Nazi interrogator. My association is to Plath's poem "Daddy" (*Ariel,* 1999), a poem that is about her love of a father who is so sadistic that she compares him to Hitler. The poem ends:

> Every woman loves a Fascist,
> The boot in the face, the brute
> Brute heart of a brute like you . . .

It seems that Stephen is again struggling to tell Levounis that love and sadism are intertwined for him, as they were for his parents. He needs help being able to recognize both feelings.

Although I have talked about the shortcomings of polarizing essentialism and social constructivism, I have also donned a social constructivist hat to discuss this case. I have used this perspective to question some of Dr. Levounis's assumptions and how they affected his work with this patient. Although my views differ from Levounis's in significant ways, it's clear that his treatment of Stephen was enormously helpful. I congratulate him on a job well done!

## REFERENCES

Grosz, E. (1994), *Volatile Bodies: Toward a Corporeal Feminism*. Bloomington, IN: Indiana University Press.

Plath, S. (1999), *Ariel*. New York: HarperCollins.

# Chapter 5

# Reflections on Self-Disclosure, Desire, Shame, and Emotional Engagement in the Gay Male Psychoanalytic Dyad

## Martin Stephen Frommer

Discussing a treatment is much easier than telling the story of one. This is true for a variety of reasons, but primary is the obvious fact that the discussant is not a character in the story being told. Discussants are heard but not seen. They do not live the relationship with the patient. Our work as therapists is much more difficult. When we conduct a treatment, we enter a complex emotional relationship and a fundamental aspect of our work involves struggling to make sense of our experience with our patients, thinking about how they affect us, how we affect them, and how we cocreate our emotional life together. In this process we may rely on various theoretical conceptualizations to help organize our experience. Regardless of the particular theoretical scaffolding we use to support ourselves, our endeavor is the same: we study our relationships with our patients so that we can help the life of the dyad and ultimately the life of the person who comes to us for help.

I should make clear that this way of understanding the therapeutic process is itself informed by a theoretical orientation which, broadly speaking, grounds itself in a two-person psychology and focuses on the relational life of the therapist and patient. This is in contrast to those theoretical frameworks which are rooted in a one-person psychology and which regard the patient as the fundamental unit of study. In the latter, the analyst is thought to be a neutral presence upon which the patient projects his or her inner life, uninfluenced, for the most part, by the therapist's subjectivity. Therapeutic perspectives which emanate from a two-person psychology, on the other hand, operate with a heightened sensitivity to the interactional elements in the therapeutic situation. (See Aron 1996, for an elaboration of the distinction between one and two-person psychologies.)

The story Dr. Levounis tells, by its very title, "Gay Patient–Gay Therapist," immediately directs our attention to a two-person perspective for understanding the therapeutic narrative which is to unfold. By highlighting the fact that this particular therapist and patient both identify as gay men, the narrator is telling us that this configuration carries some importance and will impact, if not shape, the story which unfolds. For many of us, the existence of psychotherapeutic dyads in which both members identify as gay or lesbian is so commonplace that we often take them for granted. But therapeutic dyads in which both members openly identify as gay or lesbian are a relatively recent phenomena in the history of psychoanalysis. This parallels a cultural shift which has resulted in the "coming out" and "letting in" of lesbian and gay psychoanalysts into mainstream analytic institutes, and the more open expression of experience-near analytic subjectivities which emanate from these positions.

Still, in mainstream psychoanalytic circles, the gay male psychotherapeutic dyad is often quietly, or not so quietly, regarded with a degree of skepticism or ambivalence. Consider, for example, a recent Psychoanalytic Broadcast (PsyBc) Internet discussion on homosexuality in which a prominent female psychoanalyst questioned the reasons a gay male patient would choose a therapist whose sexual orientation was known to be gay. She wondered what complicity such a hypothetical gay patient might be seeking to establish with a gay male therapist; what difficult issues such a choice might allow the patient to avoid. This question speaks to the mistrust of what goes on in psychoanalytic work when both therapist and patient are gay. It also implies a coherent distinction between gay and straight therapists, suggesting that the gay male patient who chooses a therapist of the same sexual orientation will have a therapeutic experience which is essentially different from the experience with a heterosexually identified therapist.

The subject of the gay male psychotherapeutic dyad relates directly to two major issues in contemporary psychoanalytic discourse. First, it calls forth the essentialist/constructivist debate regarding gender and sexuality: does being a heterosexual or homosexual therapist define a type of therapist? Second, it relates to the more general controversy concerning the use of the therapist's self disclosures in psychotherapeutic treatment. When a gay therapist reveals his sexual orientation to a patient, how might this disclosure influence the evolving intersubjectivity between them? These are complex questions and there are certainly no generic answers. I don't believe there is a gay male analytic subjectivity which can be distinguished from those analytic subjectivities which stem from straight male analysts. It does seem to me, however, both reasonable and relevant to ask how aspects of a gay therapist's subjectivity which emanate from his sexual identity, and its disclosure or non-disclosure in the treatment, might influence the life of the dyad.

In considering the treatment Dr. Levounis describes, it is important to recognize that this is a story about a gay male dyad in which the therapist does not disclose his sexual orientation to his patient. By calling attention to this fact, I do not mean to suggest that this is necessarily wrong or problematic, but that it must be understood as inherently relevant when we consider this treatment. There are, no doubt, many possible reasons for this particular asymmetry: The patient, to our knowledge, did not request a gay male therapist. It is not clear whether or not Dr. Levounis felt a pull from Stephen to reveal this information to him. We do not know if he actually considered the impact of disclosing or not disclosing this information to his patient, and in what ways each alternative might have felt useful or detrimental to the treatment. We do not know if Dr. Levounis is generally "out" within his training program, or whether he would feel comfortable with his patient knowing his sexual orientation. Whatever the case may be, in considering this particular gay male dyad, we need to ponder the way in which this asymmetry may have influenced the intersubjectivity between Stephen and Dr. Levounis, especially since a main theme in this narrative concerns the emergence of the patient's erotic desire for his therapist.

The gay therapist who works with a gay patient in a context in which he does not disclose his sexual orientation (for what may be sound therapeutic reasons) must often endure particular psychic pressures which result from this decision. For the gay or lesbian therapist, emotional issues surrounding the disclosure of sexual orientation in the therapeutic setting are very complex. As therapists who are gay and lesbian, we all bring a history of having had to hide our sexual orientation at some point in our lives, whether past or present, to avoid ridicule, harassment, or pain. The specific histories of our having had to sidestep questions about our sexuality, or even lie about it and our feelings about these events, come into play both consciously and unconsciously when we grapple with issues concerning the disclosure of our sexual orientation to our patients.

Sometimes gay therapists have a strong desire to come out to their gay patients. It can be painful to a gay therapist, who perhaps has had to spend significant parts of his life mastering deception in the interest of survival, to withhold information about his sexual orientation when offering that information would seem to be welcomed by the patient and promote an increased feeling of commonality and mutuality. This may be a useful disclosure for some gay patients whose developmental experience is marked by an aloneness and isolation in dealing with their homosexual identity. The gay therapist may feel vicariously identified with his gay patient, who wishes for a closer or shared commonality with his therapist, sometimes as an aspect of more complicated transference wishes. At the same time, the therapist may worry that his coming out to his gay patient may actually excite transference longings, and he worries about promoting desire in the patient through such a disclosure.

The therapist who knows something about the gay patient's experience, firsthand, is bound to convey his understanding of that experience in a way that is different from the therapist who does not, and the patient will feel that difference. The patient may experience, intersubjectively, the therapist's homosexual self and be faced once again with the sense of a secret about sexual identity that is present and yet hidden. At times, the gay therapist may rightly worry that his failure to disclose his sexuality in a treatment with a gay patient will be interpreted by the patient as the therapist's discomfort or shame regarding his sexuality, thereby reinforcing similar feelings in the patient. Occasionally, the therapist can feel a form of countertransference guilt when he senses that his patient intersubjectively experiences him as gay, but stays far away from the subject because the patient believes the therapist wishes to remain hidden. Sometimes the therapist may relate in a more distant way to the patient's material in order not to reveal his own sexual orientation.

My point is not to suggest that gay and lesbian therapists should or should not disclose their sexual orientation to their patients. Decisions of this kind, if they are to be meaningful, require that we grapple with them in the context of specific treatment situations. But it is important to recognize that issues of disclosure regarding one's sexual orientation are powerfully loaded for both gay therapists and their patients, and we need to problematize these matters sufficiently in order to grapple with them. Too often, experience-distant supervisors fail to understand the complexity of these dynamics in the emotional experience of a gay psychotherapeutic dyad, and therefore fail to adequately engage their supervisees' subjectivity when discussing how to proceed with issues around these particular kinds of disclosure. Sometimes the gay therapist in training may feel caught between what he interprets to be a "correct" or prescribed analytic stance and his intersubjective knowledge that failure to address his sexual orientation with the patient in some form can result in the treatment becoming bogged down.

It is hard to know how Dr. Levounis actually felt about not disclosing his sexual orientation to Stephen because the story of this treatment is told primarily from a one-person psychological perspective in which the focus is fundamentally on the patient. It is not the case that Dr. Levounis is insensitive to his impact on Stephen. He is clearly concerned, for example, with the interactional exchanges which take place between the two of them outside of the sessions and how Stephen may have experienced them. For the most part, however, we are left to imagine how Stephen affected Dr. Levounis. What is missing from this narrative is an elaboration of the therapist's own subjective experience in response to Stephen; the vicissitudes of his thoughts and feelings in relation to his patient, and a fuller consideration of the intersubjective influence both members of the dyad had on each other. In the absence of Dr. Levounis's own first-hand account of his subjectivity, I want to imagine what his experience might have been in relation to certain aspects of the story he tells. Here I am not so much concerned with whether or not I am accurately reflecting his particular subjectivity, as I am with creating a vehicle for discussing, more generally, aspects of subjectivity that are often present, in one form or another, in the emotional matrix between gay male therapist and gay male patient.

An interesting aspect of this treatment is that its most emotionally evocative moments, at least for Dr. Levounis, seem to occur in the encounters which take place outside of the sessions. The emotional life of this dyad, from his perspective, would seem to leave much to be desired. He alludes to the controlled, intellectual style that characterized his patient's discourse, and tells us that he was struck by Stephen's general absence of affect. He reports that he felt he could have been absent from the room without it causing any significant change in the treatment process. I imagine that he felt emotionally cut off from Stephen and somewhat frustrated in his efforts to help him be more emotionally present in the sessions. If this formulation is correct, then there is reason to suggest that it was Dr. Levounis's general understanding of Stephen's circumstance and not an actual feeling of connectedness between them that enabled Dr. Levounis to create a safe, steady, and minimally intrusive holding environment in which Stephen could begin to regain his footing.

I find myself understanding the first encounter at the gym, in which Dr. Levounis mistakenly touches Stephen, as an unconscious enactment on his part. I imagine that Dr. Levounis felt, at once, distanced by Stephen and at the same time moved by his patient's circumstance, and had a desire to reach out to him—to "touch" him, if you will—but could not find a way to do so within the emotional climate of the sessions themselves. I imagine he needed not to recognize his patient in order to give himself permission to concertize this desire and to communicate with Stephen in this different mode. This enactment functioned, then, as do all enactments: to communicate feelings which have no other available means of expression. I suspect that Dr. Levounis's touch was probably beneficial to this treatment and communicated a warmth and affection that was helpful and reassuring given Stephen's vulnerability at the time. Although Dr. Levounis does not detail his own emotional experience surrounding this enactment, it is clear that he felt thrown off by it and anxious. My own conjecture about the nature of his anxiety leads me in several directions. I wonder if issues regarding the disclosure of his sexuality contributed to Dr. Levounis's upset. Could his anxiety signal some concern that his patient will realize he is gay? Does this enactment reflect a wish that his patient know he is gay? Does his anxiety stem from his discomfort about revealing any expression of desire or feeling for his patient whatsoever? I suspect that Dr. Levounis's concern that Stephen would experience his behavior as sexually provocative reflects the possibility that he felt sexually attracted to Stephen and worried that he had communicated this to him. Whatever the case, the problem in this treatment is not in the enactment itself, but in the difficulty this dyad experiences in talking about it and other emotionally laden experiences.

The gay therapist's countertransference concerning his erotic feelings for patients is an unexplored aspect of the intersubjective experience between the gay therapist and patient. While it is generally understood that erotic countertransference of any nature may cause anxiety for the therapist (Gabbard and Lester 1995), I want to suggest that the gay therapist may be more likely to experience particular constellations of feeling in response to sexual attraction for his gay patients. Friedman (1998), a gay-identified analyst, for example, in discussing the erotic transference and countertransference in his work with a gay male patient, wonders, in relation to his having participated in flirtatious enactments with his patient, if his anxiety has to do with revealing a homosexual erotic countertransference, or if it has to do with revealing *any* homosexual feelings at all. He wonders if this would all feel different if he were a heterosexual male analyst and his patient were heterosexual and female. While Friedman is specifically addressing his anxiety in connection with revealing a homosexual erotic countertransference at a meeting of the Boston Psychoanalytic Institute, where he is the second of two openly gay candidates ever to have been admitted for training, it seems to me he is also addressing a more general issue.

As Morrison (1998) points out, lustful feelings of a male therapist toward a female patient are regarded as acceptable, perhaps even inevitable, aspects of the analyst's countertransference, and the emphasis in the literature is on maintaining appropriate boundaries with regard to such feelings. There is no analogous discussion of erotic countertransference in the context of same-sex desire which could provide a holding environment for the therapist who experiences lustful feelings toward his male patients. I think gay male therapists may be more vulnerable to feeling shame and guilt in response to their erotic countertransferences, and gay male patients often mirror this anxiety by defending against an elaboration of their own erotic transference feelings in the treatment. This can sometimes lead to gridlock in the emotional engagement between gay therapist and gay patient.

In a heterosexist and homophobic culture, if there is anything universal in the experience of gay men and women, it is the centrality of shame as an aspect of their lived experience. Shame, in this sense, is understood to be not a sometimes pathological concomitant in the formation of a gay or lesbian identity, but an inevitable experience for gay people (D'Ercole 1998). A central aspect of therapeutic work with gay patients, then, needs to include the identification and working through of that shame so that gay patients are able to conduct within themselves psychic negotiations between their shame and their desire (Frommer 1994). This often involves uncovering early developmental experiences in which the gay patient was shamed by peers and parents due to his own gender nonconformity. Early feelings of desire for other boys and men, including the boy's father, and the real or imagined rejection by them, are often powerful ingredients in this weave of shame with desire.

Gay men often evidence defenses in their early transference manifestations with male therapists which are designed to protect themselves from reliving these feelings in the treatment. These defenses may take many forms. Corbett (1993), for example, discusses early transferences which are characterized by the gay man's defensive detachment, withdrawal, and alienation, and understands them to be an effort to avoid repudiation from the analyst who is unconsciously experienced as the patient's father. Lewes (1998) discusses defensive stances in the transference with gay men which involve a prickliness and disdain for the analyst, in which the gay patient projects his own desire onto the analyst, accuses the analyst of desiring him, and then enacts the feared repudiation by relating to the analyst with contempt. No matter what the particular manifestations, the analysis of these transferences requires the therapist to find a way to engage the patient's defenses and not be put off by them. In my experience, when the therapist is successful at engaging the patient in an examination of his defenses surrounding emotional engagement with the therapist, the erotic transference and associated countertransferences are often liberated.

The therapist's own same-sex erotic countertransference may reevoke for him feelings which include shame and guilt, even though these very same feelings may have reached a successful resolution in the therapist's personal life. Erotic countertransference in the gay dyad often revolves around a father/son emotional matrix that complements the patient's transference. The therapist (as father) may experience his lust for his patient as incestuous and therefore illicit, and/or the therapist (as son) may fear his patient's repudiation were he to sense the therapist's attraction for him. The potential for these transference/countertransference dynamics often make emotional engagement within the gay male dyad precarious, especially when erotic desire is present somewhere in the relationship. The therapist may take refuge in a particular version of an analytic stance which mirrors the patient's own detachment and withdrawal and renders him more remote than is beneficial for the treatment. The therapist, as transference father, may wind up inadvertently repeating with the patient what happened between the patient and his father early on, creating a relationship that is perhaps respectful but stiff and defensively boundaried. The gay therapist may worry that his efforts to engage his gay patient's emotional distance or defensive detachment will be experienced by the patient as an effort to seduce him. This appears to be Dr. Levounis's concern when he considers the impact of touching his patient in the gym, and I imagine that what occurs in the sessions between them, after discovering each other naked in the showers, is also related to their mutual anxiety about the presence of desire in their relationship.

It is easy to immediately empathize with Dr. Levounis's anxiety regarding this event, and his worry that the treatment will somehow be strongly affected by it. Therapists, like their patients, wish to have control over what parts of themselves they wind up revealing and this powerful moment of mutual exposure embodies, on a manifest level, an inadvertent loss of control in what each chooses to show. But I want to question the accidental nature of this event and to ponder what unconscious meanings this encounter may hold for each of them. I wonder why Dr. Levounis worries that the treatment will be destroyed by this encounter. What does this encounter contain that neither therapist nor patient can consciously tolerate knowing in this relationship? I suspect it has to do with the mutual recognition of their desire for each other.

On some level, both Stephen and his therapist knew that a chance meeting with their clothes off was a real possibility from the time it became evident that they attended the same gym. Neither one of them made the decision to avoid going to the gym or brought up for discussion how or whether they should negotiate their comings and goings to avoid such a meeting. There is strong mutuality in their encountering each other naked, and there may also be a mutual unconscious collusion in their not having discussed their thoughts and feelings about sharing the same gym and the intimacies that might emanate from this fact. In this sense, this meeting has the flavor of an unconscious enactment. When Dr. Levounis inquires into Stephen's feelings about their encountering one another naked in the shower, Stephen's response is rather telling. He plays down the importance of this event, reassuring his therapist that it was "not of great concern to him," and goes on to other issues, but comments in passing that "it was inevitable," which seems to be a way of stating that at least in Stephen's mind, they both knew this was likely to happen. Although we have no way of knowing what took place in the actual interchange between Stephen and Dr. Levouis during the discussion of this encounter, I imagine that Stephen's detached, blasé attitude in speaking about this event mirrors his experience of his therapist, who asks for Stephen's thoughts and feelings, but fails to reveal any of his own.

In the following session, in connection with a dream, Stephen tells Dr. Levounis that

> The gym is a place with sexuality. Even more so for a gay person, seeing other men in various stages of undress. It is an erotically charged place and a pickup place, but it's not the type of interaction that interests me. I am not interested in one-night stands. I find the idea morally uncomfortable, but the fantasy is very attractive. I can imagine meeting someone for anonymous sex, and having very limited emotional engagement, but this is not my favorite fantasy.

When Dr. Levounis asks Stephen about his favorite fantasy, Stephen speaks of the student/teacher fantasy, but quickly (and defensively) locates himself in the role of the teacher. I understand Stephen's communications here to be layered with multiple meanings. Certainly, like Dr. Levounis, I understand Stephen to be voicing both a desire for his therapist and a fear about those feelings, but I also think that there are questions implicit in Stephen's statements. I imagine Stephen is wondering what locker rooms are like for his therapist, and if Dr. Levounis knows how Stephen feels when he's in one. I suspect Stephen would like to say, "Am I the only one in this room who experiences locker rooms this way?" I also suspect that Stephen wonders if his therapist finds him attractive, but all of this seems, at best, hidden and absorbed within Stephen's statements about himself. He does not engage his therapist in such an inquiry. One might conclude that Stephen is not ready to consciously formulate these questions to himself or to his therapist and that it is the therapist's job to maintain a holding environment in which Stephen is allowed to bring such questions into the room at his own pace. But it may be the case, as I suggest, that he already has, and that Stephen's statements require a more active emotional engagement by the therapist to help Stephen contact his own feelings and say what is on his mind. The therapist's own willingness to have emotional reactions to this occurrence—to demonstrate some disequilibrium, if nothing else—might have given Stephen more permission to be less neutral in relation to his own feelings. The therapist might have said to Stephen, "I wonder if you're wondering if the gym is a sexually charged place for me?"

We can, of course, only pose such questions comfortably to patients if we feel able to negotiate their responses. Posing such a question to Stephen might very well lead to a more direct inquiry by Stephen into Dr. Levounis's sexual desires and this might feel too dangerous, unless the therapist had some sense that he had choices about how to respond to Stephen's questions, and felt able to manage his own anxiety about the discussion proceeding in this direction. I wonder if Stephen's voicing vague dissatisfaction with therapy around this time might have been a way of voicing resentment that Dr. Levounis repeatedly requested Stephen's feelings in the treatment, while he adopted an analytic neutrality which suggested to Stephen that either his therapist was not emotionally affected by what had taken place between them or was hiding behind a particular therapeutic posture. In either case, this might unconsciously mean to Stephen that in order to maintain his therapist's respect and positive regard he needed to once again behave in a manner that mirrored his experience with his emotionally constricted and detached father. The therapist's emotional containment could thus serve to reinforce the patient's emotional constriction around his own desire and shame.

From a two-person psychotherapeutic perspective, the therapeutic relationship and the transference are always contributed to mutually by both participants in the interaction. The therapist's responsiveness becomes a primary vehicle for emotional growth and therapeutic movement within the dyad. Therapeutic action is dependent on the therapist's ability to somehow use his subjectivity in a measured way that ultimately allows him to emotionally engage with the patient in a manner that creates new experience. Often, this process first consists of repeating what has been, before new emotional ground can be broken. Although every therapeutic dyad is unique, I've tried to address certain intersubjective possibilities in the gay male dyad that create particular challenges to emotional engagement. In this sense, these are the very same challenges that gay men so often face in their lives apart from the therapeutic situation: how to allow themselves to need, love, and sexually desire another man in a context that allows for mutuality and a full range of emotional experience. It is in this sense that the gay male psychotherapeutic dyad offers the gay patient a unique opportunity to work toward these goals.

It is sad that Dr. Levournis and his patient had to part so soon. What has been reported to us is the beginning phase of a treatment which had clearly taken hold. There is no doubt that this treatment gave Stephen the "jump start" he was needing, but his dream about the long, two-hour trip was his way, I believe, of telling Dr. Levounis how much he still needed and wanted to continue this journey with him.

## REFERENCES

Aron, L. (1996), *A Meeting of Minds: Mutuality in Psychoanalysis.* Hillsdale, NJ: The Analytic Press.

Corbett, K. (1993), The mystery of homosexuality. *Psychoanalytic Psychology,* 10:345-357.

D'Ercole, A. (1998), *Psychoanalysis and Lesbians: Shame, Shame, Everyone Knows Your Name.* Paper presented at the American Academy of Psychoanalysis, 41st Winter Meeting, New York.

Friedman, C. (1998), Eros in a gay dyad: A case presentation. *Gender and Psychoanalysis,* 3:335-346.

Frommer, M.S. (1994), Homosexuality and psychoanalysis: Technical considerations revisited. *Psychoanalytic Dialogues,* 4:215-233.

Gabbard, G. and Lester, E. (1995), *Boundaries and Boundary Violations in Psychoanalysis.* New York: Basic Books.

Lewes, K. (1998), A special Oedipal mechanism in the development of male homosexuality. *Psychoanalytic Psychology,* 15:341-359.

Morrison, A. (1998), Discussion: Eros in a gay dyad. *Gender and Psychoanalysis,* 3:355-360.

## Chapter 6

# Dream a Little Dream of Me:
# A Case Discussion

### Jack Drescher

I wish to thank Dr. Levounis for inviting me to discuss this patient and for his openness in describing some difficult issues that came up in that treatment. Dr. Levounis chose to title his presentation "Gay Patient–Gay Therapist." In framing it this way, his presentation raises several issues that include the patient's sexual identity, the therapist's sexual identity, and the potential interplay of those identities in a therapeutic encounter. But a caveat is in order here. Doing psychotherapy with a gay patient is never just about psychotherapy with a gay patient.

Freud, for example, used cultural beliefs about homosexuality in his psychoanalytic discourse as a way to illustrate the concepts of innate bisexuality and libido (1905, 1920), projection and paranoia (1911, 1923), and narcissism (1910, 1914). Similarly, psychotherapeutic work with gay men today also raises many issues, some of which are being contentiously debated in many quarters of the modern psychotherapeutic world. These include the nature of psychoanalytic epistemology (Gill, 1994); essentialism versus social constructivism (Stein, 1998); questions regarding the meaning or even the very existence of analytic neutrality; the discovery of meaning versus the creation of meaning (Spence, 1982); the function of personal morality in clinical practice and the influence of the therapist's beliefs on the conduct and outcome of a psychotherapy (Marmor, 1998); the primacy of the Oedipus complex (Drescher, 1998); the meaning of a developmental line (Coates, 1997); the nature of the unconscious and the uses of countertransference (Bollas, 1987); therapist self-revelation; and the psychoanalytic understanding of dreams and affects (Spezzano, 1993). Dr. Levounis's presentation touches upon all these issues.

It should be underscored that a gay patient's concerns may be, and often are, indistinguishable from the issues that other patients bring to their therapists. All patients may talk about their emotional stress, relationship difficulties, or coming to terms with a physical illness. And although an understanding of a gay patient's sexual identity will certainly be an important issue across the course of his treatment, it will not be the only subject talked about in therapy. It was certainly not the only thing Dr. Levounis and Stephen talked about in their work together. Nevertheless, a man's gay identity will always be linked to his multiple identities of child, parent, sibling, professional, student, patient, or citizen, just to name a few (Bromberg, 1994). So although a patient's gay identity is not necessarily the primary focus of treatment in many cases, its impact upon the course of treatment cannot be overlooked nor easily separated out from his other concerns. My own clinical experience has been that a small fraction of the therapeutic time may be devoted to discussing issues related to being gay (Drescher, 1998). But having said that, there are variables. A patient deeply engrossed in coming out will be highly focused on his gay identity for much of the time. Another patient, who may have been out for a long time, perhaps less so. Therefore, it is not always possible to separate things out into neat percentages.

So what about this treatment which began after the patient returned to school following a serious and protracted illness? The first question that ran through my mind when I heard this was "What took him so long?" We heard Stephen came close to losing his life "several times" during the year he was ill, and that he also underwent multiple surgeries, including a colostomy, which was likely to have been experienced as a severe violation of his bodily integrity. Furthermore, he had a psychotic, manic episode, ostensibly due to the steroids he was taking while he was physically ill. Then, following that harrowing year, he returned to school after being told that there was a 60 percent chance that his illness had remitted. Although 60 percent might sound good to some, how did that sound to him? After all, Stephen had seen other patients sicken and perhaps die in the hospital ward where he was treated, and he was bald from the chemotherapy he was undergoing by the time he finally sought psychotherapy. So I imagine that Stephen must have used all the inner resources he could muster in order to survive this ordeal. Given the extent of trauma he described, the enormous resources he brought to bear should not be underestimated. But having survived, and then feeling that he was somewhat recovered, perhaps he felt he had no more inner reserves and so he entered treatment.

When someone waits this long to enter treatment, I also begin to wonder about the strength and nature of his premorbid character defenses and how well they served him in the past. We were told that Stephen dressed and came across as an intellectual. He also began his early sessions in an intellectualizing and detached way. His demeanor, probably cultivated as a defense, was of one who had "the air of a college professor at work." The defensive use of detachment was noted by Dr. Levounis during the initial sessions. As Stephen became more comfortable, he became more revealing. Whether this detachment preceded his illness is unclear, but it is possible that it was a long-standing character style. After all, he remembered his parents' divorce, when he was ten years old, as an unemotional "nonevent."

Sullivan's (1956) ideas about dissociation provide one way to think about emotional detachment. He envisioned a continuum of dissociative phenomena that began with selective inattention. According to Sullivan, "Selective inattention is the classic means by which we do not profit from experience" (p. 50). Or as Stern (1995) put it, "selective inattention performs the function of preserving the separation of the dissociated experience by preventing attention being paid to anything that would tend to bring that dissociated material closer to awareness . . . it screens experience rather than actively deleting it" (p. 122). Selective inattention is a normal defensive operation that makes life more manageable, analogous to tuning out the background noise on a busy street. However, in certain situations, and particularly when feelings are unacceptable in an interpersonal context, dissociative phenomena can be much more severe. In my own psychotherapeutic work with gay men, I have found that the normal need to tune things out is quite strained, and that dissociative detachment from their feelings is often quite common. Transparency, invisibility, losing one's voice, being stuck behind walls or other barriers, are some of the terms used to describe the subjective experience of dissociative detachment. However, I also think of dissociation as an adaptive experience that arises from the need to hide one's sexual feelings, both from oneself as well as from others. Colloquially, this need to hide is sometimes referred to as "being in the closet." However, this popular, cultural expression does not fully capture the wide range of interpersonal and intrapsychic maneuvering used to keep unwanted feelings out of consciousness.

From an intrapsychic perspective, a gay man may be closeted to himself. This is captured in a repeated refrain among many gay men who report, "I always knew I was gay, but I didn't want to admit it to myself." Being able to reveal one's sexual identity only in certain contexts while having to hide it in others can foster dissociative splits in everyday life. The splitting of one's identity, either subjectively or interpersonally, is referred to as multiple presentations of the self. Although splitting of the self can be adaptive, when dissociative activities are intensified in response to traumatic events, they may prevent a gay man from paying full attention to all of the consequences of his hiding activities. The closeted gay man may go to great lengths to prevent himself, and others, from knowing who he is. So if I were to hypothesize Stephen's motive for entering treatment when he did, perhaps his capacity to ward off his feelings had been strained to the limit and his defenses had broken down. Humpty Dumpty had a great fall and was consequently beginning to see pieces of both himself and his world that he was not quite prepared to see.

As he entered treatment, Stephen appeared to be a bright and cultured young man. These were traits that were probably very gratifying to him and something he didn't mind showing people. Winnicott (1965) might have called this a compliant false-self presentation. Furthermore, not only was Stephen familiar with a popularized version of psychoanalytic theory regarding the origins of homosexuality, he obligingly provided his therapist with the requisite cast of characters in his psychoanalytic morality play (Freud, 1910). He described his family as a "classical Freudian constellation with an overbearing mother and an absent father." He said his father was intrusive, perhaps sadistic, and with a poor sense of boundaries. His mother had high artistic aspirations, both for herself and for the patient, but she was a "failed artist." She was apparently also a social failure who married beneath her station. She was self-centered and manipulative. In other words, Stephen presented himself to his therapist as a perfectly average "homosexual," at least by some psychoanalytic standards (Bieber et al., 1962).

Although some might say "This family constellation was the cause of the patient's homosexuality," we do not know what causes homosexuality, or even heterosexuality for that matter. I have yet to be convinced that two people talking to each other in a therapist's office will ever discover the cause of anybody's sexual orientation. However, I do believe that a therapist and patient can together discover what homosexuality means, either to the patient or to his therapist, and possibly to the patient's family and social milieu. So I contend that what Stephen was initially telling Dr. Levounis was that he already had a theory of etiology which he was using to make sense of his own homosexuality. That is to say, Stephen entered treatment believing he was gay because of inadequate or bad parenting.

I call Stephen's narrative of "an overbearing mother and an absent father" a theory of pathology. Blaming parents for causing homosexuality is a routine enterprise in the general culture. Consequently, it is also an etiological belief that is rather common among many gay men and women. Some patients appear to derive comfort from narratives like these, in which the explanations for their own homosexuality are embedded in their (dysfunctional) family dynamics.

I would argue that it is an important piece of clinical information when a patient adopts a pathological, etiological theory of homosexuality to make sense of his feelings and his life experience. What does it mean if a gay man believes such a theory? How does his etiological theory resonate with the way he thinks about himself and about his sexual identity? The answers may lie in the clinical material. In Stephen's case, he believed there was something wrong with him because he was gay. That is how I heard the morality tale he told about his early gay relationship with Victor. Victor treated Stephen in a humiliating way when he had public sex with his girlfriend. Victor and his fiancée having "loud sex to everybody else's amusement" could be understood as an interpersonal maneuver of a closeted, gay man trying to hide his homosexuality. For a closeted man like Victor, heterosexuality was something to be flaunted, while homosexuality, embodied in his relationship with Stephen, was to be treated in a secretive and shameful manner. Stephen, in participating in that relationship, accepted, believed, and participated in that meaning of homosexuality as well.

Stephen's other feelings about being gay could also be heard as he described his coming out experiences to his family members. When listening to coming out stories, I assume, as a matter of course, that the patient is usually talking about some of his own feelings about being gay. The gay man who is coming out and struggling to define his gay identity can only do so by coming to terms with a wide range of accepting and rejecting internalizations, identifications, and introjects. When Stephen wrote to tell his father that he was gay, his father wrote back: "That's not what I would want. I have gay friends in the service, but it's different when it's your son. But that doesn't change the way I feel about you." The father seemed to be saying that "Homosexuality might be fine for other people, and I can even accept it in my friends, but I don't really want it in my family." The paternal denial of any change in feelings suggests that Stephen learned some of his defensive maneuvers from his father. Despite his father's assurances that being gay was not a problem, Stephen understood that coming out did change the way his father thought about him. And because Stephen was bound to share his father's feelings, their epistolary interaction also affected the way Stephen thought about himself. He thought the money his father sent in the letter was offered out of "guilt for the paternal estrangement." Stephen held his parents culpable for creating a homosexual son. In refusing to spend his father's money, Stephen refused to accept reparations for his father's hypothetical role in causing his homosexuality. And in doing so, not only did he keep his own internalized, unaccepting father at bay, he also kept it in a tenuous relationship with his budding gay identity.

When Stephen came out to his mother at age eighteen, this was also not greeted with much enthusiasm. She experienced a "nervous breakdown" and locked herself in her room. Stephen believed she then maneuvered him into therapy. We do not know if that therapy was an attempt to get him to change his sexual identity. Perhaps it was the place where he learned the psychoanalytic theory regarding family constellations presumed to cause homosexuality, but in telling this coming out story, Stephen was telling Dr. Levounis that he also associated being gay with psychiatric illness. Szasz (1974) has articulately illustrated how some of our modern mental illnesses serve as substitutive metaphors for religious sins. Such an association emerged when Stephen had a manic, psychotic episode while on steroids. While psychotic, Stephen had to "renounce the sin that I was gay through a cleansing ritual." Being gay, is, of course, not only unclean, but as we know from Leviticus, being gay is also an abomination. And many abominations are punishable by death, and sometimes these deaths are ordained by divine retribution. The antisexual gods are vengeful indeed. Just as many gay men with HIV report feeling that AIDS was a punishment from God for being gay, many patients with other, severe medical illnesses also see their conditions as punishment for previous sins. Stephen repeatedly tested for HIV, but was skeptical about his negative results and called it "a mark that would always be there." A mark? The mark of the Cain? It is not altogether unlikely that Stephen believed his life-threatening illness was a punishment for being gay.

Religious ideas about homosexuality, of course, draw our attention to the third family player in Stephen's drama about the meaning of being gay. His sister, who regularly appears in his dreams, is now a religious fundamentalist. She herself had undergone a conversion. She not only disapproved of homosexuality, she "relentlessly preaches and prays for her brother's conversion to heterosexuality." Although we only hear a brief mention of it in Dr. Levounis's presentation, I would not be surprised if Stephen had, and is still having, an intense struggle with his own religious beliefs. In fact, one way he could have tried to shore up his gay identity before he became ill was by dissociating from internalized beliefs and values that judged his homosexuality harshly. This may have created a problem, however, for those beliefs may have helped him maintain his equilibrium during the horrific period of his illness. It is worth noting that a patient's internalized religious beliefs are rarely limited to the condemnation of homosexuality. They often include moral and ethical beliefs, as well as hope and faith that may be integral to the adaptive functioning of the adult personality. Stephen could not unilaterally rid himself of religious self-condemnation without severing his attachments to other important identifications.

Now, although there are other themes that I might touch upon related to Stephen's gay identity, I will at this point move on to the course of treatment. Stephen, an extremely obliging patient, was very cooperative in bringing dreams to his therapist. He reported his first dream in the third session. That initial dream tells us something about Stephen's state of mind when he began treatment. He was lost in staircases and elevators with his sister, "in the context of danger." Note that his sister, previously described as critically unaccepting of him, was there with him throughout the ordeal. He was in a zoo that became the hospital in which he had been treated for his life-threatening illness. Is a hospital a zoo? It might seem that way to a sick and worried patient. The hospital became like a Nazi-run institution. What is the subjective experience of a patient being treated for a life-threatening illness? Do invasive tests and procedures feel like torture? Stephen was reading Sylvia Plath in the dream. We do not hear his associations to Sylvia Plath, but mine, of course, run to suicide. Yet Stephen did not find this to be a scary dream, illustrating how detached he was from his feelings. This might also be interpreted as bravery under fire, for how else could he get through such an ordeal if not by remaining detached? He got through his illness by forging ahead and only when he was out of harm's way did he feel the danger to which he had been exposed. This dream was a sign that the treatment was getting off to a good start.

Shortly afterward, Stephen met his therapist in the university gymnasium. Dr. Levounis, a very gregarious fellow, greeted his patient before he knew who he was. In fact, because he didn't immediately realize it was his patient he was greeting, Dr. Levounis treated the whole matter in a rather unselfconscious way. Shortly after the meeting, they had their first session in a month and Stephen again brought in a dream. He was being poisoned by Richard Burton and Liz Taylor in the roles of both Edward Albee's George and Martha as well as Stephen's uncle and aunt. We see the Kleinian symbols of paranoia, splitting, poisonous envy, and ambivalence (Segal, 1974). Once again, he had brought his sister with him to the hospital and, once again, they were on a roller-coaster ride. Although he claimed to have lost his religious faith, perhaps Stephen was just not in touch with it, like so many other things from which he had detached himself. The images of being poisoned by relatives in the hospital raised the question of whether doctors were his friends or foe. He trusted his doctor back home, but didn't feel he knew his doctors in New York well enough. Stephen himself identified this as "an issue of intimacy and trust." He might also have been asking if his new therapist, Dr. Levounis, was a friend or foe. How was the patient to interpret that friendly greeting he got in the gym? After all, people who feel they have been treated badly early in life may often have difficulty distinguishing a friendly gesture from a harmful one (Sullivan, 1953).

Dr. Levounis says he didn't want to get into the sexually charged and uncomfortable topic of his extra-therapeutic encounter with the patient. Perhaps sexuality was an issue at that moment, but perhaps more so for Dr. Levounis than for Stephen. I would speculate that Dr. Levounis might have also been tempted to get away from some of the same feelings that Stephen was trying to get away from. These would include a loss of control, humiliation, passivity, learned helplessness, and fear of death. Discretion may have proven to be the better part of valor. Dr. Levounis assumed that they already had too much on their plate and the issue of sexual feelings between the patient and his therapist were going to have to wait.

Apparently, they were not going to wait too long. They met again in the gym, this time both of them naked in the showers. As Dr. Levounis put it, it was a resident's "dreaded nightmare." Certainly, to be seen as one really is, naked and stripped of all pretense, could be imagined as undermining one's professional authority. Budding therapists often wish to believe that they can remain opaque to and unseen by their patients. Interestingly, Dr. Levounis's countertransferential response was fear. What if the therapist's countertransference is also a signal from and about the patient (Racker, 1968)? Stephen, during his illness, had recently been stripped of many of the comforting illusions with which he had gone through his life. Dr. Levounis wondered to himself what the other residents would say when they found out about this incident. What was he so worried about? For one, Stephen's feelings were getting too close for comfort. And just as we earlier heard Stephen's multiple selves articulated in the reported reactions of his family members, we also heard Dr. Levounis's countertransferential struggle to make sense of his treatment through the voices of his colleagues. Some of his colleagues said that this newfound intimacy was something to work through in treatment. Others believed it meant that the treatment was over. Dr. Levounis and his patient both appeared to be engaged in parallel, developmental struggles. Both of them, to different degrees, were trying to integrate their gay identities into the rest of their lives. Fortunately, this process went well for Dr. Levounis. Uncomfortable as all this made him, he took appropriate measures to sort out his feelings and thoughts with colleagues, with his supervisor, and one would like to imagine with his own therapist. In his efforts to sort out his own contradictory feelings, Dr. Levounis made a leap of faith and chose to listen to the voice of his supervisor, whom he described as an openly gay psychiatrist. This would be consistent with efforts to integrate his own gay, professional identity. The gay supervisor showed the gay resident that issues like these are best dealt with tactfully, but openly.

The patient, however, rather characteristically reported that seeing his naked therapist was not a problem. Dr. Levounis respected the patient's need to maintain a tight lid on his feelings about his therapist, but then Stephen brought in another dream, one that showed the ongoing development of the transference. Stephen dreamt that he got athlete's foot from the gym. He said, "But it wasn't ordinary athlete's foot; it was more like leprosy. There were horrible, crusty wounds covering my feet." He associated the gym with sexuality and disease. Are the scars to which Stephen points experienced as punishing stigmata for his own sexual feelings? Is this the aforementioned mark that will always be there? The association of his sexuality to disease again linked his feelings about his sexual identity to his bout with a life-threatening illness, but there was more than that expressed in this dream. Consider Stephen's choice of disease in that dream. "Athlete's foot" is an interesting affliction to acquire, particularly if one were an unathletic boy who envied the athletic prowess of others. One might say this symbolized a growing ambivalent attitude as he moved away from defensive splitting into a more obviously ambivalent relationship toward his illness, his sexual identity, and his therapist. His therapist? Well, everyone knows that the ancient Greeks, not to mention at least one modern one, were drawn to the gymnasium. And not only did the Greeks coin the term gymnasium, the Greek word *gymnos* means naked. Although Stephen seemed initially too self-involved to see Dr. Levounis for who he was, he was beginning to pay more attention to his therapist in an interesting, albeit indirect way. At that juncture, he could not directly talk about those feelings. Instead, he described his "favorite fantasy" of a student-teacher relationship. "How nice to have a little group of boys and not necessarily have to be in physical contact." Platonic love? Greek love? Or is the patient talking about another famous Greek altogether? And what exactly was the crime for which Socrates was given the poison with which he ended his own life?

It is around this time during the treatment, as Dr. Levounis openly talked about the possibility of feelings between the two of them, that things began to change, at least in Stephen's dreams. In his fourth reported dream, Stephen's sister reappeared, but this time she was more openly preaching, and he found her behavior embarrassing. This was a significant shift in the dreams, since previously the sister was just along for the ride and was experienced unambivalently as being on his side. As his ambivalence grew, Stephen felt conflicted about her. We move from hospitals to restaurants. Was someone being fed? However, as seen in the other dreams, there was still confusion, as when "the menus were all screwed up." Did he mean to say that he couldn't read them? That they were Greek to him? He had left his car headlights on and his battery had been drained. This is why he began therapy. He feels his own resources are depleted with little hope of replenishment, or as he put it "everybody around was in small VW bugs, and they did not have enough power to start my car." The patient, now in the dream role of Diogenes, finds "a man on foot" that looked like Dr. Levounis. Having received a charge from his therapist, Stephen expressed ambivalence about the impact of that help upon him. Beware of Greeks bearing gifts. With his newfound energy, Stephen will have to take a longer journey then he anticipated as he goes on with his life after the remission of his illness. Had he already lived longer than he initially thought he would? Was he ambivalent about having survived? As the AIDS epidemic has shown, some patients find it quite burdensome to go on living when they have already anticipated their premature death.

A series of dreams led to associations to what was referred to as "three categories" into which men fall "according to their sex appeal." These categories are actually a sexual hierarchy. Sexual hierarchies refer to the ordering of sexual desires and practices as better or worse in terms of some implicit or explicit value system (Drescher, 1998). When asked directly about where the Greeks stood in this hierarchy, the patient hedged. Earlier, Stephen had found the Dr. Levounis of his dreams a source of power, certainly much more powerful than those northern European VW bugs, but perhaps Stephen's love of the ancient Greeks did not fully extend to the modern ones. The relationship between those two cultures might also constitute a hierarchy. Stephen's dreams appear to exhibit the continuing, ambivalent transference relationship he was developing toward his therapist. His scolding sister became a scolding authority figure, embodied in the medical school professor. The helping guide was also the judging guide. This is all as it should be in the development of the therapeutic relationship. As his range of contradictory feelings became embodied in one therapist, the patient concurrently became more integrated. As Sullivan saw it, there was no self without the other. When Stephen began dating, he was still not entirely comfortable with his sexuality, but he was actively pursuing a gay identity. As he did so, he reported feeling better and his therapist saw him as better. His dreams, while still anxious, were more tolerable, that is to say, he could more easily identify his own feelings in them. Interestingly enough, this seemed to occur without any reported interpretations by Dr. Levounis. Perhaps that was merely an oversight, but if it was not, perhaps these changes were being brought about by the integrating effect of the transference alone. That is to say, perhaps the patient was having a transference cure. Now, to some analysts, such cures may be less than satisfactory. However, I believe that transference cures are the product of good therapeutic holding (Winnicott, 1986).

In his final reported dream, Stephen was once again at a picnic. He was not being poisoned as in the previous picnic dream. Instead, he was being fed. His therapist appeared again and Stephen noticed that Dr. Levounis is "good-looking." His therapist is going to leave soon and as the treatment is ending, the patient is beginning to pay more attention to his surroundings. However, having noticed his therapist, perhaps for the first time, Stephen chooses to leave the therapist in the dream, saying "Why do I have to wait for the end?" Perhaps he wants to leave his therapist before his therapist leaves him. In any event, it is more grist for the mill.

In conclusion, I imagine Stephen as a patient who was seeking a mentor. In fact, he desperately needed one. Mentor, in Greek mythology, was a friend of Odysseus, entrusted with the education of his son Telemachus. In Odysseus's absence, Mentor served as a substitute father. That, of course, is the essence of transference. Now, psychotherapy is not a mentoring process, but a therapist does enter the treatment relationship with his own values and some of them do get transmitted to the patient. These include values like reliability, self-reliance, intellectual honesty, emotional honesty, freedom of expression, a hard day's work, and the importance of play, imagination, and dreams. As you have already heard, these are just some of the things that Dr. Levounis values and they were expressed to this particular patient in this particular treatment. Although Dr. Levounis did not mentor the patient in the usual sense, he did show the patient something of value, and the patient came to value what he saw and experienced during the course of their work together. I have little doubt that this patient will make use of what he learned in his all-too-brief relationship with Dr. Levounis. For it is my sense that Dr. Levounis will remain both an important and helpful part of Stephen's pantheon of internalized objects.

# REFERENCES

Bieber, I., Dain, H., Dince, P., Drellich, M., Grand, H., Gundlach, R., Kremer, M., Rifkin, A., Wilbur, C., and Bieber, T. (1962), *Homosexuality: A Psychoanalytic Study.* New York: Basic Books.

Bollas, C. (1987), *The Shadow of the Object.* New York: Columbia University Press.

Bromberg, P. (1994), "Speak! that I may see you": Some reflections on dissociation, reality, and psychoanalytic listening. *Psychoanalytic Dialogues,* 4:517-547.

Coates, S. (1997), Is it time to jettison the concept of developmental lines? Commentary on de Marneffe's paper, "Bodies and Words." *Gender and Psychoanalysis,* 2(1):35-53.

Drescher, J. (1998), *Psychoanalytic Therapy and the Gay Man.* Hillsdale, NJ: The Analytic Press.

Freud, S. (1905), Three essays on the theory of sexuality. *Standard Edition,* 7:123-246. London: Hogarth Press, 1953.

Freud, S. (1910), Leonardo da Vinci and a memory of his childhood. *Standard Edition,* 11:59-138. London: Hogarth Press, 1957.

Freud, S. (1911), Psycho-analytic notes on an autobiographical account of a case of paranoia. *Standard Edition,* 12:1-82. London: Hogarth Press, 1958.

Freud, S. (1914), On narcissism: An introduction. *Standard Edition,* 14:73-102. London: Hogarth Press, 1957.

Freud, S. (1920), The psychogenesis of a case of homosexuality in a woman. *Standard Edition,* 18:221-232. London: Hogarth Press, 1955.

Freud, S. (1923), Some neurotic mechanisms in jealousy, paranoia and homosexuality. *Standard Edition,* 18:145-172. London: Hogarth Press, 1955.

Gill, M. M. (1994), *Psychoanalysis in Transition: A Personal View.* Hillsdale, NJ: The Analytic Press.

Marmor, J. (1998), Homosexuality: Is etiology really important? *Journal of Gay and Lesbian Psychotherapy,* 2(4):19-28.

Racker, H. (1968), *Transference and Countertransference.* Madison, CT: International Universities Press.

Segal, H. (1974), *Introduction to the Work of Melanie Klein,* Second Edition. New York: Basic Books.

Spence, D. (1982), *Narrative Truth and Historical Truth: Meaning and Interpretation in Psychoanalysis.* New York: W.W. Norton and Company.

Spezzano, C. (1993), *Affect in Psychoanalysis: A Clinical Synthesis.* Hillsdale, NJ: The Analytic Press.

Stein, T. (1998), Social constructionism and essentialism: Theoretical and clinical considerations relevant to psychotherapy. *Journal of Gay and Lesbian Psychotherapy,* 2(4):29-49.

Stern, D. B. (1995), Cognition and language. In *Handbook of Interpersonal Psychoanalysis,* M. Lionells, J. Fiscalini, C. Mann, and D. Stern (Eds.). Hillsdale, NJ: The Analytic Press, pp. 79-138.

Sullivan, H. S. (1953), *The Interpersonal Theory of Psychiatry.* New York: W.W. Norton and Company.

Sullivan, H. S. (1956), *Clinical Studies in Psychiatry.* New York: W.W. Norton and Company.

Szasz, T. (1974), *Ceremonial Chemistry.* New York: Anchor Books.

Winnicott, D. W. (1965), *The Maturational Processes and the Facilitating Environment.* New York: International Universities Press.

Winnicott, D. W. (1986), *Holding and Interpretation.* New York: Grove Press.

# SECTION II:
# EROTIC TRANSFERENCE/
# COUNTERTRANSFERENCE

Chapter 7

# On Lust and Loathing:
# Erotic Transference/Countertransference
# Between a Female Analyst
# and Female Patients

Florence Rosiello

There are certain analytic axioms that influence psychoanalytic treatment. One is the notion that only women can understand other women (Freud, 1920) and, in particular, that only women should analyze lesbians. With unintentional volition, we often make a referral after speculating if the patient will work better with a male or female colleague. Still, most of us in the psychoanalytic community hold to the belief that the analyst's gender makes no difference in treatment. Feminist influence has left us with the notion that differences as well as sameness exist between all patients and all analysts and these must be appreciated without pathologizing. The current trend in psychoanalysis is to understand that our differences can mean an openness to managing our own body experiences as well as our defensive constellations. These experiences and defenses are typically tinted by cultural and biologically based gender considerations when we work with patients. This makes a great deal of sense to me, since I have always wondered if a male analyst really understands the emotional swing and bloated body experience created by female hormones and the intense need to rip off any restricting clothing and eat whatever the hell you want when estrogen is low.

To my mind, there are very different issues that arise in treatment with the female patient by a female analyst. I am speaking about the particular dynamics that arise between same-sex gender dyads which may be nearly impossible to create in a male/female analytic frame. In this paper, I will discuss specific homoerotic transference/countertransference issues which arise between female patients and a female analyst.

In the past decade, escalating attention has been paid by relational analysts to the development and clinical implications of the erotic transference/countertransference in psychoanalytic treatment. For the purpose of this essay, erotic feelings are defined as all the patient's loving, sensual, and sexual desires toward the analyst, as well as aggressive resistances that defend against erotic feelings. Of course, in truly looking at the erotic transference from a position of mutuality, analysts consider and make therapeutic use of countertransference feelings aroused in them by their patients, as well as the analysts' own created emotions and subjective experiences. In this paper, I will present clinical material on the erotic transferences of three female patients, one who identifies as bisexual, another who identifies as heterosexual, and the third who identifies as lesbian. The focus of this paper, however, will be on the erotic countertransference since it is in the erotic countertransference arena that the erotic transference often gets bogged down or eliminated.

Lately, it appears that psychoanalytic literature on the erotic transference/countertransference has been written by female analysts, and they have mostly concentrated on erotic feelings between female analysts and male patients. There are fewer papers on erotic longings between female analysts with lesbian patients (McDougall, 1986, 1995; Siegel, 1988; Elise, 1991; O'Connor and Ryan, 1993; Davies, 1994; Wrye and Welles, 1994; McWilliams, 1996; Dimen, 1997), and there is an unfortunate lack of analytic literature on homoerotic transference/countertransference when both patient and analyst are heterosexual. McDougall (1986, 1995) tends to be one of the very few exceptions. Let me give an example of what the literature contains: In McDougall's 1995 book, *The Many Faces of Eros,* she discusses homoerotic longings within a transference/countertransference enactment where she had an emotional deafness toward the patient's erotic material. McDougall thought this deafness defended her own repressed homosexual fantasies. During the analysis, McDougall has what she calls a "homosexual dream" (p. 25). On waking, she begins a self-analysis concerning her perception of denied erotic feelings toward her own mother. McDougall seems to understand her countertransference as a development related to the patient's projective identification and when she next meets her patient she interprets the patient's conflict about feeling loved by her mother.

McDougall's writings are a good example, and a rare clinical illustration, of homoerotic transference/countertransference in the analytic literature. Still, she tends to focus on transference rather than erotic countertransference and when she does, her erotic countertransference feelings are revealed through dreams or are masked or eliminated on the therapist's return to the consulting room. In other words, countertransference is subsumed under varying degrees of analytic neutrality. I have a feeling that this is very representative of how many traditional and contemporary analysts work with their erotic countertransference, whether it is with same-sex or opposite-sex patients. How does this work in a more relational treatment where there is a mutual affective participation?

To my mind, Davies's paper (1994) is one of the few exceptions of mutually discussing erotic transference/countertransference feelings (albeit toward a male patient) as her countertransference developed in the consulting room. I understand such countertransference feelings or enactments to be an expected part of the analytic process. Countertransference enactments manifest as the analyst participates in collecting data about the patient's life. These enactments are cocreated by both patient and analyst in the living-out of emotional experience within the boundaries of the analytic frame. Levenson (1992), in discussing how the analyst reveals herself in the process of gathering data about the internal workings of the patient, believes that all dialogue by the therapist, i.e., comments, interpretations, nearly anything and everything the analyst says, is a metamessage about who the analyst is. "The ultimate issue . . . is not only what the patient says about his/her life to the therapist, nor is it only what the therapist says to the patient about the patient's life: but also, what they say about themselves—however inadvertently—to each other" (p. 562). In this way, the notion of enactments places countertransference closer to the notion of transference (Hirsch, 1994). But how do we know when we've cocreated this erotic transference/countertransference material, particularly when it can be so well defended against by either the patient and/or the analyst?

Bollas (1994) states, and I disagree with him, that the "erotic transference is restricted to the analytic partnership that splits the sexes" (p. 581). He elaborates that there is a displaced manifestation of the erotic transference in heterosexual same-sex treatments, one that could perhaps best be described as a form of "rhapsodic identification" (p. 581). In this particular relationship with the therapist, the patient falls in love with both real or imagined aspects of the therapist's character and perceived life, such as how the therapist expresses ideas, or mannerisms, or their sensitivities. "The patient develops an intense inner relation to the object of identification that gains its rhapsodic character from the analyst's . . . presence" (p. 581), a type of idealized love. In the heterosexual analytic dyad, the patient becomes immersed in a fantasized involvement, perhaps a voyeuristic preoccupation with the analyst's life. "The rhapsodic identification displaces erotic states of mind even though the erotic transference [is what] organizes affective experiences" (p. 581). Is Bollas suggesting that there aren't any homoerotic transference/countertransference developments between heterosexuals that the therapist can work with? It seems to me that his "rhapsodic identification" is an early phase of a developing or budding same-sex erotic transference, not an end in itself. It is more likely that Bollas is expressing his own discomfort with homoerotic transference/countertransference material.

So then, how in the world does the therapist work with this unconscious or consciously held defense against the erotic transference in the same-sex analytic dyad? Wrye and Welles (1994) contend in their experience that patients who develop erotic transferences evoke in the therapist powerful feelings and defenses that may include "manic, depressive, obsessional, schizoid, or paranoid elements" (p. 62). They suggest that such emotions are difficult to contain for the therapist and that we often cannot permit ourselves to participate in the erotic dynamic. Feelings of merger and the desire between the analytic couple with mutual penetration wishes toward the other, may create both longing and fear in both participants.

Intolerance of erotic countertransference in ourselves may result in enactments of it through mothering responses or in arrested feelings that are kept out of awareness, bringing about an altered therapeutic process. The most powerful erotic countertransference feelings are those fused with aggression since these inhibit the therapist's experience and can completely change the course of the treatment (Wrye and Welles, 1994). It is unfortunate that Wrye and Welles focus on the analyst's aggressive countertransference reactions to the patient. Are they agreeing with Bollas that you're fighting the odds or at least working against nature's elements when you work with the erotic transference/countertransference relationship? Wrye and Welles do give good clinical examples of a heterosexual, female patient's erotic transference, but they understand the patient's narrative as "coalescing around issues of fusion, schizoid or obsessional distancing, and grandiose or manic treatment agendas" (p. 64). They add that the female patient was experienced by the female analyst as a "toxic, parasitic infant who seemed bent on, and capable of, dismantling and devouring" the analyst (p. 76). Why is the erotic countertransference so slippery when the patient is heterosexual? Is it different when the patient is gay?

Frommer (1995) began his essay "Countertransference Obscurity in the Psychoanalytic Treatment of Homosexual Patients" by stating that within the psychoanalytic literature there is an absence of the analyst's countertransference in the treatment of same-sex patients where there is sexual desire. Frommer's essay is an important theoretical contribution to the literature on the treatment of gays, but unfortunately he provides no clinical illustrations of erotic transference/countertransference.

There are a few recent publications in which a smattering of authors come close to discussing erotic countertransference to same-sex/lesbian patients, but more often the attention is on the erotic transference (Elise, 1991; McDougall, 1995; McWilliams, 1996; O'Connor and Ryan, 1993; Siegel, 1988; Wrye and Welles, 1994). It is my impression that these authors self-analyzed or discussed their erotic feelings with a colleague to obtain understanding and acceptance of sexual or loving feelings toward the patient. Again, this is a rather traditional response to working with erotic countertransference feelings in which the therapist returns to the consulting room with her own emotions intact. In addition, the therapist believed it was important that her patient not feel an erotic indifference and interpreted that her patient's "sexual interests were stimulating, delightful, precious, poignant, and safe" (McWilliams,

1996, p. 218). Why was it necessary to qualify that erotic feelings in treatment are safe? Doesn't saying something is safe in treatment mean to the patient "Don't worry, all this material we're discussing is unreal. It's just verbal dry humping; there's no chance of really getting affectively pregnant, because I won't penetrate you by taking any emotional risks." As it turned out, the patient started focusing on images of a future loving relationship with the analyst and wanted to leave treatment before analyzing it, to really "have" the analyst. Does this mean the erotic fantasy broke down? Did it become stuck on the patient's actually loving the analyst with her hopes of the treatment ending?

In an unpublished paper by Dimen titled "Bodies, Acts, and Sex: Thinking Through the Relational" she wrote about an erotic transference/countertransference development where she felt a female patient was about to unconsciously enact the therapist's erotic feelings by developing a destructive relationship outside the treatment. In this particular treatment, the patient had a history of cultivating disastrous relationships with men when the erotic transference/countertransference manifested itself in the treatment relationship. Dimen interpreted this to the patient in the hopes of stopping the patient's acting out. In other words, Dimen told the patient she had sexual feelings about her and said she thought the patient had in the past unconsciously enacted the erotic transference/countertransference feelings in destructive relationships with men. To my knowledge, this is the only paper where homoerotic feelings were disclosed by the analyst to the patient in the hopes of developing treatment.

With the exception of Dimen's unpublished paper, analytic literature indicates that the erotic transference and countertransference feelings are altered through the analyst's interpretations into a more workable or sexually-neutered transference alliance, or that treatment is ended either by the patient or the therapist, which is what Freud suggested at the beginning in his 1915 paper on transference love.

Kaftal (1994), in his paper on treating gay men, suggests that the heterosexual therapist subtly signals ambivalent feelings about homoerotic fantasy. He warns that transferential fantasies need to be opened up and expanded before understanding and interpretation begins since "A simple push to move more quickly to the interpretive phase is more than enough to suggest [to the patient] that emotional expression and erotic phantasy are not entirely welcome" (p. 9). This is a different treatment warning from the traditional analytic stance: Kaftal is saying be careful about interpretation diluting the erotic transference/countertransference into just unreal or real feelings and fantasies, or leading too quickly into discussions on infantile longings since this may lead to a premature ending of the erotic transference or of the treatment itself in order to be with the therapist.

Why is the erotic countertransference so difficult to work with, especially with the same-sex female patient? Butler (1995) wrote an important paper, "Melancholy Gender-Refused Identification," in which she discussed "the foreclosed status of homosexual love that never was" (p. 156). Butler goes on to say:

> For it seems clear that, if the girl is to transfer the love from her father to a substitute object, she must first renounce the love for her mother and renounce it in such a way that both the aim and the object are foreclosed. Hence, it will not be a matter of transferring that homosexual love onto a substitute feminine figure, but of renouncing the possibility of homosexual attachment itself. Only on this condition does a heterosexual aim become established as what some call a sexual orientation. Only on the condition of this foreclosure of homosexuality can the scene emerge in which it is the father and, hence, the substitutes for him who become the objects of desire, and the mother who becomes the uneasy site of identification. (p. 169)

Butler uses the word "foreclosed" to mean a

> preemptive loss, a mourning for unlived possibilities; for if this is a love that is from the start out of the question, then it cannot happen and, if it does, it certainly did not; if it does [anyway], it happens only under the official sign of its prohibition and disavowal. (1995, p. 171)

The heterosexual individual then disavows a constitutive relationship to homosexuality. Then, if this is so, what does it mean to erotic transference/countertransference feelings within the heterosexual therapist and same-sex patient dyad?

I have never struggled with the beginnings of a paper in the way I have with this one. I felt as if I were all over the place, way too fluid. I couldn't come up with an outline to save my life. I put off writing it for months because I was "thinking." I told nearly everyone who would listen that I was writing it, almost to the point that I would introduce myself and within moments launch into the struggles I was having with this paper. Then I realized, it's as if I'm coming out by writing about homoeroticism in heterosexuality. Do lesbian and gay analysts professionally present themselves as such or do we all have sexuality secrets? Are there professional or personal risks? Isay (1996) has suggested that gay therapists should acknowledge being homosexual when patients ask. Not disclosing compromises the truthfulness of the analytic relationship. However, Isay adds that such disclosure is complicated by shame. Is this just true about the therapist's sexual identity, or does shame relate to most sexual issues and feelings that arise in psychoanalysis and psychotherapy?

Lately, I have been giving some thought to whether or not we, as analysts and therapists, put our own emotions at risk when we treat patients. We ask our patients to question what they feel, analyze their experiences, and let us guide them—and maybe this is an emotional risk or seduction into the unknown parts of the patient's self. How can we do that if we aren't prepared to take a similar sort of risk? This got me to thinking about the risks I've taken in psychoanalysis and the risks I haven't. To my mind, taking a risk as an analyst means putting our own emotions on the line, of disclosing our own feelings at times, of stretching the boundaries of the analytic playground through emotional risk without being out of control.

I recently found an illustration of this in a class I was teaching at an analytic institute. I found myself intimately discussing my feelings about my work with patients, as well as my subjective experiences and countertransference. I was pleased at the innermost responses the candidates returned about their work and themselves. In the last meeting of the semester, we were discussing our thoughts about the readings and one of the candidates said she loved the class because it made her question her work and herself. Then she added she also hated me for having made her do that, meaning she hadn't intended to give so much of herself emotionally in and to the class. My having taken risks about my own feelings made her feel a desire to meet me at the threshold.

### Clinical Illustration of a Female Bisexual Patient

Pauline came to treatment to discuss her conflict about her sexuality. She has only been in heterosexual relationships, yet she believes she is bisexual and would like to fulfill her desires with a woman. She is one of six children from a Roman Catholic family. A female child, born dead eighteen months before Pauline was born, was also named Pauline. When she was five, Pauline and an older brother experimented with mutual masturbation without penetration. Pauline feels this was disgusting and sex as an adult, with men, has retained a vulgar edge for her. Pauline's longest relationship of seven years was with a verbally abusive man who shared her alcoholism. Since becoming sober nine years ago, she has only had "crushes" on women.

Pauline related an interesting memory about her mother. She remembered being about six years old, riding alone with her mother in their car. She said it was one of the few memories she had of being alone with her mother without the other children. Pauline stared at her mother as she drove in an attempt to get her to respond in some way to a multitude of stories and questions she was asking. Her mother was preoccupied and eventually told Pauline to be quiet. They drove on in silence with Pauline feeling humiliated at her mother's rejection and obliviousness to her desire. It's not surprising that Pauline is a rather isolated and emotionally withdrawn adult.

I remember in an early session with Pauline that she talked about a lack of any sex in her life. I asked if she masturbated. She didn't, saying it took too long and she got too tired before climaxing. "Don't you use a vibrator?" I asked. She giggled with discomfort and titillation and seemed thrilled at our topic. In the next session, she announced that she had gone to the Pleasure Chest shop in Greenwich Village and purchased a large dildo, not a vibrator, that had all sorts of special features and used it the night before our session. She felt pleased I'd given her permission to have this sexual experience. I realized that I was somehow involved in her fantasy, either as overseer, voyeur, participant, or maybe as the prey and she agreed.

At this point, she became intensively curious about my life. What did I do on weekends? Who were my friends? Was I married? She thought not, and hoped I had female lovers. Monday morning sessions were full of her questions about my weekend. I consider Pauline's fascination with my life to be an example of Bollas's "rhapsodic identification." However, a patient's preoccupation need not stop here if the therapist can allow or tolerate a further unfolding of the erotic transference as it can organize affect and create intimate experiences.

Pauline became increasingly flirtatious in the successive sessions. Adam Phillips declared "Flirtation keeps things in play, and by doing so lets us get to know . . . [people] in different ways." "[Flirtation] plays with, or rather flirts with, the idea of surprise . . . [it] confirms the connection between excitement and uncertainty, and how we make uncertainty possible by making it exciting" (1994, p. xii). Pauline took her flirtation to courtship and started bringing small presents from the store where she works and began writing letters and calling between sessions. I asked if she was trying to emotionally seduce me; she thought so and punctuated this session with a long letter. "To answer your question from Friday," she said, "the feelings I have for you are sexual, which scares the hell out of me to tell you that. I fear that it will disgust you to know my attraction is sexual."

I am certainly not disgusted by Pauline's sexual desire and have told her so. She appeared less humiliated on hearing that. Perhaps she has learned that I can be engaged through her presentation of erotic material. Through my work over many years, I have slowly come to the realization that I speak a very passionate language. Words that to me feel warm and intimate, are sometimes experienced as seductive, enticing, and alluring to others. Patients quickly learn their analyst's language and seem to know what topics spark an analyst's interests, whether it's narratives about aggression, separation/individuation, sex, or whatever. Often patients will consciously or unconsciously engage the analyst by evoking such topics, and of course, vice versa. Pauline's engagement of my attention is a different experience than she had riding in her mother's car as a child. I feel quite comfortable with Pauline's sexual wishes and fantasies. She came to treatment with a longing to be with a woman and, for now, I have become the object of her desire. I assume her sexual longings will become more and more explicit as we continue to work together, and that I will feel attracted to her in the erotic transference/countertransference matrix. What concerns me is the possibility of the patient's unconscious enactment of the erotic transference/countertransference outside the treatment, i.e., Dimen's clinical illustration. If Pauline develops a relationship with a man or a woman, is this an erotic transference/countertransference enactment, is it an expression of the patient's maturation, or is it a regression?

What I find curious in treating Pauline is the lack of conflict I experience regarding my erotic countertransference. I do not feel troubled by Pauline's sexual longings. Our work has a very intimate, warm quality in that I feel very emotionally engaged and related to her stories and memories. Pauline's sexual desires and my comfort with them are a part of our mutual relationship that allows for an unfolding of both the patient's and the therapist's creativity and opens opportunities for emotional risks. Pauline has desires for women, as do my lesbian and heterosexual male patients, and I am, therefore, an object of her desire.

### Clinical Illustration of a Female Heterosexual Patient

Simone began treatment eight years ago after she found out her husband had a brief affair. Years passed with the two of us struggling with her failed career as an interior designer in relation to her husband's business success. Treatment was uneventful, easy, I thought, and Simone was funny and entertaining and I enjoyed her visits. She was also quite beautiful with large saucer eyes, blonde hair, and a lovely smile. This was a psychotherapy case and the transference was rather calm and maternal for many years, much the same as she described her life in Kansas as a child. Her mother sang in the church, her father was a teacher, and her only sister was her closest friend.

About four years into the treatment, Simone decided to take a temporary assignment as a secretary at a construction company. She had never been exposed to this environment, where her boss cursed up a blue streak and screamed at clients. The receptionist was openly having an affair with the boss's partner, who videotaped their sex and showed it to the men at the office. Mobsters showed up for private meetings with the boss and sexual harassment in the office was expected and casually accepted or elicited, and on and on. It was as though squeaky clean, church-going Dorothy from Kansas had stumbled into a licentious den of inequity.

Simone was fascinated, frightened, and mesmerized with their behavior. Sessions became weekly recounting of unusual relations between co-workers, which she told in a hilarious way. The two of us would roar with laughter as she described feeling like Michelle Pfeiffer in the movie *Married to the Mob.* She then began talking more specifically about her boss, Tony. He was a big, gruff, burly, but good-looking Italian guy who was becoming charmed by Simone's innocence, appearance, and humor. They began having lunches together and then drinks after dinner and finally he told her he was falling for her.

At the same time, Simone was very busy being a corporate wife in her husband's career. His boss began inviting them to the Hamptons for weekends and after one evening meal, Simone found herself followed into a bedroom by her husband's boss. He professed a sexual desire as he pulled her onto the bed and attempted to seduce her. She decided that something sexual seemed to be in the air, kismet or karma, and after telling her husband's boss she wasn't interested in his advances, a few days later she let Tony know she was receptive to his (Tony's) advances.

In her treatment, Simone's stories had heated up. I anticipated the coming attractions of her narratives and found myself musing and fantasizing about the upcoming events outside the hour. When Tony finally propositioned her, she came to the session and asked what to do. I asked if she wanted my consent to have an affair and she said yes. After an exploration of her desires and fears, and after discussing how she would be living a secret life, she decided to have an affair with Tony and asked if I would help her through it. I told her I would always help her and she interpreted this as permission. At this time, I wondered about the homoeroticism inherent in triangulations, specifically about those in Simone's decision. Certainly, when Simone went to bed with her lover, she took her thoughts about his wife. In a sense, theirs would be a very full bed and I assumed I would be present in some form as well.

Simone began a very passionate affair with Tony and her relationship with me became equally steamy. It often felt like we were mutually visualizing porno flicks as she narrated weekly events with her boss. We were both becoming sexually aroused by her stories. In Benjamin's book, *The Bonds of Love* (1988), in the chapter titled "Woman's Desire," she writes that the developing child wants more than a plain satisfaction of need, instead each specific "want" is an expression of the child's desire to be recognized as a subject. "What is really wanted is a recognition of one's desire; what is wanted is a recognition that one is a subject, an agent who can will things and make them happen" (p. 102). Desire is often framed by gender—women are frequently the object of desire in that someone else, the subject (often the man, in heterosexual relations) gets pleasure, and the object of desire (usually the woman) gets sexual enjoyment from pleasing the subject. Being the subject of desire, however, would mean that a woman had her own wants.

My own fantasy about how I am perceived is that I have my own wants. This is conveyed in the way I dress, my manner, sensitivities, how I use language, and my attitudes—all of these have a sexual component or edge. Benjamin suggests that the " 'real' solution to the dilemma of woman's desire must include a mother who is articulated as a sexual subject, one who expresses her own desires" (1988, p. 114). This was true of my relationship with my mother, and now in my relationship with Simone as she began to identify with a female therapist who has her own desires.

Simone wanted to be able to want. She wanted sex, she wanted to be sexual, and she wanted to have an affair. She was the subject of desire, and through my recognition of her desire, I became a coconspirator. Yet, because I facilitated her becoming a subject, the real affair was with me since I had also facilitated her subjectivity. And the same for me, since this facilitation was out of the realm of men and their objectifying selves.

Benjamin (1988) suggests that it is "recognition of the other that is the decisive aspect of differentiation" (p. 126). In recognition, a sense of self and other evolves through an awareness of shared feelings and experience, as well as the sensation that the other is external and dissimilar—a mutual recognition that provides a point of self-differentiation. When we have erotic feelings toward another person, we desire, want, and experience the other as being inside and outside us. It is as though our minds and bodies are made up of aspects of the other and this often gives us a sense of wholeness as well as a differentiation of self in relation to the other. The erotic transference can be a powerful arena that can help many patients differentiate.

In erotic unions between men and women, it has been my experience that while men may desire a loss of self in an erotic relationship, they are least likely to tolerate too much of it. It is more usually women who can merge with the other temporarily. Yet, merger is a core issue in lesbian relationships and often results in sexual bed-death. A merged relationship defuses the shared, mutual power of two individuals engaged in the erotic fantasy of being swept away by the other, and often results in a lessening of erotic feelings.

Very quickly into the affair, Simone's boss arranged an apartment for the two of them and let her decorate it. They would meet there frequently during the week and perform an unusual sexual interaction. Tony did not undress himself, nor did he entirely undress Simone, but he would instead perform oral sex on her. This is a rather different outcome of a heterosexual affair where typically it is the woman who performs oral sex or where the man penetrates the woman. She was happy with the arrangement and so was he. To my mind, it was Tony who was objectified by this woman's desire.

Still, was Simone in more control than I knew, both outside and in the treatment? Were her stories of their meetings meant to seduce, dominate, control, and/or objectify me? Was Tony performing my part in his surrender to the subject? Simone wasn't sure, but said I was definitely in the room when they were together. I remember feeling uneasy when she said this. Just how large was my part? How much was I colluding or not colluding? I felt caught up in the events at this time and I couldn't seem to interpret the transference successfully. Yet, what kind of reality would an interpretation of this enactment have? More and more, I felt like a participant in her stories and as though I was being masturbated in the sessions. Or, was I was manipulating her, like Svengali. With whom was Simone having sex?

As she shared her sexual fantasies with Tony in the office, and with me in the sessions, she spoke about an experience she had as an adolescent. She and a very close girlfriend had taken to spending time talking as they lay on the friend's bed. As they shared intimacies and secrets they found themselves fantasizing and telling the other of their sexual as well as nonsexual desires. She said they both began to feel aroused and eventually began affectionately touching each other.

In a matter of time, their thinking and talking about sex had become action as they progressed to kissing and then sexual exploration and eventually mutual masturbation. She then confessed to recently having masturbated to the fantasy of two women together and when I asked if she meant us, she said yes.

In Simone's mind, she was imagining having sex with me. On the one hand, I could consider her feelings to be an unreal erotic transference experience. We weren't really having sex and we weren't going to, and one way I could understand her reactions would be to attribute them to infantile longings. And, while I wouldn't rule out such an interpretation, I didn't feel it was enough in my relationship to Simone. Our affiliation seemed more complex, more mutual, more intimate, and the sexual stimulation that we both felt in relation to her narratives was very real. As long as we didn't engage in the action of sex, did that mean there was no sex between us? What constitutes a sexual relationship? Is actually having sex, real sex? Or, is imagined sex, real sex, too?

In an as yet unpublished paper, Kaftal posed the question "What makes sex, sex?" I feel this question relates very much to my experience with Simone. For instance, is sex in transitional relating, such as in the analytic relationship, different from imagining having sex with someone? Is imagining having sex the same as really having sex? Some people might answer "yes" and others might say "no" to that question. But the next query might be: Is phone sex, sex? Many of us have an immediate answer to that question, and to my mind, phone sex is sex. So bear with my "yes" answer, "phone sex is sex," for a moment as the questioning continues: How does phone sex differ from imagined sex if imagined sex is not sex? So where do we draw the line, what makes something sex?

The answer has to do with the intention of the people involved. If we think that imagined sex is helpful in dealing with the patient's other issues in treatment—for example, a patient's sexual feelings are defending against other nonsexual feelings, i.e., aggression, intimacy—then sexual feelings between therapist and patient are diffused. In other words, the sexual feelings between both individuals are imagined and unreal. What about the experience of two individuals in the same room, bedroom, backroom, who are jerking off together? Isn't that sex? If the room is a consulting room and one of the individuals is a sex surrogate and if there is a clinical reason for the other person to jerk off or masturbate, is it sex? Or is it the same as just jerking off?

In psychoanalysis or psychotherapy, there is a whole different rule for physical actions. In both, our actions are verbal and there must be a matter of intention for both people, and then there is how we read these intentions. What constitutes sex is not fixed in any certain way. In this moment in our current society and culture, what really matters to us is what we really do—not just what we intend to do. For instance, when someone asks "Do you really love me?" although it matters what you say, it matters more what you do. It's the way we understand what sex means, what meaning system we use to understand sex, that matters. In my mind, there a certain kind of mutuality in what constitutes sex. For instance, sex need only be a sharing of similar sexual stimulation or experience at the same time. For me, it was sex between Simone and me and it is my interpretation that for Simone it was sex for her, too. Simone and I coconstructed or created our sexual feelings for each other, with each other. It's not because I uncovered a clandestine closet that was full of secret fantasies that she'd always had and psychotherapy brought it to the surface, rather we created these sexual feelings together, and maybe I started them.

Certainly, my experience with Simone felt this way when she talked about her affair and about her sexual fantasy to be with me. We weren't really having sex, but sexuality had become the theater for getting the point across between us, we were definitely sharing emotional intimacies. Our mutual recognition, the encounter of our separate selves, had become the context for desire.

I then told her that I had wondered for a long time about the extent of her sexual fantasies about me, particularly since I had recently become aware of mine about her. I continued saying that we were involved with each other in many ways and levels, and our relationship felt deeply intimate, sexual, and loving. Simone and I had developed and shared a mutuality of affect and a sense of the other as entirely engaged and saturated. Mitchell (1988) remarked, "There is perhaps nothing better suited for experiencing and deepening the drama of search and discovery than the mutual arousal, sustaining, [of] . . . sexual desire" (p. 108). Our intimate feelings climaxed and were maintained after my disclosure of this particular countertransference vulnerability. Benjamin states that "Women make use of the space in-between that is created by shared feeling and discovery. The dance of mutual recognition, the meeting of separate selves, is the context for their desire" (1988, p. 130).

Tony showered Simone with gifts and she delighted in showing me all of them. On her birthday, he gave her beautiful pale pink roses which she brought to the session and left with me, saying she could not take them home because of her husband. Interestingly, her husband, around this time, began pressuring her to have a child. He began a subtle seduction of spending more time with her, he bought her a sexy teddy, began dominating her in bed, and penetrating her in the way Tony did not. (Simone and her husband had a history of satisfying sex until he became overinvolved in his new job.) Although she felt seduced back into his bed, Simone thought her husband could not possibly raise a child because he had been so isolated in his own childhood. Nonetheless, she let herself be swept away and immediately became pregnant. Tony promptly fired her.

Throughout the pregnancy, Simone became very interested in finding a way to raise the baby without having her husband too involved. She thought he had no experience with children and she wasn't too sure about her own abilities. She decided I would help her raise the baby by telling her what to read and catching her if she did something wrong. In a way, the erotic transference was facilitating Simone's sense of herself as powerful and she experienced my penetrating qualities as offering her a new intersubjective perspective on what she could want or desire. She wanted an inner space in which her interior self could emerge.

She missed her session one week, called me from the hospital, and brought the newborn baby in the next week. He was colicky and she was having trouble nursing, which she showed me during the session. I realized that as soon as the baby fussed, she pulled him off her breast and stopped feeding. I also realized that I was seeing Simone's exposed breast. Next week, the baby looked horrible and she complained he cried all the time. I told her not to take him off the breast entirely, but to let him breathe a little and feed him until he was full. Next week, he was much better and she sobbed, saying she had been starving him, and I think she was. I was now deemed an official parent. Each week for the next year, she brought the baby in to session and nursed him at some point. At the end of the session, she would hand him over to me while she went to the rest room and he and I would play together for a bit. In a way, we were married in our transference/countertransference enactment and we had a child, and like some couples with children, the sexual tension was somewhat reduced as we focused on the baby.

Had the erotic transference just become maternal? I don't think so because there was still such a powerful erotic component in our relationship. In sessions, we discussed the emotional closeness we felt with each other, and Simone told of an ongoing internal dialogue where she imagined telling me her feelings about everything that happened or everything she wished would happen to her. At times she questioned her heterosexual identity and wondered if she might be bisexual, saying a woman had more emotional potential with another woman, than with a man. In a footnote in *The Bonds of Love,* Benjamin states

> Ideally, in the psychoanalytic process, analysand and analyst create a transitional space, in which the line between fantasy and reality blurs and the analysand can explore her own inside. The analytic relationship then becomes a version of the space within which desire can emerge freely, can be felt not as borrowed through identification but as authentically one's own. (1988, p. 127)

In this treatment, Simone and I were maintained in our subject to subject space. In our relationship, there was a recognition between self and other self.

### Clinical Illustration of a Lesbian Patient

June has been in psychoanalysis for four years now and the transference has until recently been lustfully erotic. I receive multiple letters per week from June, many of them with drawings of the naked torso of a woman who she says is me. Often she speaks about her wish to watch me have sex with a man and/or a woman while she looks on and masturbates. She frequently fantasizes about parts of my body and tells me details of how she will arouse me sexually. June often wistfully looks up from the couch stroking her chest bone as she relates her sexual desires. Recently she told me the following joke:

" 'Doctor, Doctor, please kiss me.' The doctor, she said, answered, 'No, no, I can't.' 'Please, Doctor, kiss me.' The doctor replied, 'I can't kiss you, I shouldn't even be lying on the couch with you.' "

June was quipping about her awareness of our mutual erotic transference/countertransference relationship. I have repeatedly asked her what meaning she makes of sexually arousing me, and she has interpreted that our mutual sexual stimulation is akin to actually having sex.

June doesn't believe in making love, rather she takes pride in "fucking like a man." She recounts affairs where she has seduced a woman, usually one who identifies as heterosexual and married, has sex with her and leaves while the woman is still naked in bed. Is this an analogy of our relationship? I asked her. She thought so and said it expressed her desire to control me—an enacted triumph over her fear of abandonment/wish for merger and achievement of intimacy through sexuality.

A few months ago, June's transference turned from lust to loathing. June had been obsessing about getting a new job and feeling very out of control. Concurrently, I began experiencing a deadness in the treatment, a countertransference reaction I had successfully interpreted in the past. However, this time, the more she obsessed, the more I felt sleepy and angry at her for making me struggle to stay awake. Sessions seemed to drag on and even though I tried to interpret the emptiness in the hour/in her/in me, how her obsessions were burying/defending her, nothing brought the dead back to life. Finally, after a few weeks, I just couldn't tolerate it or her any longer and grappling with my grogginess, I angrily told her to stop it. I said, "I hate your obsessionalism, I hate feeling sleepy, and I hate being controlled. You're treating me exactly the way your mother treats you—killing me with deadness and obsessionalism. You're trying to make it impossible for me to work." In a fury, she called me a "fucking cunt" or variations on that theme for the remainder of the session. Throughout the day, June called my office, leaving additional messages about my being a "fucking cunt," and threatened to take a break from treatment. I called her back, told her she had to come back, that she was in psychoanalysis and not finishing school and she couldn't take a break. She kept cursing at me, but agreed to return. Maybe in her mind she wanted an opportunity to berate me to my face.

In the subsequent sessions, my name seemed forever linked to "fucking cunt." Had the erotic transference just been a defense for an underlying aggression waiting to erupt? Or, had we both created a mutual narcissistic injury in the other and were both seeking revenge? June had wounded and obliterated me through her obsessionalism, which made me feel unnecessary, and I had not contained or successfully interpreted June's underlying feelings about envy, control, and abandonment.

Mitchell (1988, 1993) asserts that sexuality is an essential human experience because it is a powerful vehicle for developing and maintaining relational dynamics—and the same is true of aggression. "Aggression, like sexuality, often provides the juice that potentiates and embellishes experience" (1993, p. 165). Both aggression, as well as sexuality, can be fundamental organizing elements among multiple self-organizations. "It is universal to hate, contemplate revenge against, and want to destroy those very caregivers we also love" (1993, p. 170).

In the next few sessions, my subjective experience and countertransference was of hating June for hating me. I wanted the return of her sexual attention and love. I wanted her to stop her aggressive feelings, just as I had previously wanted her to stop her obsessionalism. Who was dominating whom, who was exploiting whom, who was possessing whom? Then June wrote in a letter,

> Give me ambition. Real ambition. I don't wanna be sent off to track down a piece of cheese in a labyrinth. I'm scared of you because you're in the world and I think you like it. How do you know where I am?

June envied me for my place in the world and in her life, and I felt envy about her skill in controlling me. I told her this and added that I really did not know exactly "where she was" and I should have been much kinder to her. I then asked if our mutual aggression felt comforting to her—I wondered aloud if we had both taken sanctuary in the other's powerful involvement. With hindsight, it seems that our aggressive feelings deepened our relationship in that we now knew the other could not be easily frightened off when we showed the worst parts of ourselves.

She then wrote a note that said:

> As time goes by, as time will do, we get closer, not further apart.
> So it fucking only makes sense that I'd wanna stay with you.
> That's the fucking nature of a relationship. The more you do the
> more you want to do. A relationship wouldn't be pleasurable if
> all you had to do was push a button. The downside of a human
> relationship is that you just can't eat a person, smoke, inject, or
> snort them. I wish I could just come in there with a lighter and a
> pipe and, by God, I'd like to smoke you. But when I tried that
> you nearly died in the process when you felt clouded over by my
> obsessions. I think a relationship is like breakfast cereal in that it
> sort of satisfies the desire to smoke or eat people.

In the transference/countertransference matrix, June and I enacted
her early relationship to her mother. In a sense, I became a participant
in the reenactment of an early trauma and became June's abuser. It is
within such disruptions and the ensuing repairs that relationships and
analysis progress. In *The Clinical Diary of Sandor Ferenczi,* Ferenczi
said,

> I have finally come to realize that it is an unavoidable task of the
> analyst: although he may behave as he will, he may take kind-
> ness and relaxation as far as he possibly can, the time will come
> when he will have to repeat with his own hands the act of murder
> previously perpetrated against the patient. (1932, p. 52)

He added that the deepening of any relationship is promoted when the
analyst acknowledges her own mistakes and limitations—since this
aids in mutual forgiveness. Ferenczi was one of the first analysts to
realize that the patient observes and reacts to the analyst's countertransference, as the analyst enacts a role framed by her own character
traits in response to the patient's resistance. In so doing, the analyst
becomes a distinct and real person whom the patient genuinely affects and is affected by.

In one of June's most recent notes, she wrote, "It fascinates me that
there is no gun at my head, yet I return day after day, week after week
to you."

# REFERENCES

Benjamin, J. (1988), *The Bonds of Love: Psychoanalysis, Feminism, and the Problem of Domination.* New York: Pantheon Books.

Bollas, C. (1994), Aspects of the erotic transference. *Psychoanalytic Inquiry,* 14:572-590.

Butler, J. (1995), Melancholy gender-refused identification. *Psychoanalytic Dialogues,* 5:165-180.

Davies, J.M. (1994), Love in the afternoon: A relational reconsideration of desire and dread in the countertransference. *Psychoanalytic Dialogues,* 4:153-170.

Dimen, M. (1997), *Bodies, Acts and Sex: Thinking Through the Relational.* Paper presented at First Annual Lecture Series, "Contemporary Approaches to Gender and Sexuality," Psychoanalytic Psychotherapy Study Center, New York, September 26.

Elise, D. (1991), When sexual and romantic feelings permeate the therapeutic relationship. In *Gays, Lesbians and Their Therapists: Studies in Psychotherapy,* C. Silverstein (Ed.). New York: W.W. Norton and Company, pp. 52-61.

Ferenczi, S. (1932), *The Clinical Diary of Sandor Ferenczi,* J. Dupont (Ed.) (trans. M. Balint and N.Z. Jackson). Cambridge, MA: Harvard University Press, 1988.

Freud, S. (1915), Observations on transference love. *Standard Edition,* 12:157-171. London: Hogarth Press, 1958.

Freud, S. (1920), The psychogenesis of a case of homosexuality in a woman. *Standard Edition,* 18:145-172. London: Hogarth Press, 1955.

Frommer, M.S. (1995), Countertransference obscurity in the psychoanalytic treatment of homosexual patients. In *Disorienting Sexualities,* T. Domenici and R. Lesser (Eds.). New York: Routledge, pp. 65-82.

Hirsch, I. (1994), Countertransference love and theoretical model. *Psychoanalytic Dialogues,* 4:171-192.

Isay, R. (1996), *Becoming Gay: The Journey to Self-Acceptance.* New York: Pantheon.

Kaftal, E. (1994), *Some Obstacles to the Heterosexual Analyst's Introspection.* Paper presented at the 14th Annual Division 39 Spring Meeting of the American Psychological Association, Washington, DC, April 14.

Levenson, E.A. (1992), Mistakes, errors and oversights. *Contemporary Psychoanalysis,* 28:555-571.

McDougall, J. (1986), Eve's reflection: On the homosexual components of female sexuality. In *Between Analyst and Patient,* H. Meyers (Ed.). New York: The Analytic Press, pp. 213-228.

McDougall, J. (1995), *The Many Faces of Eros.* New York: W.W. Norton and Company.

McWilliams, N. (1996), Therapy across the sexual orientation boundary: Reflections of a heterosexual female analyst on working with lesbian, gay and bisexual patients. *Gender & Psychoanalysis,* 1(2):203-221.

Mitchell, S.A. (1988), *Relational Concepts in Psychoanalysis: An Integration.* Cambridge, MA: Harvard University Press.

Mitchell, S.A. (1993), *Hope and Dread in Psychoanalysis.* New York: Basic Books.

O'Connor, N. and Ryan, J. (1993), *Wild Desires and Mistaken Identities: Lesbianism and Psychoanalysis.* New York: Columbia University Press.

Phillips, A. (1994), *On Flirtation.* Cambridge, MA: Harvard University Press.

Siegel, E. (1988), *Female Homosexuality: Choice Without Volition.* Hillsdale, NJ: The Analytic Press.

Wrye, H.K. and Welles, J.K. (1994), *The Narration of Desire: Erotic Transferences and Countertransferences.* Hillsdale, NJ: The Analytic Press.

# Chapter 8

# Cross-Gendered Longings and the Demand for Categorization: Enacting Gender Within the Transference-Countertransference Relationship

Barbara Tholfsen

MARTY: I'm always trying to please people. Is that common? I've heard that that's common for incest survivors to feel that way.

THERAPIST: I wonder what you're looking for with that question.

MARTY: It's important to feel not . . . unique. In group, the stories are all different, but the feelings are the same.

THERAPIST: I think there's some concern that I'm going to see you as a freak—as ultra unique.

MARTY: I want to be reassured that I'm not alone. It's comforting to see that I'm not alone. I can consider myself lucky when I see it that way. The shame is crippling; my secret desire to be a woman. To say that, to hear myself say that is really something. It's almost . . . it gives it less power, but that shame thing covers a little. Are we done?

THERAPIST: We actually have some more time. Is there some reason you want this to be the end of the session?

MARTY: I lie here and I talk about it and I think: Is it all worthwhile? Is this another crapshoot?

THERAPIST: You're wondering whether I can help you.

MARTY: Are you taking notes?

THERAPIST: Yes.

MARTY: Can I expect you to come up with your own conclusions?

THERAPIST: Is that what you would like? [He sighs and then there is silence.] How am I being difficult?

MARTY: It's hard to pin you down. I want that a lot. That concrete definitive answer.

THERAPIST: How would it feel if you got that definitive answer from me?

MARTY: Part of me says "relief." Part of me would say "She's full of shit."

TED: Yesterday my wife brought home flowers. She just left them there on a counter. I put them in a little vase. This is something I shouldn't be doing . . . I still have a need to do these things, but how will it be read? . . . People will say it's not masculine. So I say—should I avoid it? Should I say that's the way I am and I'll do it? Is this a gender identity problem? People who cook—the greatest chefs might be men. If I cook because I'm hungry or to be creative or I make wedding cakes . . . What do you do? Where do you draw the line? Where are the demarcation lines?

I'm in a turmoil because I don't want to do these things that might put me in a different category; which may make me convinced that there is something strange about my personality that I don't admit to. I don't allow myself free rein. I restrict myself. I'm afraid of what people will say or what it will confirm in my own mind about me. As I stuck those flowers in the vase today, I thought if I left it to Linda, she would have let the flowers lie. But she goes to baseball games. I don't. It's like I have the feminine part and she's got the masculine part to some degree. Or am I a female in a male body or is she a male in a female body? I don't know . . . I feel like now I don't have anything I'm excelling at . . . I feel like a robot.

I am at an impasse with Marty and Ted. It is a familiar place. I have felt stuck like this with other men who have presented with overlapping concerns about gender and sexuality. I long to feel empathic, helpful, flexible; but instead I feel pushy, impatient, judgmental. I'm uncomfortable, confused, unsure of what's going on and so is the patient, but there seems to be no way out of the confusion. It's like I'm choking on some kind of epistemological double bind that the patient and I have constructed as a team, but it's constructed out of several different languages and the patient only knows one of them. Maybe I know two.

Men with concerns about gender often ask, with both desperation and ambivalence, to be categorized. They frequently ask, "How freakish am I?" or "How abnormal am I?" which often translates into "How masculine and/or heterosexual am I?" My unstated, but conscious response to the pressure from patients to categorize them can be dismissive. I want to say, "All your suffering would cease if you would just see that men who are primarily attracted to other men are about as widely dispersed on the masculine/feminine scale as those who are primarily attracted to women." I want to say that men who are primarily attracted to women have dreams in which they have breasts, or have sex with men, and fantasize about feeling sexy in heels. I want to say, "Let's figure this out together. There is no normal. Forget normal. I am not the judge of what is normal in the room." Whether I say this or imply it, the result tends to be the same: he continues to try to get me to tell him what he fears is true and fixed and shameful about himself, and I resist doing so. He comes to believe that I am holding back what I really (objectively) know, perhaps out of a desire to protect him from the "awful truth." I start to embody this "awful truth" for him, this fixed system of men and women and nothing in between, gay and straight and nothing in between. I know he's really gay, but I won't tell him. I know that he's a woman trapped in a man's body, but like him, I cannot face it.

I think one reason Marty and Ted and I get stuck like this is that we think about gender and about knowing quite differently. Men who present with overlapping concerns about gender and sexuality tend to believe in a fixed, binary view of gender in which men should be men and women should be women (Shapiro, 1991). Marty and Ted each ask for "objective" answers to questions about how his genitalia (sex) and his gender (what we expect from people based on sex in a particular culture) are related. Each assume that there is some "natural" way gender and sex and sexuality must be related and that I, as his hired expert on psychological health, must know what that relationship is. But I, the "expert," come from a feminist/psychoanalytic/postmodern tradition that tends to consider concepts like "objective," "natural," "masculine," and "feminine" illusory.

Historian Mary Jo Buhle (1999) notes that "feminism and psycho-analysis developed dialogically . . . in continuous conversation with each other" (p. 3). During this development, there were times when feminists and psychoanalysts conceived of gender and objectivity in much the way Marty and Ted do. At other times, both groups questioned the dichotomies of objective/subjective and masculine/feminine, finding ambiguity in both gender and in knowing. Psychoanalysis was born out of Freud's fascination with the hysterical symptoms that women were exhibiting at the turn of the century (see Benjamin, 2001).[1] There was no "physical" cause for the blindness, the seizures, the inability to walk or talk that these women complained of. Their bodies bound psyche and soma into an undifferentiated mass that challenged the body/mind, subject/object dualism of the day. Freud listened and came up with, in Chodorow's (1989) words, a "wounding . . . blow to human megalomania." Freud made it "impossible to think about the self in any simple way, to talk blithely about the individual" (p. 154). He stated baldly in 1905[2] that there was no such thing as pure masculinity or femininity—"either in a psychological or a biological sense" (Buhle, 1999, p. 31). Chodorow (1989) sums it up this way: "According to Freud, then, we are not who or what we think we are: we do not know our own centers; in fact we do not have a center at all" (p. 154).

In the years that followed, Freud fled this psyche/soma, objectivity/subjectivity uncertainty and used gender to cap the fragmented, splintered world of knowing he had found. In what Muriel Dimen (1997) calls "a failure of nerve" he "dissociated what he knew" (p. 533) and created a "highly differentiated," centered, integrated mechanistic self that was "distinctly male" (Buhle, 1999, p. 355). By the 1950s, psychoanalysts had embroidered this stance into some of the most detailed, binary, rigid, inflexible, pseudo-scientific, contradictory (and I must say goofy) stereotypes of what men and women should be—ever.

Women had vaginal orgasms if they developed properly (the clitoris being too "masculine" to be properly "feminine?") and penis envy if they didn't (and if they did). Men were aggressive and therefore masculine if they developed properly and "defending against passive, feminine and masochistic wishes" (Greenberg, 1991, p. 60) if they did not. At first, feminists responded with parallel stereotypes (men have womb envy; women are more relational), but by the late 1970s, they began to question the whole inflexibly dualistic setup (see Buhle, 1999; Grosz, 1995). Feminists began to question whether anyone can successfully be "masculine" or "feminine." Gender was no longer seen as a "sinecure for any of us." In Shapiro's words, "we are all passing" (1991, p. 257). Gail Bederman (1995) spells out this point of view clearly and succinctly:

> At any time in history, many contradictory ideas about manhood are available to explain what men are, how they ought to behave, and what sorts of powers and authorities they may claim as men. Part of the way gender functions is to hide these contradictions and to camouflage the fact that gender is dynamic and always changing. Instead, gender is constructed as a fact of nature, and manhood is assumed to be an unchanging, transhistorical essence consisting of fixed, naturally occurring traits. (p. 7)

This feminist/postmodern take on gender is illustrated in a cartoon that pictures two children standing in front of a picture of Adam and Eve. One child says to the other, "Which one is the man and which one is the woman?" The other child says, "I don't know, they don't have any clothes on" (Shapiro, 1991). Such a cartoon is actually a pretty good representation of a toddler's view of gender. Before we have understood the biological differences between men and women, we "know" that hair length and clothing style are as fixed as a penis or a vagina.[3] The language of the toddler as she or he learns her or his grammar for the first time, is rigidly dualistic: Good and bad; fair and unfair; strong and weak; right and wrong; pretty and ugly; normal and abnormal; sick and well; male and female. Working analytically, one comes across these dyads operating problematically in adults, both inter- and intrapsychically. Often, in analysis and psychotherapy, this binary way of looking at the world or feeling about oneself begins to shift, but the problems that can be associated with internalizing a rigid notion of gender as pairs of fixed opposites are not always acknowledged. In some treatments, they are still propped up.

Things have been changing. For the past fifteen years, many analysts have set about deconstructing the gendered, binary, biological language of psychoanalysis: with passive and active standing for male and female, and heterosexuality and homosexuality standing for gender health versus gender pathology. Taking a critical look at how concepts as basic to psychoanalysis as "health," "self," "body," "identity," or "integration" get constructed (see Hoffman, 1991; Mitchell, 1993; Silverman, 1994), analysts find themselves questioning all of the old psychoanalytic assumptions about gender and identity: Is there really a link between identifying with the "right" parent and developing a "healthy, evolutionarily determined desire to reproduce" (Schwartz, 2001)? Do boys who identify with their mothers really tend toward gender identity "disorders"? Is there any fixed relationship between gender identity and sexual preference (Burch, 1993)? Must an adult really develop a single integrated gender identity to be considered "healthy" (Dimen, 1991)? Maybe it is the attempt to develop a single integrated gender identity which creates psychopathology (Goldner, 1991). Under this kind of scrutiny, psychoanalytic categorization based on gender has lost its theoretical base and most psychoanalysts have "set aside their search for . . . characteristic family history, structural conflicts, internal object relations or psychological developmental lines than lead to . . . same sex . . . sexual attraction" (Magee and Miller, 1997).

Knowledge is thus seen as "less encompassing" rather than more (Grosz, 1995). Knowing, expertise, and objectivity are now viewed with a psychoanalytic skepticism traditionally reserved for a patient's free associations, dreams, and slips of the tongue. Transference is no longer seen merely as distortion on the part of the patient that the "objective" analyst interprets to the "subjective" patient. The countertransference is no longer seen as a neurotic stumbling block that an analyst must work through and expel in order to maintain objectivity. The transference/countertransference relationship is seen as a place where patient and analyst cocreate enactments, where subjectivities merge and interact (see Mitchell 1988, 1993). Words seem poor tools to describe these spaces (Harris, 1996) and analysts often resort to metaphors of paradox when making an attempt:

> the solution to the problem of splitting is not merely remembering the other poles but being able to inhabit the space between them, to tolerate and even enjoy the paradox of simultaneity. (Dimen, 1991, p. 348)

> It is . . . what each of the patient's selves does *with* each of the ana-
> lyst's selves that makes transferential experience usable. . . . As
> the patient's dissociated self experience becomes sufficiently
> processed between them . . . the patient reclaims . . . his sense of
> dynamic unity—what I call "the capacity to feel like one self
> while being many." (Bromberg, 1998, p. 310)

This repositioning in respect to objectivity and knowing can also
be seen among feminist theorists. Elizabeth Grosz reflects on Luce
Irigaray's reconception of knowledge:

> Irigaray's work thus remains critical of such traditional values as
> "truth" and "falsity" . . . she does not present a more encompass-
> ing knowledge, but rather a less encompassing knowledge . . . her
> texts are openly acknowledged as historical and contextual, at
> strategic value in particular times and places, but not necessarily
> useful or valid in all contexts. . . . She shows that there are al-
> ways other ways of proceeding, other perspectives to be occu-
> pied and explored . . . the fact that a single contested paradigm
> (or a limited number) governs current forms of knowledge dem-
> onstrates the role that power, rather than reason has played in
> developing knowledge. (1995, pp. 41-43)

Many therapists working today attempt to bring these new ways of
thinking about gender and knowing into their consulting rooms—to
look beyond the manifest in ways that are, in the end, quite Freudian.
Aware of multiple meanings, shifting identifications, camouflage,
breakage, splinter (Butler, 1990), analysts hesitate warily before the
gendered language of psychoanalysis and do a double take. Freud
scratches a breast and gets a penis. Melanie Klein scratches a penis
and gets a breast. If you call the object a phallic mother and move on,
you may be missing a lot. If you turn over the object, you may find another dimension where gender, genitalia, and sexuality are related to
each other like elements in a dream—where gender can camouflage
your patient's transference distortions or your own.

### Marty

Marty approached treatment asking whether he had "gender dysphoria." Recently divorced, primarily attracted to women, Marty had

wondered since early adolescence whether he "should" have been a woman. He connected these wonderings to childhood memories of a mother he described as strikingly beautiful:

> My mother used to rock me until I would go to sleep on her shoulder. (This went on) until I was four or five. There was a lot of nudity. She would go to the bathroom with the door open. She'd scold me with her vagina in my face with a little, short shirt on. And thinking about all this with the transexuality, it's connected.

Marty was fascinated by talk shows about transsexuals and aroused by magic shows that showed a woman being cut in half. He sometimes dressed in women's clothes to promote sexual excitement while masturbating or just to feel more relaxed when at home doing chores. This was always done in private and he would more often than not throw the clothes away, hoping to prevent himself from repeating the behavior. Though it became clear that Marty was highly ambivalent about hearing my "definitive answer" to his questions about who he "really" was, I felt the pull, both from him and from myself, to give us one. Just as Marty wanted a definitive answer from me, I wanted a definitive place to sit in the room with him. I wanted to ease my own discomfort with ambiguity. I wanted to ease his terror. What were my options? A clinician specializing in sex change operations, the treatment prescribed for gender dysphoria, could have agreed with Marty that the task at hand was to determine whether his gender just didn't properly match his genitalia. Questions would focus on how "female" Marty feels in order to determine how strong his "feminine" identity is. Such a clinician might even figure into the equation his own guess as to whether he, as a man, might feel attracted to Marty (after the operation of course!) (Stone, 1991). But Marty seems quite "masculine." Wouldn't the paradoxes begin to show? Second thoughts (Eigen, 1996) and suicide are common after the operation. Would it be stretching much to make a comparison between going to a surgeon for help with gender problems with going to a dermatologist for help with problems of race (Shapiro, 1991)? Marty also approached his treatment with questions about whether his wish to be a woman might mean he was gay. At times, I longed to "help" him find that his "woman trapped in a man's body" approach was just "a disguised form of homosexuality" (Shapiro, 1991, p. 252). I wanted to say, you are gay, straight, or "bi"; let's figure out which and get over this societally induced idea that being gay is shameful. I could only take this stance with Marty if I assume that (1) gender identities have fixed predictable relationships to sexual preferences; (2) that preference for same-sex or opposite-sex relationships is more important to defining a person's identity than any other sexual preferences; and (3) that sexual preference is a matter of finding one of two or three fixed niches to fit into (see Schwartz, 1995). Although I can't assume these three positions comfortably, it's also uncomfortable sitting with Marty's shame. Caught between my discomfort and Marty's, I want to rough ride over the meaning of his concerns, fears, conflicts, and pain on the road to liberation. Somehow I know if I do this, I'd be like a frustrated Freud saying to a patient suffering from hysterical blindness, "Get off it, you can see!" So I don't answer him when he asks me if he's gay. Like a good psychoanalyst, I explore the conflict and move on.

Similar problems crop up when I take the postmodern approach. If I promote too assuredly a view of gender as "basically" flexible and ambiguous, it becomes difficult to explore the ways Marty and I (and all of us) enact gender as if it isn't. If I imply that living gendered is as simple as "seeing" the emperor's new clothes, I also imply that Marty and I are capable of interacting in some gender-free space where we both can "pass." With my stance of knowing better than he that his feeling of being out of gender is a symptom of his inflexibly held gender ideology, I subtly request that he stop enacting his conflict about gender within the transference relationship and that he ignore my part in such enactments. I "dissociate what I know" and forget that my own conscious and unconscious gender configurations affect the treatment in ways in which I am and am not aware. I pretend that there is no intersubjective part for me to play in transference enactments of Marty's concerns about gender. I forget the extent to which my own, more inflexible positionings as to gender are camouflaged from myself.

Bederman again:

> The ideological process of gender—whether manhood or womanhood—works through a complex political technology, com-

posed of a variety of institutions, ideas, and daily practices. Combined, these practices produce a set of truths about who an individual is and what he or she can do based upon his or her body. Individuals are positioned through that process of gender, whether they choose to be or not. Although some individuals may reject certain aspects of their positioning, rare indeed is the person who considers "itself" neither man nor woman. And with that positioning as "man" or "woman" inevitably comes a host of other social meanings, expectations, and identities. Individuals have no choice but to act on these meanings—to accept or reject them, adopt or adapt them—in order to be able to live their lives in human society. (p. 7)

## Ted

Though Ted didn't present with concerns about gender, it eventually became clear that such concerns were a major reason he subjected himself to what was a difficult experience for him: analytic psychotherapy three times a week. Ted didn't have a sexual relationship or move out of his parent's home until he was in his mid-thirties and had had only one sexual partner: his wife. Now in his forties, he spoke of missing the more active sexual relationship that they had had in the first few years of their marriage. He wanted sex more frequently than she did—this was becoming a problem. About six months into the treatment, Ted began to speak vaguely about fears that he was sexually attracted to men. Indirectly, he began relating these fears to parallel concerns about gender. My approach was to sidestep the gender issue altogether, exploring Ted's pleas as interpersonal or intrapsychic problems in a way that said gender is not the true problem here. I tended to focus on the rigidity evident in his thinking about gender and how this rigidity permeated his feelings and thoughts about everything, not just gender. My assumption was that the ability to move "between qualities of greater rigidity and greater fluidity" (Sweetman, 1996) with respect to gender is "healthier."

However, as I avoided gender, Ted circled in on it. In one session, Ted talked about "categorizing" people by gender. He talked about men who are "car-oriented. That's a masculine thing. Then there are ladies who like trucks. This gender demarcation thing gets to be very interesting because as I go through life I see people who don't fit into categories." He adds, "I can categorize a couple of females" and then describes women at work who exhibit what he considers to be masculine behavior and dress. He expresses disapproval of a man at work who wears an earring, and then says: "I put people in these categories. Everyone has a place. Everyone has a category." In response, I ask him if he has tried to categorize me. At first he says no, that I'm an enigma like Mona Lisa, but then he says: "You want a reading? You want me to tell you what I think?" I reply affirmatively, and he says, "I don't want to be embarrassing." I respond by saying, "embarrassed for me or embarrassed for you?" He answers at length:

> Me being embarrassed about how I see you. It might not be anything how you see yourself or how you really are . . . Let me see . . . Your hands. Well, you have a wedding ring on. You have rather large hands. You have a squarish face. You don't seem to be ultra feminine, but you're definitely a woman. I think you're very kind and sensitive to people's moods. That's why you do what you do. No jewelry. I don't think I've ever seen you wear earrings. No make-up. No lipstick. You don't fuss with your hair to any great degree. It's just there, which is fine. You're not beautiful, but you're not ugly either. You're fine and you seem to wear very dark clothes all the time. Today gray. Once in a while you touch it up with some red, but not too often. Always conservative shoes. No high heels. Maybe if you go to a party you look different, but meeting with me it's fine. It would be a distraction if you were different. I might even find you attractive, more than I do at the present time, and that could be a problem. I don't know. Does that make any sense?

I nod and he continues:

> I don't know. I wonder if you wash your windows and if you vacuum your floors or if you have someone who does it. Who puts the light bulbs in? I don't think you climb way up there. You're wearing a wedding ring. Maybe your husband likes to vacuum.

He talks about his fascination with television programs about cross-dressers and pushes me to tell him what this fascination means.

He asks me to "rate" him like he "rated" me. He says, "Do you see me as masculine, feminine, somewhere in-between? How far in one area and how far in another?" He then free associates about gender and sexuality and television talk shows about transsexuals until the time is up. He has left me no chance to answer and I feel relieved, but the relief is telling. Ted is asking me to use my own personal gender rating system to rate him, and I want to keep this (very non-postmodern) part of myself hidden.

Ted did not let me hide. He was clear that there were two people in the room. In this case, two different sexes and the implication of multiply or at least ambiguously gendered selves. He made it clear that no matter what my theories about gender are, I carry unconscious and conscious gender processes, both rigid and fluid, that are reflected in my tone of voice, body language, clothing, language, affect, etc. It is understandable that Ted would "rate" me with respect to gender and to expect that I would "rate" him, too. Within each moment we are each positioning ourselves with respect to gender. His experience of how I position myself at a particular moment might be different from another person's or from my own "rating" of myself. Contradictions and ambiguities may clutter up these rating systems to the point where they make little sense, but to deny that each of us consciously and unconsciously rate ourselves and others with respect to gender is to deny the obvious.

### Marty

Just a few weeks into the treatment, Marty began discussing an experience he'd had the night before. A woman he had recently met offered to give him a massage for free. She was a licensed massage therapist, who "needed the practice." As she was married and because she behaved "professionally" when she came to his house, Marty felt shame when he began to feel aroused during the massage. Since Marty knew I was taking a very low fee because I was in institute training and "needed the practice," I wondered whether Marty was talking about shame he felt about sexual feelings he had in sessions with me. I asked if he ever felt aroused during our sessions. Marty paused and then changed the subject, talking about his mistrust of a woman at work. When I connected this to his possible mistrust of me following the question that I had asked, he had what seemed to be a dissociative experience, and said he felt "almost" like he was "having an LSD trip." When I asked him to say more he said, "My face feels large. There's a feeling I would get when I was a child. There's a similar, like a suffocating kind of large swollen feeling. Boy, I don't know what that's about." In the next session he talked about leaving treatment. I asked why, and after a pause Marty wondered aloud about why I had asked "that question" in the previous session. I told him some of my reasoning. Seemingly changing the subject, Marty then described a "dysfunctional" relationship he had had with a woman years before. She had loved him and would "do anything" for him. He had taken advantage of her and now felt ashamed about how he had treated her. Ignoring the sadistic aspect of this story, I focused on his fear of getting entangled in another "dysfunctional relationship" with me.

In the next session, Marty talked about a previous treatment in which the male therapist seemed to have difficulty maintaining boundaries. Later in the session, Marty told me a dream:

> You and I were talking about friends being friends and it was warm, and nice. I kept waking up with a powerful erection and I don't get a lot of erections now. My libido is not that strong. For some reason I put the two together.

Later he said that the erection was actually "sparked" by another dream about a transsexual he had had the same night. He said that although the erection was "sparked" by the dream, the erection was the all-important thing, "not the dream." Marty then talked about another long-past "dysfunctional" relationship with a woman and about a male friend who had recently betrayed a confidence related to Marty's cross-dressing. Throughout the session, it was the erection that continued to preoccupy Marty and he eventually said, "My male performance is important to me because so many of my fantasies have involved being a woman." In the next session he discussed a history of physical fights with his mother when he was an adolescent, including one in which he pushed her down and broke her shoulder. He spoke again about his mother's intrusive sexualized behavior with him as a child, and we explored the possibility that when I asked whether he felt aroused in sessions, this had reminded him of his mother's sexual intrusiveness.

A dream I had while working on this paper led to associations about my work with Marty:

> I'm young in the dream, just out of college and at a new office job. I'm in the ladies room with another woman. We are each sitting in a stall and she is telling me about a game that is played every year at this office. Eventually, I'm hanging out over the top of the stall talking to this woman from above (I must be standing on the toilet seat). Some time during this friendly, easygoing chat, the woman opens her fly or lifts her dress and shows me that she has a penis. My first reaction is self-protective. A man is exposing himself to me in a ladies room and I don't want to be victimized or humiliated. How can I humiliate him instead? So I say, "It's not such a great penis. I don't see why you'd want to go showing it to people." Then I start to look anxiously at his face and figure out how I could have missed the fact that "she" was a he. Where did I go wrong? How was I fooled? There must have been some sign in "her" face that "she" was a man. And now I see it, yes, I see that she is a man. Her features are heavier than a woman's. Her hair is like straw. As "she" now begins to look more male, I feel more oriented, less anxious. Then the scene changes and I'm in the office playing the game she/he had told me about earlier. Anxious once again, I am sitting at a card table practicing with another woman. I play for a while and eventually it doesn't seem that hard. It's like Trivial Pursuit and I get some answers right. So again, I start to feel less anxious. I think, "This isn't so bad. I can play this." Then, as I sit there, I remember what has just happened in the ladies room. I realize that I may have misinterpreted the whole interchange. I realize that I may have felt vulnerable with the man in the ladies room because I saw the interchange as one between flasher and victim, but as I look back on it I see that the man was taking a risk in order to tell me something personal about himself. He was actually making himself vulnerable to me. So I start to feel guilty. I wish I could take back my hurtful words. I am going through this change of heart as fellow office workers begin to explain the game to me in detail. As I try with difficulty to pay

attention, they tell me that I will have to make up questions for the game and that I'll be given two words that are related to each other in some analogous way—like a pun—and each must be in one part of a two-part question. This makes me nervous. This sounds hard, and I've always been somewhat befuddled by puns. Then someone hands me a piece of paper and tells me I've been assigned to a team. On the paper are two or three number/letter combinations (like L4 or H2) and I say, "Oh, I must be in the L4 team" and they say, "No, no, no. Teams do not have letter and number combinations!" But I'm still confused. I don't really get it. I look around for help and I notice something I hadn't noticed before: everyone in the room is a woman. I'm about to comment on this when I remember that the man dressed as a woman is not a woman. So I hold back on saying anything about the gender of the people in the room. I consider the possibility that the man doesn't want anyone to know he's a man. Maybe he just told me. Maybe he wants to pass.

My associations to this dream included: memories of "take back the night" rallies in the seventies, when women would tell stories of successful attempts to turn the tables on flashers and subway gropers; memories of feeling frightened and angry as a young therapist when male patients would sexualize the therapeutic relationship; my guilt in response to Marty's dissociative experience when I asked him if he felt aroused in sessions; and the thinking and reading I had been doing about gender ambiguity. Marty had described his childhood relationship with his mother as one in which sexuality was used to dominate and humiliate. He described his adolescent relationship with her as stormy and violent, and adult sexual relationships with women in which he is dominating and self-serving. Was I then, by sexualizing the therapeutic relationship with Marty first, beating him to it in order to protect myself from feeling defeated in a dangerous gender game with confusing and changing rules and roles? Was my too-early reference to a sexualized transference with Marty sparked by the same aggression and fear I experienced in the dream when my co-worker exposed himself or herself to me in the ladies room? Did I have to buy the stereotype "women typically violate boundaries less often than men" (Maroda, 1999, p. 80) in order to violate this particular boundary? Did a tendency of mine to expect men (and not women) to sexualize a relationship as a way of asserting control help me dissociate from what I knew—that women (and I) can do the same? Was it only by dissociating this aspect of myself from myself that I was able to construct, with Marty, a reenactment of particularly nasty aspects of his relationship with his mother? Is this an example of gender functioning as camouflage?

Women as subordinator (mother) of the vulnerable (child) must be a powerful internally gendered relationship for all of us. Do I dissociate from woman as sadist because it's too frightening to dwell too long on this particular dyad? Is it easier to associate masculinity with sadism and femininity with masochism and allow our opposite associations to be expressed in misogynist or feminist intellectual acting out that implies women are either inferior to men or superior, more victim or more victimizer, more nurturing or less rational, more relational or less aggressive?

Associations to my dream also included the word "fag," which in England means cigarette and in this country is a pejorative term for gay men: two separate meanings made analogous by medieval witch burnings. (Gay men were said to have been used to feed the fires in which the witches were burned.) This association reflects power relationships in which gender is used to punish, and annihilate, but in ways both inside and outside the "woman as victim of male domination" stereotype. Women and men both, this association reminds me, made up the burners and the burned in medieval Europe. Gender relationships shift, according to historical circumstances, class and race relationships, who is involved in a given relationship, life circumstance, momentary shifts in mood or motive, or shifting identification. There is a moment in the dream when I almost understand this. It is the moment when I realize that the man in the ladies room was not necessarily a threat to be feared, but that his behavior was an attempt to reach out to me or make himself vulnerable to me. This is a familiar experience; a moment when I realize I have mistaken one kind of relationship for another; a moment when the transference is apparent, when I can see my tendency to assume a relationship to be binary (with room only for one-up and one-down). Suddenly there is room to consider more ambiguous configurations.

And yet, what does one do with all this room? Ambiguity is uncomfortable, disorienting, a little scary. Of course, pretending that reality is unambiguous—that I can clearly differentiate between myself and my patient, between one of my selves and another, between masculinity and femininity—that's also pretty uncomfortable. But ambiguity is worse. Or is it? In the dream it is both differentiation and ambiguity that are uncomfortable. All the binaries are there: win/lose, correct/mistaken, virtuous/sinful, smart/dumb, ignorant/educated, male/female, victim/victimizer. I don't want to be a victim or a loser. I want to be a winner. I want to understand the rules of the game like my office mates seem to. It's not just that I want to feel smart and win, I also don't want to feel so out of it and alone. But the rules, which seem so orderly, so differentiated one from the other to my office mates, in the end, don't make any sense to me. I try to understand them, but I am befuddled by them. I feel vaguely dissociated: half in my memory of the incident in the ladies room, half in the game trying to concentrate so I can understand. In the end, all I have is guilt because I made a "mistake." I am comfortable only at the beginning of the dream, when female is female. I'm beside (unable to see "her") or I'm on top (looking down on "her") and the game is outside.

Marty and Ted feel that they are trying to pass for something that they should be but are not. They feel vaguely out of gender (Dimen, 1991) and they feel alone. They have mixed feelings about asking me to categorize them as gay or transsexual because, on the one hand, there's hope that a category would help them feel less anxious, less confused about themselves, and less alone; but on the other hand, they sense that categories carry with them stereotypes that are too confining and unambiguous to describe the way they really feel about themselves. Rather than sit in the ambiguity, however, Marty and Ted choose to hold onto the certainty that can be found in stereotypes. Though I claim to "know" how ambiguous gender "is," I also have difficulty sitting in the ambiguity I find. I try to escape in a different direction. Rather than clinging to Marty and Ted's unambiguous reality of gender stereotypes, I try to escape to the unambiguous reality of "corrected, 'purified,' unbiased" (Grosz, 1995, p. 41), ungendered knowledge. That is a position as untenable as Marty's or Ted's. So this is how we get so stuck. Marty and I or Ted and I take on incompatible approaches to gender and sit on opposite sides, neither of us wanting to enter the space between. What we all fail to realize is that there is no escaping this space. Marty and Ted can pretend that if they try hard enough they can be masculine or feminine and not just pass or I can pretend that if I try hard enough, I can sit outside of gender and smugly feel "right," but in "reality" there is no doing either. That stuck feeling I get with these men, that discomfort, frustration, and unease; that is gender. It is only by resisting the urge to escape the discomfort, by living through the stuck feeling and noticing how it feels, that we can explore what gender is and does to each of us. We are all passing. In that sense, Marty and Ted and I are not alone. We just don't "know" it yet.

## NOTES

1. Also see Breuer, J. and Freud, S. (1895), Studies on hysteria. *Standard Edition* 2. London: Hogarth Press, 1955; and Freud, S. (1905), Fragment of an analysis of a case of hysteria. *Standard Edition,* 7:1-122. London: Hogarth Press, 1953.

2. See Freud, S. (1905), Three essays on the theory of sexuality. *Standard Edition,* 7:123-246. London: Hogarth Press, 1953.

3. See Kohlberg, L. (1966), A cognitive-developmental analysis of children's sex role concepts and attitudes. In *The Development of Sex Differences,* E. Maccoby (Ed.). Stanford, CA: Stanford University Press, pp. 82-172; Maccoby, E. and Jacklin, C. (1974), *The Psychology of Sex Differences.* Stanford, CA: Stanford University Press; and de Marneffe, D. (1997), Bodies and words: A study of young children's genital and gender knowledge. *Gender and Psychoanalysis,* 2(1):3-33.

## REFERENCES

Bederman, G. (1995), *Manliness and Civilization.* Chicago: The University of Chicago Press.

Benjamin, J. (2001), Between body and speech: The primal leap. In *Storms in Her Head: Freud's Women Patients Revisited,* M. Dimen and A. Harris (Eds.). New York: The Other Press, pp. 31-63.

Bromberg, P. (1998), *Standing in the Spaces: Essays on Clinical Process, Trauma, and Dissociation.* Hillsdale, NJ: The Analytic Press.

Buhle, M. (1999), *Feminism and its Discontents: A Century of Struggle with Psychoanalysis.* Cambridge, MA: Harvard University Press.

Burch, B. (1993), Gender identities: Lesbianism and potential space. *Psychoanalytic Psychology,* 1(3):359-375.

Butler, J. (1990), *Gender Trouble: Feminism, and the Subversion of Identity.* New York: Routledge.

Chodorow, N. (1989), *Feminism and Psychoanalytic Theory.* New Haven, CT: Yale University Press.

Dimen, M. (1991), Deconstructing difference: Gender, splitting, and transitional space. *Psychoanalytic Dialogues,* 1(3):335-352.

Dimen, M. (1997), The engagement between psychoanalysis and feminism: A report from the front. *Contemporary Psychoanalysis,* 33(4):527-548.

Eigen, M. (1996), *Psychic deadness.* Northvale, NJ: Jason Aronson.

Goldner, V. (1991), Toward a critical relational theory of gender. *Psychoanalytic Dialogues,* 1(3):335-352.

Greenberg, J. (1991), Countertransference and reality. *Psychoanalytic Dialogues,* 1:52-73.

Grosz, E. (1995), *Space, Time, and Perversion: Essays on the Politics of Bodies.* London: Routledge.

Harris, A. (1996), Animated conversation: Embodying and gendering. *Psychoanalytic Dialogues,* 1(3):361-383.

Hoffman, I. (1991), Toward a social constructivist view of the psychoanalytic situation. *Psychoanalytic Dialogues,* 1(4):74-106.

Magee, M. and Miller, D. (1997), *Lesbian Lives: Psychoanalytic Narratives Old and New.* Hillsdale, NJ: The Analytic Press.

Maroda, K. (1999), *Seduction, Surrender, and Transformation.* Hillsdale, NJ: The Analytic Press.

Mitchell, S. (1988), *Relational Concepts in Psychoanalysis.* Cambridge, MA: Harvard University Press.

Mitchell, S. (1993), *Hope and Dread in Psychoanalysis.* New York: Basic Books.

Schwartz, D. (1995), Current psychoanalytic discourses on sexuality: Tripping over the body. In *Disorienting Sexuality,* T. Domenici and R. Lesser (Eds.). New York: Routledge, pp. 115-126.

Schwartz, D. (2001), Words and bodies: Dereifying sex after a reading of the case of Frau Emmy Von N. In *Storms in Her Head: Freud's Women Patients Revisited,* M. Dimen and A. Harris (Eds.). New York: The Other Press, pp. 185-199.

Shapiro, J. (1991), Transexualism: Reflections on the persistence of gender and the mutability of sex. In *Body Guards: The Cultural Politics of Gender Ambiguity,* J. Epstein and K. Straub (Eds.). New York: Routledge, pp. 248-279.

Silverman, D. (1994), From philosophy to poetry: Changes in psychoanalytic discourse. *Psychoanalytic Dialogues,* 4(1):101-128.

Stone, S. (1991), The empire strikes back: A posttransexual manifesto. In *Body Guards: The Cultural Politics of Gender Ambiguity,* J. Epstein and K. Straub (Eds.). New York: Routledge, pp. 280-304.

Sweetman, A. (1996), The changing contexts of gender: Between fixed and fluid experience. *Psychoanalytic Dialogues,* 6(4):437-459.

Chapter 9

# Gay or Straight?
# Why Do We Really Want to Know?

Linda I. Meyers

Issues pertaining to sexual orientation, while always deeply personal, are most profoundly constructed along traditional lines by cultural factors. The dilemma—gay or straight—appears most frequently in treatment in its interrogative form: "Am I gay or am I straight?" The question is imbued with an urgency considered self-evident by the patient and the therapist. Why? Why do we really want to know? What can the answer mean for the patient? What does it mean to the therapist? What does the necessity of an answer illuminate about Western notions of sexuality?

## *"The Question" in Culture*

Inherent in this paper's thesis is the supposition that we are unable to clinically comprehend what we do not culturally comprehend. The cultural, like the psychological, is rarely manifest; it must be made visible before it can become comprehensible. Three approaches come to mind: the first method, most familiar to psychoanalysts, is the analysis and deconstruction of language; the second, most familiar to anthropologists, is the contrast and comparison with other cultures; the third, an integration between the cultural and the psychological, can be seen within the developing metapsychology of psychoanalytic theory. The way we use the question of sexual orientation with patients beautifully illustrates the importance of an integrative comprehension.

Judith Butler (1991, p. 17), a queer theorist attentive to the importance of language, shows us how the ostensive polarity of the terms "straight" and "gay" dissolves upon closer inspection. She asks, "What do we use as the determinant of its [sexuality's] meaning: the phantasy structure, the act, the orifice, the gender, the anatomy?" If a woman has sex with men, but achieves orgasm only through fantasies of other women, is she straight or is she gay? Or consider a male transvestite whose preferred sexual partner is a woman; sexually he functions like a man but he looks like a woman. If he were to feel like a woman, dress as a woman, yet choose sex with a woman, would he be a psychological lesbian?

The anxieties that are raised by Butler's simple question are ameliorated by a belief in the existence of confined categories. The straight/gay dichotomy is particularly seductive because it proffers stability; choose and the issue is closed. The psychological needs of the individual are supported by the misconceptions of the culture. We'd rather believe that if you're gay now, you were gay before and you'll be gay later. If you were gay before, but now you define yourself as straight, you're just "trying to pass"; and if you're gay now, but say you were straight before, you just weren't ready to accept the truth. The edict in our culture is "let's just decide and get it over with."

Ambivalence—an inevitable, normal human condition—is not well tolerated in Western, particularly American, culture. Ambivalence and anxiety nourish one another, creating the entropic, circular condition which language is meant to penetrate. The more ambivalent the issue, the greater the anxiety, and the greater the impetus to create and name binary categories, false or otherwise.

The term *homosexual* was first coined by the medical establishment in 1869; *heterosexual,* its presumed counterpart, was labeled years later. While the term *sodomite,* the homosexual's predecessor, had no female counterpart, the term homosexual required an opposite and the category *lesbian* was created (Halperin, as cited in Lesser, 1995). Obviously, homosexual, in its vagueness, induced an anxiety necessitating the relief of a new category. However, the desire and the behavior meant to inform these distinctions always existed; the labels and stigmatization are modern social inductions.

The more powerful the anxiety, the more tenaciously we cling to the category.

The history of psychoanalysis' nosology reflects the anxiety. Classical psychoanalysis, conceived in the Darwinian era, needed a strict and discerning taxonomy in order to be respected as science. Patients, of necessity, were *diagnosed;* that is, they were pathologized and categorized. Although Freud (1905) professed the existence of an inherent bisexuality, that did not mean he believed bisexuality was "normal." He believed that sexuality, and particularly homosexuality, needed to be sublimated for the benefit of society. The drive may be normal but the behavior was pathological. It wasn't until 1973 that attempts were made to remove homosexuality from the American Psychiatric Association's DSM-II manual. Psychoanalysts protested vociferously (Bayer, as cited in Drescher, 1995).[1] In the 1980s, an attempt was made to retain the perception of homosexuality as pathology but the burden was transferred from the psychoanalytic establishment to the pathology of the patient; hence, the category of ego-dystonic homosexuality was created. We claimed to no longer think of homosexuality as pathology, but if patients did, we were completely understanding and willing to "cure" them.[2] By 1987, I suspect, more as a reaction to its untreatability than a true change in beliefs, homosexuality as pathology was finally removed from the nomenclature.

In our society we use specific categorical distinctions to ameliorate ambiguity and to allay anxiety. True androgyny is too uncomfortable. However, this anxiety is a cultural, not a biological manifestation and the categorical distinctions are cultural constructions. A meaningful presentation of cultural comparisons is beyond the scope of this paper. However, for illustrative purposes I will briefly mention the *hijra* of India and the Sambia of New Guinea. For a more comprehensive investigation, I point the reader to Gilbert Herdt's edited volume, *Third Sex, Third Gender: Beyond Sexual Dimorphism in Culture and History* (1994).

The hijra are an Indian cult whose members are considered not men, not woman. They begin their lives as males, but claim power through emasculation. The surgical removal of all genitalia is generally self-performed and represents the final initiation into the cult. Hijras dress as women and demonstrate through their ritual dances and comportment the "hot, erotic, aspects of female sexuality that . . . transforms them into sacred, erotic, female, men" (Nanda, in Herdt, 1994, p. 375). In the Hindu view, the Supreme Being has male and female sex organs; hermaphroditism is idealized.

According to Kakar (cited in Nanda, 1994) the anxiety in the Indian culture is assuaged by a third sex. He offers a classical psychoanalytic interpretation. Mature Indian women eroticize their relationships with their sons because of the sexual deprivation they endure with their husbands. The sons distance the engulfing women and eventually become the sexually depriving husbands. The hijra help the men contain their anxiety by acting out the actual castration.

Similarly, the Sambia of New Guinea defend against castration anxiety by the institutionalization of "homosexuality." This is not a contradiction for the Sambia, nor is it necessarily "homosexuality" as we conceive of it. Male individuation, supremacy, and agency are achieved through dependence on semen and exclusive relationships with men. At initiation, boys are wrested away from the women's sphere and their male identity is secured through powerful initiation rituals. First and second stage initiates are fellators. Third-stage pubescent boys are recipients of fellatio, inseminating prepubescent boys. Although there may be erotic attachment, after marriage eroticism transfers to the wives. It is interesting to note that the "stronger" idealized warriors are allowed to continue homoerotic practices even though they are married.

The Indian hijra and the Sambian men are presented as examples of nondichotomous sexual categorization. In these cultures, sexuality is, as Schoenberg describes (1995) "a fluid, dynamic process which assumes different forms at different times" (p. 220).

### *"The Question" in Psychoanalytic Theory*

I had mentioned earlier that the evolution of psychoanalytic theory also reflects changes in culture. These changes have had an impact upon our clinical approach and conception of sexuality. In contemporary, relational theory, the human need to develop and maintain relationships has replaced drives as the major motivation and cohesive force within the psyche. Therefore, the intersubjective world created by the patient/analyst relationship has become paramount to psychoanalytic theory and application.[3] This shift from the intrapsychic to the relational has profoundly affected the way analysts think and apply themselves in their work. The postmodern emphasis on subjectivity that has infiltrated anthropology, literary criticism, history, etc., has not neglected psychology. It is interesting to note that this movement, best represented within psychology by psychoanalysis, developed side-by-side with a burgeoning research in neuroanatomy and brain physiology.

One clear manifestation of the shift to the subjective can be seen in our new attitude toward countertransference. The so-called "neutral" analysts are out; not because they're passé but because they never existed. Today, analysts are encouraged to explore and apply all of their feelings and reactions to their understanding of their patients. The term countertransference has expanded meaning. No longer limited to the analyst's residual pathology, it is now meant to include the subjectivity the analyst brings to the treatment, the subjectivity stimulated by the treatment, and the subjectivity induced by the patient.[4]

How does this theoretical shift affect the gay or straight dichotomy? The current recognition and use of countertransference forces the therapist to grapple with his or her own conflicts and anxieties about homosexuality. She can't simply retreat to the safety of cultural reductionism.

The recognition and utilization of countertransference is particularly salient when the patient is grappling with questions of sexual orientation. The following case is intended to elucidate the value of the theoretical shift. I have used the question "Am I straight or am I gay?" and its permutations to organize the case material and to highlight the underlying subjectivities. As you can see by now, I believe this question is artifice; a culturally constituted binary that falsely implies the existence of two discrete choices. As you will see, it was used by me to achieve distance from my patient. It allowed me to safely locate myself in the cultural mainstream, outside the anxiety and travails of my patient's exploration. The patient, Mary, through the question "Am I straight or am I gay?" identifies my perch and attempts to dislocate me from the security of the moral highground. She forces me out into the margins of our culture into the fray of her personal experience.

## *"The Question" in Treatment*

### *I Ask Myself, "Is Mary Gay?"*

Mary, my analysand, first came to see me upon her return to college after a year off for a "breakdown." It was three years before I learned that her escape from school was precipitated by an attraction to a female classmate. Mary's reticence to reveal this pertinent piece of information was not particularly remarkable. She offered very little information about her past, frustrating me in my efforts to discern the etiology of her extreme anxiety and guardedness. Mistrust and caution were the key descriptors of our work. Nevertheless, she clearly wanted my help. She was in a great deal of psychic pain, but there was an unverbalized, yet strong message to stay back. This "please help me but don't get too close" communication was familiar from my past experiences with trauma victims. I began to wonder, and then later in the treatment, seriously suspected, that Mary had been a victim of early sexual abuse. The most probable perpetrators were her mother and her maternal grandmother. Although Mary had no definitive memories of her own abuse, her mother knows that she, herself, was abused by Mary's grandmother, and while claiming no memories that she abused Mary, thinks it is quite possible that Mary may have been abused by her grandmother. The fact of this probability had complicated the transference, countertransference, and the issues around Mary's sexuality. Its importance was seductive and distracting.

Mary made it clear that she needed to control the sessions; she would decide when and what I should know. This was not done aggressively. Her eyes would look inward and she would hide behind a gauzy vagueness, or she would erect a smoke screen of obsessional concerns. My vision was obscured while hers was clear and focused. She watched me vigilantly, attending to every nuance of expression and gesture, calibrating every inflection of voice and semblance of mood. I could not escape Mary's scrutiny. Mary's mother's behaviors and moods were unpredictable. Mary must have learned to watch her very carefully. I was very uncomfortable. I felt as I imagined Mary's mother felt, and I also felt Mary's fear. Vigilance is exhausting. I wanted to push her away. I longed to put her on the couch but that was out of the question.

I contemplated whether to tell Mary that I was feeling put under the microscope. Perhaps I should have, but it felt important at the time to not seem intimidated. I did not want Mary to feel too powerful. I suspected it would have scared her and further intimidated me. I avoided the issue by trying to get her to do self-reflecting, history-seeking, analytic work. It was a theoretically sanctioned effort to escape the present by attempting to get her to focus on her past. It didn't work. I was increasingly aware of wanting to leave the room. I felt like a butterfly in a net; would I be pinned to the wall or would I be admired? Either way, I was captive. Mary had stripped me of my psychoanalytic modus operandi; with little else at hand, I was forced to contain my anxiety. I'd sit quietly, unnoticed, in my chair. I did not realize until later that I was anxious because I was being sexually aroused. I suppressed those feelings and occupied my thoughts with the most salient question, "Is Mary gay?" "Is she gay?" I kept wondering. The apparent sensibility of the question provided a cognitive puzzle and a rational distraction. It was calming. If I needed a cognitive focus, the more relevant question—it eluded me at the time— would have been, "Why am I aroused?" What does my arousal tell me about our relationship, about Mary, about myself?

### I Ask Myself, "Am I Gay?"

Mary, having mastered the art of hiding while appearing present, recognized my arousal before I was aware of it myself. It unnerved her. Mary believed many of the women she encountered were sexually aggressive and seductive. If they were conscious of their behavior, they were less dangerous to Mary than if they were unaware. She preferred the conscious to the unconscious manipulation but never doubted that attempts were being made to manipulate and use her. Her beliefs were not only a complex manifestation of projected desires and fear of victimization, but also, at times, intuitively astute and accurate readings of the situation. My position was difficult, as I could not assess the accuracy of Mary's perception. I did not want to be another out-of-touch, inattentive, unprotective authority; nor did I want to validate misperceptions. As long as I remained hidden and disconnected from my own desires, my abilities to accurately intuit hers were dubious. Fortunately, Mary, as with many patients, knew what she needed and knew how to get it from me. (If I would not come out, then Mary would go in.)

Mary became extremely confrontational. She was convinced that my touching my hand to my neck was an erotic gesture; that the crossing and uncrossing of my legs was evidence that I was getting "hot"; or that I had chosen my dress specifically with her in mind.

The spotlight was on me. I tried to deflect it onto her. "What," I asked, "would it mean to her if I did desire her?" She was having none of that psychoanalytic evasion; she simply answered, "You do." There was no place to hide. I became increasingly self-conscious and annoyed. I wondered if I could scratch an itch without it being construed as seductive? Finally, my defenses began to waver; did I want to seduce Mary? I may have been experiencing an induction of her childhood feelings, but what of my own feelings? What about my desire? There was no doubt I would have had less difficulty with my erotic feelings if my patient were a gay man, or even a straight man. Unnerved by my obvious defensiveness, I tried to retreat. I began to ask myself, "Am I gay?" By a variation of the superstitious logic that regulates the binaric plucking of daisy petals, if the answer was "no" then my desire was negated. This was a distraction that allowed me to continue to disavow my wish for homosexual love.

When I finally began to imagine loving Mary, I conjured sexual scenes in which she was genitally dominant and I was the cared-for, appreciative receptor. I could feel her strength and caring. My fantasies allowed me to experience her in the way she could—and eventually, I hoped—would someday, be sexually with the right partner. It was quite different from the actual, but minimal, experiences she had had with men, or from her probable childhood history with women. At this time, she was sexually inactive; she masturbated rarely and never achieved orgasm. My fantasies were gratifying scenarios because they provided a positive love map for Mary and, importantly, expanded the interrelational space. A secure place had evolved where the two of us could comfortably rest together. I now felt safe with Mary. In time, my fantasies shifted from genital sexuality to a different kind of intimacy: a deep, warm feeling of closeness; a shared knowledge that required few, if any, words to communicate; a longed for symbiosis that may not be possible in heterosexual love. I felt a pervasive sadness that I recognized as mourning. I was mourning the absence of homosexual love and felt envious. These fantasies and feelings were very different from those I had experienced with my male patients. Mary had helped me push through personal and cultural defenses and imagine a sexual world of positive homosexual love and desire.

*Mary Asks Me, "Are You Gay?"*

It had been my resistance to my feelings, not the feelings themselves, from which Mary had protected herself when I was denying the erotic countertransference. I was unwittingly increasing her fears of being manipulated and misused. She could not risk closeness with a woman who was split off from herself. In a certain sense, Mary had succeeded in "outing" me, inducing a countertransference experience which Drescher (1996) parallels to the actual internal experience of people struggling with same-sex desire. Once this happened, the transference began to shift and we experienced the full force of Mary's sexual desire. No longer was I the evil woman who wanted to misuse her, rather I had become the vulnerable loving object of her desires. Having been split off from my seductiveness, I began to worry if I had worked carefully enough with my countertransference. Perhaps I had just shifted the quality of the seduction from venal to loving? Anxious again, I reminded myself that I had tried to keep a delicate balance between being neither seductive nor rejecting. I'd let Mary know that I thought she would be a wonderful lover, but I periodically reiterated the boundaries implicit in our relationship. I tried to assuage her disappointment by explaining how much more useful I was to her in this capacity than I would be as her lover. Once again, I was retreating behind normative, psychoanalytic interventions. Rational responses to a "hot" erotic transference can be like cold water on a severe burn—momentarily cooling, but not particularly curative. My words were useless. Mary, however, was tenacious. The erotic transference persisted. She did not doubt that with time and patience on her part we would eventually be "together."

If my suspicions of early abuse were correct, then the erotization of the relationship was the only protection she had against abandonment. If I didn't want her, then I didn't love her, and, therefore she was of no use to me, and I would leave her. If, however, I wanted her then I wouldn't leave her; as such, our relationship was obviously destined to be sexualized. I felt as trapped as Mary did. I was preoccupied in trying to discern how I could disentangle caring, erotic desire, acting out, and Mary's fears of abandonment. The question of my sexual orientation had gradually lost its relevance for me but it remained paramount for Mary. She wanted to know, "Was I straight or was I gay?"

*Mary Says, "You Want Me to Be Gay."*

With my acceptance of my own and Mary's sexual feelings, her concerns of abandonment abated but what remained of them she used in resisting her same-sex desire and in the service of her own culturally supported homophobia. Mary's erotic desires were no longer dictated by her fear of women. She spoke frequently of her romantic interests in women. When I reflected and supported her feelings, she accused me of pushing her into society's margins: "How could you care about me and want me to be gay?" Mary was trying to extricate herself from her own homophobia by giving it to me. Crespi (1995) speaks of the need to mourn lost heterosexuality. This was work needing to be done. As McWilliams (1996) notes, it is difficult terrain. The temptation is to mitigate the issue by dissolving sexuality into the totality of the person, which can be interpreted as an attempt to deny the uniqueness of the patient, and negate the importance of affiliation. Mary needed to mourn the loss of her heterosexual ideal, but she also needed to locate herself. She needed a reference group and self-objects that reflected an image she could embrace. She needed to negotiate her own balance between self and culture. Defining herself as homosexual exacerbated the conflict. Feeling herself a victim in her childhood, forced into a precocious autonomy, she consciously identified with and tried to glamorize the hard working gas station attendant or the waitress who was on her feet all day. These were the people that carried society, but were unappreciated and exploited by the upper classes. In moments of disappointment and despair, she shamefully admitted that her Ivy League education and superior intellect entitled her to more. No one was going to keep her down. She would not be a lackey her whole life. She equated the gay life with an underclass and she projected that prejudice on to me. To Mary, embracing homosexuality was forfeiting her rights to my lifestyle. She wanted the nice house and the husband and children. She'd decided that I wasn't gay and my support of her homosexuality amounted to a rejection and subjugation; she wasn't good enough to be part of the mainstream.

The working through of Mary's homophobia signaled an end to this phase of the treatment. She became aware and appreciative of the heterogeneity in homosexual culture and began to imagine affiliation without having to sacrifice her hard-fought individuality. The "question" was no longer needed by either of us and was no longer asked. Mary had begun to date and experiment sexually. I realized that I was only hearing of her relationships indirectly, in an off-handed way. When I confronted her, she admitted she was afraid I'd be jealous of her new woman, her youth, and her sexuality. I knew then that our dynamic had moved into oedipal territory.

## Summary

The question "Am I straight or am I gay?" functions as a lightning rod that attracts individual and cultural anxieties. It is a question that galvanizes the attention of the patient and the therapist, refracting and filtering their associations and seemingly less significant conflicts, through its culturally constructed lens. Caught up in the clinical moment, we accept the apparent validity of this question without attempting to fully deconstruct its meaning. We sit with our patients and labor this issue, wishing to make the quintessential interpretation as if it could reveal some essential truth about their nature. In fact, this question and its permutations are intended not to reveal but to obscure. It masquerades as a "natural," "human" need for identity and connection while it subtly seduces us from the more difficult, insightful, and substantive emotions at the heart of human relationships. As I hope Mary's case illuminated, if we focus on this question, we end up perpetuating anxiety and unwittingly playing out the heterosexual bias of contemporary Western culture. Our psyches have incorporated the misuse of the gay/straight dichotomy. Of course, psychoanalysis cannot stand outside of culture. However, the emphasis in contemporary theory on the subjectivity of the therapist, paradoxically provides us with a greater observing ego. Today, we are better able to confront anxiety, tolerate ambiguity, and shed the cultural defenses our discipline has helped to construct.

## NOTES

1. See Bayer, R. (1981), *Homosexuality and American Psychiatry: The Politics of Diagnosis.* New York: Basic Books.

2. This was concretized in the DSM-III as the diagnosis of ego-dystonic homosexuality. For the history of these diagnostic changes, see Krajeski, J. (1996), Homosexuality and the mental health professions. In *Textbook of Homosexuality and*

*Mental Health,* R. Cabaj and T. Stein (Eds.) Washington, DC: American Psychiatric Press, pp. 17-31.

3. See Mitchell, S. A. (1988), *Relational Concepts in Psychoanalysis: An Integration.* Cambridge, MA: Harvard University Press.

4. See Racker, H. (1968), *Transference and Countertransference.* Madison, CT: International Universities Press; Levenson, E. (1983), *The Ambiguity of Change.* New York: Basic Books; Hoffman, I. (1983), The patient as interpreter of the analyst's experience. *Contemporary Psychoanalysis,* 19:389-422. Reprinted in *Relational Psychoanalysis: The Emergence of a Tradition,* S. A. Mitchell and L. Aaron (Eds.). Hillsdale, NJ: The Analytic Press, 1999, pp. 40-72; and Stern, D. B. (1997), *Unformulated Experience: From Dissociation to Imagination in Psychoanalysis.* Hillsdale, NJ: The Analytic Press.

## REFERENCES

Butler, J. (1991), Imitation and gender insubordination. In *Inside/Out: Lesbian Theories, Gay Theories,* D. Fuss (Ed.). New York: Routledge, pp. 13-31.

Crespi, L. (1995), Some thoughts on the role of mourning in the development of a positive lesbian identity. In *Disorienting Sexualities,* T. Domenici and R. Lesser (Eds.). New York: Routledge, pp. 19-32.

Drescher, J. (1995), Anti-homosexual bias in training. In *Disorienting Sexualities,* T. Domenici and R. Lesser (Eds.). New York: Routledge, pp. 227-241.

Drescher, J. (1996), A discussion across sexual orientation and gender boundaries: Reflections of a gay male analyst to a heterosexual female analyst. *Gender and Psychoanalysis,* 1(2):223-237.

Freud, S. (1905), Three essays on the theory of sexuality. *Standard Edition,* 7:123-246. London: Hogarth Press, 1953.

Herdt, G., Ed. (1994), *Third Sex, Third Gender: Beyond Sexual Dimorphism in Culture and History.* New York: Zone Books, pp. 21-81.

Lesser, R. (1995), Objectivity as masquerade. In *Disorienting Sexualities,* T. Domenici and R. Lesser (Eds.). New York: Routledge, pp. 83-96.

McWilliams, N. (1996), Therapy across the sexual orientation boundary: Reflections of a heterosexual female analyst on working with lesbian, gay and bisexual patients. *Gender and Psychoanalysis,* 1(2):203-221.

Nanda, S. (1994). Hijras: An alternative sex and gender role in India. In *Third Sex, Third Gender: Beyond Sexual Dimorphism in Culture and History,* G. Herdt (Ed.). New York: Zone Books, pp. 373-417.

Schoenberg, E. (1995), Psychoanalytic theories of lesbian desire: A social constructionist critique. In *Disorienting Sexualities,* T. Domenici and R. Lesser (Eds). New York: Routledge, pp. 65-82.

Chapter 10

# On Homoeroticism, Erotic Countertransference, and the Postmodern View of Life: A Commentary on Papers by Rosiello, Tholfsen, and Meyers

Karen J. Maroda

Dr. Florence Rosiello's paper, "On Lust and Loathing: Erotic Transference/Countertransference Between a Female Analyst and Female Patients," was not only the longest of the three papers to be discussed, but certainly the most intellectually and sexually provocative. I was impressed with her powers of observation, especially her frank self-observations, yet equally amazed at the small impact these insights seemed to have on her overall approach to her patients. Dr. Rosiello's main point is that the erotic countertransference often hinders the treatment due to the therapist's discomfort or shame over having sexual feelings toward a patient. She points out that denial of erotic countertransference has the effect of subduing or even eliminating the erotic transference. I quite agree with her statements on this point, as well as her contention that a relational perspective implicitly calls for more admission of participation on the therapist's part, even when it occurs in the area of eroticism. The dilemma we face is how to interact with the patient about the erotic aspects of the relationship without being seductive or blurring the boundaries.

Clearly speaking as one who is quite comfortable with her sexual feelings, she asks, "Why is the erotic countertransference so difficult to work with, especially with same-sex female patients?" My own opinion on the difficulty in handling erotic transferences, be they heterosexual or homosexual, is the fear/wish that they will be acted on (Maroda, 1997, 1999a,b). This can be especially true regarding disclosure of the erotic countertransference. Many analysts fear that once a disclosure of erotic countertransference has been made, the likelihood becomes greater that some type of sexual acting out will occur, although I have tried to illustrate that this fear is not substantiated by the details of patient sexual abuse documented by Gabbard (1996). The point I have made repeatedly is the critical importance of whether or not the patient was *seeking* the information from the analyst, and whether or not the analyst restricted him or herself to precisely what the patient wanted to know (Maroda, 1994, 1999a).

So even though I agree with much of what Dr. Rosiello says regarding the necessity of acknowledging, and even, at times, revealing the erotic countertransference, I was quite taken aback by some of the things she actually said and did. For example, in her discussion of her patient Pauline, Rosiello describes Pauline's mother as unresponsive and rejecting, often foreclosing any conversation at all by simply telling her to be quiet. Rosiello is far more active with the withdrawn and socially isolated Pauline, presumably to avoid repeating the sins of her mother. When Pauline says she has no sex life, Rosiello asks if she masturbates. I have no problem with this question. However, when Pauline answers that masturbation is too much work and she quits before reaching orgasm, Rosiello responds with, "Don't you use a vibrator?" Not surprisingly, Pauline becomes quite sexually stimulated by this question and immediately runs out and buys a dildo, which she uses before the next session. My question when reading this material was, "Does Dr. Rosiello realize that she has just planted a fantasy in Pauline's mind of her analyst masturbating with a vibrator?" If this was done deliberately, then to what end? Certainly, this goes far beyond affirming Pauline's need to have sex and, in fact, encourages her to think about sex with her analyst.

Rosiello goes on to describe the other signs of Pauline's subsequent overstimulation, including her relentless pursuit of details of her analyst's private life, sexual and otherwise. Pauline is also now openly flirtatious. Rosiello does not say how she herself responded to all these questions and flirtations, but this is a regrettable omission. Did she continue to sexually stimulate her patient, or did she hold more closely to the boundaries of the professional relationship? Having titillated her patient, did Rosiello provide even more stimulating personal information or did she refrain from further blurring the boundaries between a personal and professional relationship? I fear that she did continue to reveal intimate details of her life to Pauline, because Pauline upped the ante by then bringing small presents to her analyst, suggestive of more stimulation and a continuing courtship.

In the ongoing juxtaposition of what Dr. Rosiello seems to know about herself, and what she does with that knowledge, she says, "I have slowly come to the realization that I speak a very passionate language. Words that to me feel warm and intimate, are sometimes experienced as seductive, enticing, and alluring to others." Good, I say to myself. She knows she can be very seductive, even if she is not aware of it at the time. I congratulate her on her willingness to see this about herself, yet I am frankly amazed at how little impact this self-awareness seems to have had on her decisions with regard to Pauline. Does she or doesn't she realize that her seduction of Pauline began with the question about using a vibrator? Or does she realize it, and feel that this is a legitimate opening up of the sexual feelings between them? I would like to know more about what happened between Rosiello and Pauline. Rosiello describes their relationship as warm and very intimate, but it is hard to imagine that stormy periods of frustrated sexual desire would not also be present.

I would be reluctant to make strong statements regarding Rosiello's seductiveness if it were not for her own admission of it, and the evidence presented not only in the case of Pauline, but in the subsequent case history of Simone. In describing Simone's affair with her boss, Tony, Rosiello says, "It often felt like we were mutually visualizing porno flicks as she narrated weekly events with her boss. We were both becoming sexually aroused by her stories." Implied in this is a significant amount of graphic detail, which I think is gratuitous in any treatment situation. This behavior is rationalized by a quote from Benjamin regarding the need for "recognition of desire."[1] Although I am in agreement with both Benjamin and Rosiello that desire must be recognized and affirmed, this is very different from creating a highly charged sexual atmosphere in an analytic session where the patient is encouraged to describe the intimate details of her sex life. Affirmation and voyeurism are not the same thing.

Rosiello also mentions that her own style of dress, use of language, and personal manner have a sexual edge. What does this mean exactly? Is her style of dress overtly sexually revealing or provocative, or does she merely dress stylishly? Is she openly flirtatious or merely emotionally available and engaging? Does she typically have very intense sexual transferences and countertransferences with her patients, or are the three cases she reports atypical?

In her continued discussion of Simone, Rosiello asks all the right questions and is dead-on in her observations. She says she knows she is involved in an enactment with Simone, knows that Simone was imagining having sex with her, and then proceeds to declare that they were, in fact, having a type of sex. She says, "For me, it was sex between Simone and me and it is my interpretation that for Simone it was sex for her, too. We created these sexual feelings together, and maybe I started them." To me, this was an astounding admission. Rosiello said everything I was thinking about her relationship with Simone and assumed she was denying. This therapist doesn't appear to be denying anything that is going on between her and her patients, save the potential destructive consequences of her actions. Just when I thought the whole sexualized relationship with Simone had reached outrageous proportions, Rosiello reports that Simone has a baby, which she nurses in her sessions for the next year.

Next comes her discussion of the sexually aggressive June, who calls her a "fucking cunt" with abandon. When the sex talk between them abates and June becomes obsessively boring, Rosiello lets her have it, again demonstrating her self-awareness by admitting that she had underestimated the effect this would have on June. She says she should have been kinder. I found myself wondering if the only thing that keeps Rosiello's attention for very long is graphic sex talk or some other form of seduction. She concludes her paper quite abruptly, failing to provide any overarching view of what she saw as effective, desirable, therapeutic, or dangerous in her three cases. Her last words are a quote from June referring to her amazement that she keeps on coming week after week. Is this meant as some affirmation of the treatment? Are we to assume that what goes on between them must be therapeutic if June keeps on coming? Or is Rosiello equally amazed that June continues to come?

I am sorry that I do not know more about how Rosiello thinks that these sexual enactments with her patients are therapeutic. As I said previously, I agree with many of her basic notions about the need for handling erotic transferences, and countertransferences, better than we do. I agree that most therapists, including myself, could be much more comfortable with these situations than we are. However, Rosiello's blatant sexual play and seduction of her patients goes way beyond anything that I can condone in the name of allowing room for the erotic transference to emerge and be worked through. I cannot imagine that her admitted form of having sex with her patients would ultimately be therapeutic. How long does the "sex" go on, and how does she manage to move out of this form of relating to explore other important topics in the treatment? What keeps her patients from expecting that actual sex will eventually replace the virtual sex they are having, especially since the boundaries have become so blurred? Do many of them respond like spurned lovers and leave in a rage? Or do they never terminate and stay for the sex with her? Do they stalk her outside of the sessions? These all seem like potential consequences of her behavior.

I try to keep an open mind regarding creative options for engaging patients, particularly those who are difficult to engage, and am happy to consider anything within reason that has some therapeutic potential. However, patients baring their breasts in sessions, having unending periods of graphic sex talk, and being openly seduced by their therapist constitute a level of sexualization that I cannot condone and I feel such behavior is inappropriate. It also concerns me that so many of the provocative exchanges between Rosiello and her patients were initiated by her, rather than by the patient. It makes me wonder how much of what transpired between analyst and patient was actually countertransference dominance rather than a flowering of the erotic transference.

Barbara Tholfsen, in "Cross-Gendered Longings and the Demand for Categorization: Enacting Gender Within the Transference-Countertransference Relationship," addresses an issue that remains controversial for the very reasons that she presents in her paper. On one hand, if we can name something it becomes more real. It provides form and definition. On the other hand, once something has been named it begins a move toward reification, toward rigidity. I find it interesting that both

Marty and Ted practically beg their therapist to name what they feel is wrong with them. Tholfsen is understandably reticent to do this. First of all, how can she know for certain? Second, even if she felt confident about some conclusion regarding these men, would it really be helpful to label them? She is understandably reluctant to label them as freakish or abnormal. She talks about the bind she is in when they desperately want to know what she really thinks and she wants them to give up the notion of diagnosing themselves, in favor of accepting and exploring who they are.

I am sympathetic to Tholfsen's concerns. She knows what her patients may not appreciate—that we know precious little about how our sexual identities, sexual preferences, and gender identities are formed. When our patients ask us for explanations, we are truly at a loss much of the time to provide them with any certainty. What we mostly know is that these things rarely change. Marty is not likely to lose his interest in women's clothing or his fantasies of becoming a woman, no matter what treatment he undergoes. Tholfsen is reluctant to encourage his thoughts of sex change, given what she knows about the depression and suicide rates following reassignment surgery. She wonders if seeking surgery for gender dysphoria might be akin to seeking out a dermatologist for race dysphoria (shades of Michael Jackson). This analogy can be extended further to include longings to be beautiful, taller, shorter, smarter, or richer. How much do we encourage our patients to take any action in their lives, especially if it includes major surgeries? How much do we accept about who we are and how much can we change, both internally and externally? What are the potential consequences? How do we determine what transformations are possible versus what must be grieved as unattainable? Perhaps the vivid imagination of the transvestite should remain just that, a capacity for fantasy and fantasy-based play that can only be fulfilling if left to the world of fantasy. When it comes to gender-changing, it may be a case of being careful what one wishes for.

Tholfsen makes another important point when she talks about Marty's shame. In part, he wants to know what she really sees when she looks at him because he fears that she shares his feelings of loathing and disgust. This is what needs to be discussed in depth, rather than Marty's gender or sexual identity. However, it may be true that both Marty and Ted need to have their therapist admit that they are not normal, meaning not like most other men, even if the therapist herself is uncomfortable with this, simply because they know this to be true. Part of the reason they are obsessed with what is male and what is female, what is heterosexual and what is homosexual, is because they are conflicted in these areas. Most people take their sexuality and their gender for granted. Marty, Ted, and many others do not. So, in an odd way, both these men may be seeking a form of empathy and understanding from Tholfsen when they insist on some definitive feedback from her. They need to know that they have real problems, that they are not just being silly or being sissies. They are in real conflict and in real pain over their identities. They know that most men do not suffer the way they do.

Ted wants Tholfsen to "rate" him on his gender, and she admits that we all do this. We size each other up on any number of variables, including our femininity or masculinity. Tholfsen says Ted is rigid on the issue of gender, yet he perseverates on it because he has unanswered questions. Not fitting the masculine stereotype, he worries about how people see him and asks Tholfsen to give him a reading, presumably because he trusts that she will be honest. Who else can he ask? Who else can he admit these things to? Perhaps a description of what she sees when she looks at Ted would help him in his quest to define himself. Perhaps then he could settle into a reality-based vision of himself and get relief from his fears of how he is seen by others. Tholfsen says that our postmodern version of reality may be too ambiguous to bear. I might add that it is too ambiguous to be helpful.

When patients such as Mary and Ted are ardently seeking feedback, perhaps we fall into our own postmodern trap when we refuse to respond honestly. There is a difference between callously hanging a label on a troubled patient that will only arm him with a new insult versus compassionately helping him draw a portrait of himself that is real and that he may one day accept.

Linda Meyers says early in her paper, "Gay or Straight? Why Do We Really Want to Know?," that being "gay or straight" is a cultural construction. If we are speaking purely about language, about the use of labels, then I would have to agree. What is not socially constructed is whether a person prefers to have sex with the opposite sex, same sex, both, or neither. She says, ". . . implicit in the binary is society's belief in sexual stability; choose and the issue is closed." It has always struck me as odd that heterosexuals, for the most part, are quite comfortable with their label, and also with their sexual stability. Why is it that gays often take such offense to being labeled as gay when straights do not? Doesn't it have more to do with the fact that for many people, gay and straight, gay is a dirty word? And if we who *are* gay, regardless of our sometime attraction to members of the opposite sex, refute this naming of our preference, aren't we implicitly stating that we share the view that there is something wrong with being gay?

I have argued elsewhere (Maroda, 1997) that it is one thing to accept that sexuality, along with gender identification, runs along a continuum, and another to deny that most people ultimately fall into one of two categories when it comes to sexual preference. To postulate two general categories, each containing a broad and diverse array of personalities, styles, and modes of sexual expression, is not nearly as restrictive and depersonalizing as many postmodern theorists would have us believe. Again, do heterosexuals feel pigeonholed by their designation? They do to the extent that we all feel the societal pressure to behave in certain ways (which I do not deny can be oppressive). So I am not saying that societal expectations cannot be oppressive. I just do not agree that the designation of "gay or straight" is as oppressive as it is made out to be. What makes being gay oppressive is not the expectation that we are sexually attracted to the same sex, and rarely intensely attracted to the opposite sex. What makes being gay oppressive is what society says about the meaning of being gay. Society says we are immoral, we are sinful, we are degenerate. Straight people should hide their children from us. Now *that's* oppressive.

Meyers presents her patient, Mary, who is intent on finding out whether or not Meyers is "straight or gay." True to her theoretical and clinical position, Meyers does not answer Mary. Instead, she ponders the question "Is Mary gay?" and then asks the same about herself. I couldn't help but wonder how she could disavow these categorizations and then use them when trying to understand Mary and herself, but she does effectively explore her erotic countertransference to Mary, showing us how her initial discomfort with Mary gave way to her realization that she was sexually aroused in response to her.

Meyers astutely concludes that what Mary is really seeking is for Meyers to be comfortable and honest with herself and her feelings. She says, "When I was denying the erotic countertransference, I was unwittingly increasing her fears of being manipulated and misused." I couldn't agree more. Mary simply wanted to know that Meyers wasn't afraid of what she might feel for Mary, so then Mary could trust her and feel free to express and explore her own feelings. I also agree with Meyers that the question of "Am I straight or am I gay?" can serve to hide an underlying and more important question, but this can be true of any question. That is why we typically discuss such a question and its meaning before deciding to answer or not. Yet I believe that the underlying meaning when a patient asks the analyst, "Are you straight or are you gay?" often involves wanting to know that we have the courage to admit who we are and how we feel, whether society approves or not. This can pave the way for our patients to do the same.

## NOTE

1. See Benjamin, J. (1988), *The Bonds of Love: Psychoanalysis, Feminism, and The Problem of Domination.* New York: Pantheon Books.

## REFERENCES

Gabbard, G. (1996), Lessons to be learned from the study of sexual boundary violations. *American Journal of Psychotherapy,* 50:311-322.

Maroda, K. (1994), *The Power of Countertransference: Innovations in Analytic Technique.* Northvale, NJ: Jason Aronson.

Maroda, K. (1997), Heterosexual displacements of homosexuality: Clinical implications. *Psychoanalytic Dialogues,* 7(6):841-857.

Maroda, K. (1999a), *Seduction, Surrender and Transformation: Emotional Engagement in the Analytic Process.* Hillsdale, NJ: The Analytic Press.

Maroda, K. (1999b), *What's Love Got to Do with It? The Perversion of Desire in the Analytic Relationship.* Paper presented at the Division 39 Spring meetings, April, New York, NY.

Chapter 11

# The Analyst's Erotic Subjectivity: A Reply to Karen Maroda's "On Homoeroticism, Erotic Countertransference, and the Postmodern View of Life"

Florence Rosiello

In Chapter 1 of Maroda's book, *Seduction, Surrender, and Transformation* (1999) she says,

> Our reluctance to admit what we actually do and say when we are working with our patients remains the norm. Worse than that, however, is the tendency to *omit* the mention of interventions that might be controversial. That is, even when clinicians are talking about what they actually do, they frequently fail to include a behavior that they fear being censored for, such as, taking a patient's hand, or disclosing their feelings. The absence of honest discussions of technique has naturally created a most unfertile ground for innovations. (p. 11)

Maroda adds that even with the excitement over new developments in the two-person psychology of the relational theory, analysts are "still reluctant to talk about technique, and there is a regrettable resistance to changing what we do to accommodate our new paradigm . . . if reconceptualizing the analytic relationship doesn't translate into technical changes, how important can these theoretical changes be?" (p. 12).

### Synthesis

One of the paradigmatic changes that has developed, particularly in contemporary theory, is the use of the analyst's countertransference in treatment. Most frequently, countertransference or the analyst's subjectivity is used to inform an interpretation or an insightful response to the patient. Self-disclosure of countertransference is most commonly not provided, although the analyst may decide it is indeed useful and disclose it to the patient. Contemporary psychoanalytic literature is currently focusing on the advantages and disadvantages of self-disclosing, with many authors determining that some analysts are better able to work with self-disclosure than others.

One of the reasons I wrote "On Lust and Loathing" was to openly disclose homoerotic countertransference. In the third paragraph I said, "The focus of this paper . . . will be on the erotic countertransference since it is in the erotic countertransference arena that the erotic transference often gets bogged down or eliminated." I meant to provide my insights to my own interventions and interpretations to three female patients who had developed erotic transference. Only a few of my patients have developed erotic transference and when I write I usually refer to these few. Most of my patients do not have erotic transference feelings. The question of why erotic transference/countertransference does or does not develop between a patient and an analyst is of particular theoretical interest to me.

In wondering and writing about development of erotic transference/countertransference, we have to question "who did what first," according to Maroda. She makes a good point when she asks if my treatment of these three female patients was influenced by "countertransference dominance" and not "a flowering of the erotic transference." To my way of thinking, I cannot really separate the development of my patient's transference from my countertransference—both are mutually constructed by patient and analyst. I don't have to make sure that an erotic transference developed first in my patient, because I don't believe it could possibly just originate in the patient—I'm involved even when I don't know it. Similarly, my countertransference or my subjectivity is also created within the relational mix with ingredients from my patient's transference/subjectivity. Transference and countertransference are not linear. They develop together and are indistinguishable from the whole.

Aron (1996) states, "the term countertransference obscures the recognition that the analyst is often the initiator of the interactional sequences, and therefore the term countertransference minimizes the impact of the analyst's behavior on the transference" (p. 77). Aron continues:

> The relational-perspectivist approach I am advocating views the patient-analyst relationship as continually being established and reestablished through ongoing mutual influence in which both patient and analyst systematically affect, and are affected by, each other. A communication process is established between patient and analyst in which influence flows in both directions. This implies a "two-person psychology." (p. 77)

The essential notion of a two-person psychology is that we make meaningful intersubjective spaces that cannot be broken down into a linear model where one thing causes another. For practical purposes, the analyst may have to think who started it, but still thinking about who started it is a question of perspective. Psychoanalysis is something that is lived forward and understood backward. Similarly, the erotic transference is something lived forward and understood backward, and how we understand it is determined by perspective.

Winnicott (1960) said, "there is no such thing as an infant" (p. 39) and by that he means there is mutual influence between mother and infant even in the womb. I would say there is no such thing as just transference or just countertransference, they are mutually constructed and both are so thick that the analyst can't sit around and wonder "Is it the patient's or is it mine?" Countertransference dominance is subsumed under mutual construction—if it is not, where are we in the development of a two-person psychology?

### The Analytic Frame and Boundaries

Maroda repeatedly appreciates my insights but bemoans that they have no impact on my behavior. Part of her contention is that I blur the boundaries of the analytic frame. She writes that I have selective insight and self-awareness and that my understanding of internal dynamics doesn't extend to my patients. This seems a rather limited interpretation of my treatments on Maroda's part and not very realistic.

My insights and awareness, whether about myself or about my patients, originate from a different subjectivity than Maroda's. Each analyst can only bring his or her own subjectivity to bear on the clinical situation—these differ, one from another, particularly in terms of what each analyst feels to be primary. We are all influenced by who we are in how we organize our analytic frame. For instance, lesbian and gay analysts have a different frame than I do, given their own experiences with homophobia. Analysts of color have a different theoretical frame, given their experiences with racism. I try to keep my own and these other analysts' theoretical paradigms, both traditional and contemporary, in mind when I work with patients. Likewise, I hope that other analysts will consider a relational, mutually constructed, theoretical frame influenced by sexuality in their own work, as well.

Would a theoretical frame influenced by sexuality just blur the boundaries of treatment, as Maroda suggests? Just what are those boundaries? Who set them? Have they changed since the beginning of psychoanalysis? Are they different for analysts who are of different theories, of different generations? Are they different for analysts who live in different cultures, or different for analysts who live in cities rather than in the country are: our boundaries fluid, elastic, rigid, changing? Who tells us what they are? Our institute instructors, our supervisors, our analysts? I think we can all agree that we don't agree on analytic boundaries, some people may have similar analytic boundaries, but I bet they disagree somewhere along the line.

### Clinical Illustrations

I mentioned earlier that I discussed three female patients in "On Lust and Loathing," Pauline who identified as bisexual, Simone who identified as heterosexual, and June who identified as lesbian. In addition to my essay serving as a clinical illustration of erotic countertransference, it also contains lengthy, clinical examples of three different patients. Clinical illustrations are more the exception than the rule in a contemporary psychoanalytic literature which tends to focus on theory, as any new approach would. Essays include vignettes of patient experiences or analyst subjectivity, but rarely include clinical illustration—Dimen (1997) and Pizer (1998) being exceptions who do present both analyst and patient clinical illustrations. "On Lust and Loathing" is a clinical, relational-perspective essay that focuses on erotic countertransference supported by interactions with three female patients who developed erotic transference dynamics. Maroda criticized my treatment of these patients, arguing that I "created a highly charged sexual atmosphere in an analytic session where the patient is encouraged to describe the intimate details of her sex life. Affirmation and voyeurism are not the same thing." Affirmation and voyeurism are not the same thing since it is the voyeur who watches another from a secret position. The restrained analyst does the same thing and keeps mum about it. I addressed sexuality with Pauline, Simone, and June. I have not been mum—to the contrary, I have written my experience with these patients. So I will now present my patients in more detail since Maroda focused on them in her criticism.

## Pauline

Pauline has been in treatment for three years at a frequency of four times a week. She began her analysis sitting up, but after a few months I asked her to move to the couch. When Pauline sat in the chair, from the first session on, she slithered over the cushions, the armrests, fondled the carpet by her feet, slid her hands up from her shoes to her shoulders in what felt like constant movement over her body. She spoke to me with her head tilted, her eyes never looking at anything but me. Before leaving every session, she would stand in the doorway, put on her coat, walk back and forth between the chair and the door (I open the door at the end of all sessions), and would finally exit. She would then turn around at the threshold for one last long look before she left. If a patient acts in such a manner from the first session onward, does that mean she started it? Does it mean that I did because I already existed in the room? I don't much care who started it, and that's why I said, "maybe I did" because mutual construction of emotions and influence eliminates countertransference dominance or transference dominance.

Within a few weeks of treatment, I asked Pauline to begin using the couch for my own relief as well as an attempt to get her to concentrate on her analysis. Now, on the couch, she still slithers and wears short cropped shirts that rise well above her waist when she stretches her

arms above her head. Although Pauline was sensual when I first began treating her, she was not sexually active. She identified as bisexual although she had never slept with a woman. Although she had sex
with men, she never experienced an orgasm. She rarely dated men
and those she did date were eliminated after a few meetings. She did
maintain erotic crushes on unattainable, heterosexual women. My
question about her sexual life or lack thereof, and why didn't she use a
vibrator when she was vibrating visibly in her sessions, seemed natural. Perhaps Pauline was stimulated by this question, but what did it
matter given the state of her already existing stimulation? Maroda then
questions whether or not I knew I "*planted* [italics mine] a fantasy in
Pauline's mind of her analyst masturbating with a vibrator?" Certainly
I knew that, but to my way of thinking, the purpose of treatment is to
create fantasy—fantasy bridges experience, real or dissociated. Fantasy links the multiple layers of the self. In this case, sex for Pauline
was dissociated and my comment about the vibrator addressed a movement of experience, a communication along a network of dissociated
islands, dissociated aspects of the self. Pauline didn't know she was ad-
vertising sex—my question opened up this discussion, it helped her become more creative in talking about it, in conceptualizing it within herself, as a part of herself, about herself as a sexual being.

In the time we've been working together, Pauline has "come out," a
long, complicated, painful experience, and now identifies as lesbian.
She has begun dating available women who also identify as lesbian
and she climaxes during sex with them. She has also been promoted
at work and is earning close to six figures. She is finally attending a
much-desired, though enormously feared, film course. She is attempting a more realistic relationship with her parents. And, recently,
she told me she thinks I'm straight and likes me anyway.

### Simone

Maroda was right that Simone's treatment was full of graphic details
of her boss's sexual interest in her. Was it gratuitous and destructive
as Maroda judged it to be? It was graphic data from my perspective,
not just detail, and more important, it was resistance. I don't think it
was sinful as Maroda infers. Sinful would be destructive and what developed between Simone and me was not sinful, unless talking about

sex is considered so. For Simone, sex got a little dirty with her boss—but I don't think that's a sin either and discussing it with one's analyst is expected when it is within an analytic frame and boundaries that include sexuality. So, in Simone's treatment, did she start the sexual feelings between us when she spoke about her boss's transgressions? Or, did I start the sexual feelings between us because I let her talk about her boss's transgressions?

Again, to my way of thinking, Simone's erotic transference and my erotic countertransference were mutually constructed—not linear, not cause and effect. In "On Lust and Loathing" I stated "We created these sexual feelings together, and maybe I started them," but how would anyone know who truly starts any dynamic first? Certainly, I did not suggest that Simone breast-feed her baby in our session, she just did it; I realized I had seen her breast after she did it and of course we discussed it. But, I remember during our discussion that this experience of a "naked breast-feeding" was nothing compared to Bollas's (1994) essay about a male patient who sexually aroused himself on Bollas's couch and climaxed during the session.

Simone left treatment when she became pregnant with her second child and after she and her husband bought a house in another state. I hear from her by phone on rare occasions and she sends me pictures of her children at Christmas. She says she is happy with her life and her marriage and remembers her affair with her boss as a last hurrah before motherhood. At the time our "sex talk," according to Maroda, communicated Simone's dissociated fears about not being sexual, about becoming a nonsexual mother, like her own mother. This was interpreted to Simone. Her sexual fantasy toward me and my acknowledgement of mine toward her, meant to her an acceptance and recognition of being a sexual subject concurrent with being a mother who still had sexual desires. Our mutually developed fantasies united aspects of her self to other aspects of her self—a creative dynamic that helped Simone eventually bridge two desires—sexuality and motherhood.

## June

Maroda wonders if only "graphic sex talk or some other form of seduction" keeps my attention and she asks the question "Are we to assume that what goes on between [June and myself] . . . must be therapeutic if June keeps on *coming?*" [italics mine]. Certainly, in June's treatment, her loathing of me when I could not tolerate her emotional emptiness led to her talking about her desire to become more intimate, I surmise her emotional emptiness and her resulting verbal aggression were a resistance against her erotic desires to begin with. From the beginning of June's treatment, she spoke about her attraction to me. Although I did not feel a mutual attraction, I have always felt very emotionally related to June, as though I have always known her. Perhaps that feeling is erotic, or perhaps the feeling of having always known her is better defined as loving June.

I have used June as a clinical example in quite a few essays on erotic transference/countertransference, perhaps four or five essays all told. Her treatment and her development over the years are chronicled in these essays (Rosiello, 2000). June recently has been promoted in an office job she took a few years ago. A year ago she began a relationship with a woman with whom she seems to have fallen deeply in love. They are discussing living arrangements and long-term commitment. This is June's first serious relationship in seven years, outside our treatment relationship.

I would credit June most for helping me struggle with my idea that the purpose of treatment is to create fantasy. I recently wrote a paper dealing specifically with how fantasy bridges experience, particularly dissociated experience. The paper begins with June discussing her fetish toward amputees and her pigeon phobia. Our use of fantasy had allowed her to admit her fetish (we were four years into treatment) and to elaborate on her phobia (which I had known about from the get go). In my opinion, dissociated fantasy, sexual or otherwise, fuels creativity and bridges isolated aspects of the self with other self aspects, allowing an inner communication to move along a network linking isolated islands of the self.

Now, in June's treatment, as she discusses her relationship with her lover, which I also understand as an expression of transference developments, she has been attempting to define what love means to her. This from a patient who used to curl up under the kitchen sink and cry for hours when she first began treatment, who couldn't imagine being more than a waitress, and who could only consider being sexual in a ménage à trois because she needed the buffer of another individual. I will cite what she has written because I think it shows her inner growth from dissociated affect to acceptance of her own desires within her self:

> Love is the mutual enjoyment of one another, and an awareness of that mutuality, an awareness of the awareness. It's an "I know you know that I know, and we both know" situation. Love provides a context for parts of the self. . . . In thinking about love, I keep returning to the importance of mutuality, and the awareness of that mutuality. Mutuality in love engenders trust; trust engenders love. As trust grows our capacity to take love expands, and our desire to give love also increases.

Recently, an editor at a publishing house read a few excepts of June's other notes to me that I've quoted in other essays. The editor was impressed with June's writing ability and thought she was quite talented and should write more and publish. I related this to June, who has always harbored a wish to become a writer. When June first started writing notes to me, she only used lower case, no capitalization of any kind, no punctuation, no paragraphs, and no signature. A disjointed self at odds. Now she writes in full sentences, her ideas are thought through, she is more creative, more daring in what she risks saying to me, and through me.

I like what Maroda says about mutuality (1999) and I think it applies to my work with June, Simone, and Pauline, "The essence of mutuality lies in the analyst's co-participation and emotional honesty. . . . I find it unfortunate that so many people have interpreted mutuality primarily in terms of positive emotions, giving short shrift to the primitive and aggressive impulses" (p. 29).

I assume these primitive impulses include sexuality.

## REFERENCES

Aron, L. (1996), *A Meeting of Minds: Mutuality in Psychoanalysis.* Hillsdale, NJ: The Analytic Press.

Bollas, C. (1994), Aspects of the erotic transference. *Psychoanalytic Inquiry,* 14:572-590.

Dimen, M. (1997), *Bodies, Acts and Sex: Thinking Through the Relational.* Paper presented at First Annual Lecture Series, "Contemporary Approaches to Gender and Sexuality," Psychoanalytic Psychotherapy Study Center, New York, September 26.

Maroda, K. J. (1999), *Seduction, Surrender, and Transformation: Emotional Engagement in the Analytic Process.* Hillsdale, NJ: The Analytic Press.

Pizer, S. A. (1998), *Building Bridges: The Negotiation of Paradox in Psychoanalysis.* Hillsdale, NJ: The Analytic Press.

Rosiello, F. (2000), *Deepening Intimacy in Psychotherapy: Using the Erotic Transference and Countertransference.* Northvale, NJ: Jason Aronson.

Winnicott, D.W. (1960), The theory of the parent-infant relationship. In *The Maturational Processes and the Facilitating Environment,* D. W. Winnicott (Ed.). New York: International Universities Press, 1965, pp. 37-55.

# SECTION III:
# GENDER IDENTITY AND CREATIVITY

# Chapter 12

# Gender Identity and Creativity

## Joyce McDougall

This paper is intended as a modest contribution to conceptualizing the construction of gender and sexual role identity as well as its role in creative activity.

Whether we are considering homosexual or heterosexual object orientation, there is no evidence that a psychic representation of core gender identity is inborn. Core gender and sexual role identity are shaped in large part by the experiences of early childhood and the parental discourse on sexuality and sexual role. Freud himself emphasized that the objects of sexual desire are not innate—they have to be "found."

Some forty years ago, in my very first attempt to write a psychoanalytic paper, I gave a lecture to my Paris Society titled "Homosexuality in Women"; this paper was based on a small number of analysands and I drew conclusions that, as a young and inexperienced analyst, I believed could apply to female homosexuality in general. As the years went by, my increasing experience, both with my ongoing self-analysis and what I learned from my lesbian analysands, led me to conclude that the generalizations I had proposed in my lecture were inappropriate and applied only to the analysands quoted in that paper. However, the lecture was subsequently included as a chapter in a 1964 book published in France dealing with various aspects of female sexuality, and was later translated into English (McDougall, 1964). In view of the fact that at that epoch, psychoanalytic studies on female homosexuality were extremely rare, in the ten years that followed, my debutante research was reprinted at the request of different editors, sometimes with minor additions or subtractions. Thus I am frequently credited with having published a number of papers on female homosexuality.[1]

However, the criticisms stirred up by this outdated paper have given me much food for thought and have helped me reflect on certain clinical and theoretical impasses in my early attempts to understand the complexities of sexual orientation. I was saddened to hear recently from an American colleague that I was cited somewhere as believing that "lesbian sex is fictive and illusory."[2] I probably did believe at the time that paper was written that being homosexual must involve some denial of sexual differences as well as confusion about one's gender identity and illusions about one's sexual partner! When my 1968 book *Plaidoyer Pour une Certaine Anormalité* was requested for an English version (McDougall, 1978), this same paper (which does not figure in the French edition) was expressly asked for by the editors who wanted an extra chapter. As though this weren't enough for an immature piece of work, it was then included in a volume on "sexual deviations" sometime in the late 1970s. Thus this one pathetic paper is today frequently presented as a number of different papers by certain colleagues and often accompanied with the mention: "McDougall who has written extensively on lesbian issues!"

However, at least I can comfort myself that, at the time I wrote the paper, in spite of being inexperienced and inundated with bad theory (our analytic teachers of that period regularly referred to homosexuality as a "perversion" and a symptom that should be "cured"), my countertransference was apparently not too noxious for the three analysands quoted therein. Two of them still keep in touch with me; both assumed homosexuality as their orientation, one has herself become a therapist and the second is a gifted artist. The third patient married a man who shared her ambiguous feelings about sexual desire but both very much wanted children—and I get news of these grown-up children from time to time.

In this paper I have chosen the case of a female patient in order to explore to what extent family circumstances and the unconscious wishes of her parents may have contributed to her adult sexual orientation, as well as the role these played in her creative activities. Before coming to a phase that took place in the sixth year of our work together, I shall give a brief account of her family background.

## *Initial Interview*

Mia came to see me some eight years ago. I opened the door of my waiting room to a woman in her early forties, attractively dressed in a gray pantsuit. She began by saying she had an important post in the Ministry of Cultural Affairs and that she was charged, among other duties, with writing cultural surveys of literature and art, but that the quality of her work was falling off. She then went on to say that she was lesbian and was desperately unhappy following the breakdown of a fifteen-year love relationship with Cristina, a French actress—and that this was the main reason she was having difficulty in working. The break in the relationship was precipitated by Mia's discovery, a year earlier, that Cristina had begun a secret love affair with a young Englishwoman, Nathalie.

> I'm so unhappy—as if my life is no longer worth living. Cristina and I have been lovers for so many years and I trusted her completely. She seemed to need me as much as I needed her. She was the total background to my life. Nothing has any meaning without her. She says she can't give up her affair with Nathalie but that it changes nothing as far as our relationship is concerned. It's just an adventure.

She added that Cristina is approaching sixty and had stressed her age to support her right to have this "extra-marital" affair. The "culminating insult," as Mia put it, was Cristina's suggestion that she might enjoy meeting Nathalie and thought that the three of them could establish some kind of ménage à trois. This released a flood of violent quarreling during which time Mia had thoughts of committing suicide. Finally, she had taken her courage in both hands and precipitately left the apartment for which they had shared all costs over the past fifteen years. Much of Mia's furniture was still there and Cristina did everything to prevent her taking from her belongings away. Mia continued:

> That's more than a year ago, yet I still cry every night and still feel totally lost. I try to work on the book I'm doing for the Ministry, but I can't concentrate; I try to play my piano and I start crying. Nothing helps. Cristina keeps begging me to come back,

saying she doesn't want to live without me; that I'm childish and moralistic to have created this rupture for such a minor matter. It's like an unbreachable gap in understanding between us. I've been living an illusion all these years. I can't go back—and I can't go forward either. I can't bear the pain of knowing she loves another woman. Why is it so unbearable? I wonder if I shall ever love again. Why is it such a life and death matter? Can I be helped?

I felt very moved by Mia's pain and her questions. I also found myself thinking back over former patients who had faced similar catastrophic ruptures, in both heterosexual and homosexual love relations, and how the hurt partner often rushed into a new relationship with the hope of avoiding the pain. Mia, on the other hand, was eager to understand why the loss of Cristina was so intolerable to her and why she could not even imagine herself meeting a new lover.

Toward the end of our initial interview, I reviewed what she'd told me and said it seemed as though she'd left some very important parts of herself with Cristina—her capacity to love, her joy in her work, as well as the pleasure she took in writing poetry and in playing music. I then explained briefly what a psychoanalytic engagement involved and said it might help her understand the painful process of mourning and why she was not yet able to take back the many precious parts of herself that bound her to Cristina.

She looked quite surprised and said that this would give her food for thought, then asked if she might see me once more. At our second interview she said, "When I left your office the other day, I felt that a new world might open up inside me." She also told me on this occasion that her mother, who was in her eighties, was dying of AIDS. My shock was visible and she explained that she and her sisters had only just received the verdict: the HIV virus was traced back to some years ago when her mother had received a blood transfusion during a minor surgical intervention—it was contaminated blood. Mia would now have to arrange, somehow, to find time to see her mother regularly, and give her support to face the treatment and the fear of death. Within the next few weeks we had a few scattered sessions in which Mia referred continually to the gravity of her mother's condition as well as to her recurring pain over the loss of Cristina. (I began to sense that the two losses might have something in common and wondered if Cristina had been invested as a maternal figure for Mia.) She also brought a couple of dreams in which she played the role of a child who had lost her way.

At the end of our first year of intermittent sessions, Mia asked whether I could manage to see her on a regular basis and in spite of her frequent absences due to her professional occupations. We are now in the eighth year of our analytic voyage and my interest and fondness for this patient are such that I have usually managed to replace the innumerable sessions she has had to miss because of her work, and she has made the same effort, accepting to come very early in the morning, late in the day, and so on.

I shall briefly describe certain elements of Mia's childhood background insofar as they may shed light on her adult sexual orientation. Most of these details came to light in the first few weeks of our therapeutic voyage, although other essential events that had been totally forgotten only came on the analytic scene as the years went by.

### Mia's Family Background

Mia's mother is a retired lycée professor and her father a government administrator. She has a sister ten years older than herself (whose name also happens to be Cristina!). When Cristina was nine years old, her mother gave birth to a stillborn child—a boy. The following year her mother became pregnant again—and Mia arrived. When Mia was five, another sister (Suzanne) was born. The two sisters are married with children and Mia is very attached to her nieces and nephews.

Mia recalled that, when she was nine, her father received a post some distance from the town where they lived and only returned home on the weekends, a situation that continued until Mia was sixteen. She felt his absence keenly during those seven years and her belief that her mother needed special support from her became acute during this long period. Mia always suspected that her father had a lover in his place of residence but she has no evidence of this. Her sisters are skeptical about this belief and, in addition, unlike Mia, neither of them has the feeling of having been abandoned by their father, or that their mother was depressed throughout those years.

In her early twenties Mia left France to take up a teaching post in Los Angeles and remained there for several years. During a return visit to France (she was then in her late twenties), her father died suddenly. She recalled vividly the scene: her sisters and her mother were talking with the hospital doctors about the measures to be adopted in an attempt to save him, thus she was alone with him at the instant of his death. She sobbed uncontrollably for hours, to the concern of the other members of the bereaved family.

> It was in Los Angeles that I had my first serious love affair with a woman. Up till then I'd had various sexual adventures with different boys but those encounters never meant anything to me—just the feeling that I was doing the right thing; it took some time— and courage—to admit to myself as well as to my mother that I could only love a woman. Mother was most understanding and said I should follow my heart. . . . Of course, I could never have told my father about it! That would have been too much for him to take. In any case, after my father's death I decided to return permanently to France—and that's when I changed professions.

Mia seemed to indicate that in some tragic way her acceptance of her lesbian identity had become associated with her father's death, but it took several years before the implications of this link could be analyzed, thereby enabling Mia not only to freely assume her sexual orientation but also to write her first novel. (I shall return later to this important phase in our psychoanalytic voyage.)

During the early years of regular work together, we had many occasions for exploring hitherto unacknowledged feelings of dependency and separation anxiety. The first noticeable reactions to fantasies of abandonment came through transference manifestations. Mia knew in advance, as all my analysands do, that I was always absent at the time of the Paris school vacations, but it was necessary to remind her of this on every occasion. Each impending absence released a number of anxiety dreams whose themes tended to reveal an alarming disinvestment of her value as an individual. Moreover, she frequently had unusual somatic manifestations during my absence. She would catch colds or flu whenever I was away, and on two occasions suffered from alarming cardiac symptoms. At my insistence, she consulted a leading cardiologist who declared that there was no cardiac pathology. I then learned that Mia's cardiac troubles were not new—they had begun shortly after her father's death. As Mia slowly became convinced that her somatizations were a reaction to separation and loss, she came to question seriously, for the first time, the emotional events that may have surrounded her birth and her place in the family.

### The Dead Boy

On a couple of occasions following a dream, and later a fantasy, concerning a dead child, I asked Mia what she thought may have been the attitude of her parents toward her birth following so closely the death of their son. She treated the notion that this fact could have had any importance with total denial.

> I was sure I was my mother's favorite. I did more to help her than anyone else—and also in a way I was my father's special child too because I was the only one who was keenly interested in intellectual pursuits; he was proud of my academic success.

Then came a dream in which a child was killed and Mia was to be charged with the murder. My immediate reaction was to ask whether it was a little boy or a little girl who died in this dream but I checked this impulse and was pleased when Mia herself said, "Now this time I have to find out what effect that baby's death may have had on my life."

As a result, she decided to ask her sister who was ten years old when Mia was born, if she recalled anything about her birth. Cristina replied:

> My goodness, how could I forget it! But I was always careful not to talk to you about it. Well, Mum and Dad were both convinced the new baby would be a boy, then on the day you were born Dad called me into his study and said "I've some very sad news for you—it's a girl." And he burst into tears.

This led to much construction and reconstruction concerning Mia's vision of her role in the family. Among the different fantasy constructions, she uncovered a feeling of guilt at not having fulfilled her parents' wish for a son and came to connect this with her determination from a very young age that she must do everything she could to "make mother happy." She recalled innumerable efforts to comfort her mother during the seven lonely years when her father was working away from home. She came to question whether she had attempted to take over her father's role by caring so intensely about her mother's welfare. After acknowledging the importance this had always occupied in her inner psychic world, she went on to tell me that in her love relationships she thought exclusively of her partner's pleasure, sexually and otherwise. She added that her lover Cristina had often complained that Mia was too insistent on their sexual relationship and that she much preferred to sleep. Out of love for Cristina, Mia accepted the partial abstinence that had marked the last years of their conjugal relationship and was therefore all the more shocked and hurt when she discovered the existence of Nathalie.

We also came to understand that, under the pressure of the unconscious belief that she should have been a boy and that she was supposed to play her father's role to her abandoned mother, she had fought all her life for her right to be a girl. Apart from her identification to the "father-lover" who brings sexual gratification to the "mother-woman," Mia was extremely critical of her homosexual acquaintances who were notably masculine in their dress, attitudes, and manner. When I asked her the reason for this intolerance, she came to the understanding that she had fought since childhood against the fantasy that she should have been a boy, and had done everything in her power to protect her feminine identity. This was a powerful factor in her giving active support to many political issues, particularly when they involved the ill treatment of women or the problems of children who were the victims of sexual abuse.

### The Little Sister

In the same way in which Mia had repressed all knowledge of her childhood pain and confusion about being born a girl to parents who desired and expected a boy, she also had difficulty in recognizing—and reconstructing—what she had experienced at the time of Suzanne's birth. From time to time she would mention quarrelsome relations with her little sister (whom she always referred to as Sue) which puzzled her. When I asked her if she recalled any jealousy at the time of Sue's arrival in the family she said, "Not at all! I cherished my little sister and was always concerned for her welfare." Yet certain dreams and reports of quarrels and disagreements with Sue tended to reveal the opposite. She slowly recalled how she had become withdrawn around the time of Sue's birth, and how, in her early school years she had closed herself off from the others for hours, reading and listening to music. She also fell in love with another little girl when she was six, only to discover that the intensity was not shared. It seemed that this first experience of love outside the family circle was an attempt to give to another what she desperately desired for herself, as well as trying to resolve her pain around the birth of Sue. We gradually found further evidence that Sue's birth had been a profoundly traumatic event, particularly since their father had shown considerable interest in the new baby. Mia finally admitted that she thought Sue had been her father's real favorite and came to envisage herself as a lonely little girl with Mother and Cristina on one side and Father and Sue on the other.

A typical incident that occurred a couple of years back confirmed these reconstructions. Mia had lunched with Sue and her two children and came to her session later that same day saying that she had tried to talk to Sue about their ambivalent relationship, which had become increasingly evident after the death of their mother some two years earlier:

MIA: I got home from Sue's and was preparing to come here when I discovered I'd lost all my papers: my identity card, my car papers, my credit cards. My first thought was that they must have been stolen, then I realized that I'd left them at Sue's place. I phoned her and explained where I thought they were. She searched everywhere and said they weren't there. Somehow I don't trust her.

JM: As though she's stealing your identity once again?

MIA: Oh, I'm sure you're right! She said she spent thirty minutes searching through every room where I'd been. Why do I still maintain such an infantile attitude toward her? [Mia was so anxious that she couldn't pursue this important question and went on.] So where did I lose the papers? I've looked everywhere in my place and they're not there.

At the end of the session she said, "What shall I do without my papers—I'm leaving for China in three days and I've no time to replace them." Then, rather unexpectedly, a little like a child—which did not in any way resemble her usual adult manner—she said piteously, "What would you do in such a situation?" I said, "Well, if your papers haven't been stolen, then unconsciously you know where they are. I'd go back home and let myself wander without reasoning, to any place that comes to mind with the hope that I might find them." She said, "Is that a psychoanalytic theory?" I replied that I didn't think so, but that it sometimes worked.

Later that evening, I found a message on my telephone recorder saying,

> I did what you said and without reasoning I went through the pockets of a raincoat that I had not worn and there I found my papers and identity cards. I must have put them there absent-mindedly when I was wondering whether it might rain. Please accept my grateful thanks. See you in a couple weeks' time.

Two major events occurred in our third year of working together: the first was Mia's meeting with Suzanne (the same name as Mia's little sister), who was to become her lover. The second was her mother's death.

### Mia's New Companion

Mia met Suzanne at a meeting of professional women concerned with the ill treatment of women in Bosnia and North Africa. Suzanne is a lawyer six years younger than Mia. They were attracted to each other intellectually, and each learned that the other had lived through the painful rupture of a long-standing love affair. Mia was, for the first time, able to contemplate forming a new relationship, although with many misgivings, and the two women eventually decided to live together. After a few months of conjugal life, there were quarrelsome exchanges between them, largely stimulated, according to Mia, by Suzanne's extreme jealousy over Mia's constant preoccupation with her dying mother. She encouraged Suzanne to consult an analyst in order to preserve their relationship. Mia later reported that Suzanne had become much more agreeable to live with since beginning her analysis and they now formed a more loving couple.

### Mother Dies

A year and a half later came the mother's slow and painful death. Mia went through a normal period of great sadness and much reminiscing, alone and with her sisters. There were disputes among the sisters regarding the handling of the small legacy—in particular, the three sisters now owned in common a country house which had been in the family for many years. Sue and Cristina both claimed they needed the country house more than Mia since they had children whereas Mia had only herself to look after. Mia began to explore and try to deal with the conscious and unconscious resentments that she detected in her two sisters toward her lesbian orientation. During this difficult period, she was also able to sort out many different projections and settling of accounts with the past that added to the intensity of these quarrels and she began, very sensitively, to explore the competitive feelings of the three sisters toward their mother. Our work also enabled Mia to analyze more fully her narcissistic need for the omnipotent fantasy that she alone could "repair" mother, and she came to better understand why she had showed more devotion and given more time to visiting the dying woman than her two sisters had done. Her view of the family constellation at this point presented the two sisters as married with special responsibilities while she was in some sense "married" to their mother and therefore had special responsibilities toward her.

After the mother's death, the daughters were advised to sue the doctors responsible for the contaminated blood through which the mother had contracted AIDS. The case was thrown out by the medical legal authorities who said that people of that age were not entitled to compensation. But Suzanne, in her capacity as a lawyer, fought the legal decision, claiming that it was a scandalous outcome, that a woman in excellent health might well have lived on into her eighties, etc., and she won the case. The daughters received compensation, but Mia cried throughout the following session, saying that this money did not bring her mother back and in fact she thought she would give the money to AIDS research.

## *The Novel*

As Mia slowly came to terms with the loss of Cristina and the place that she had held in her life, she began to write her first novel: her autobiographical story. This was a breakthrough in that her former published works were essays dealing with sociocultural themes, whereas this, she knew, would be different from anything she had written before. When the novel was completed, she exclaimed (to my shock), "Now I must destroy it because I would never dare publish it." In exploring my strong countertransference reaction I realized that, in a sense, Mia's novel was akin to a literary baby that we had created together and here she was preparing to abort it! We spent many a session trying to understand the destructive impulse which led to her expressing concern that her colleagues in the Ministry, mostly men, would be shocked by the revelation of her lesbianism. I helped her examine these projections from all angles and, as a result, she finally decided to send the manuscript to one or two publishing houses, expecting rejection. In fact, the manuscript was eagerly taken up by a well-considered publishing house. There was some dissension about the title the book was to receive: Mia wished it to have a title referring to human passion and the pain involved in broken love relationships, but the editor was adamant—the novel was to be titled in such a way that it referred to love relations between women.

When Mia finally received the page proofs, to her surprise a subtitle had been added which caused her further irritation. The editor's additional title read "marginal lovers." As Mia put it, "This ridiculous subtitle suggests that my novel is focused on lesbian secrets whereas its central focus is on the drama of treachery and the emotional turmoil that follows any fracture in human love relations."

The book received considerable success, including laudatory reviews and a request (which Mia accepted) to be interviewed on Radio France; she steered the interview as she put it "toward myself as a female writer rather than a female homosexual."

It seemed to both of us that our analytic voyage had made great headway and when Mia asked whether it might one day draw to a close, I proposed the possibility of terminating "perhaps in a year's time"—which may have precipitated the following dream. The new material that came to light led to my noting the session rather fully.

### The Broken Plate

MIA: I dreamed about you for the first time in a long while! You were entertaining many guests in your home. Your place was a magnificent manor with exquisite gardens and trees everywhere. Somebody who was supposed to be your husband was looking after things. I had broken a beautiful plate and I am looking for you, so I can give you the broken pieces that I am holding in my hands. I don't remember the end of the dream, but I know it was a happy feeling, as though, in spite of my having broken the plate, this would be a peaceful matter between us. [Mia went on to say that she didn't understand the dream at all and could not associate to any of its elements.]

JM: [thinking to myself that the plate might represent something belonging to me that she wished to break—or some broken parts of herself that required mending, perhaps related to the tentative idea of our work terminating sometime in the near future, I said] And the broken plate?

MIA: I'm not someone who breaks plates. I'm a very careful person.

JM: Only my things? And only in a dream?

MIA: [She laughed.] Wait a minute—I've just thought of something. *Mon Dieu!* I haven't thought of this in years! I was—er—about six and I was helping my mother set the table because we were expecting guests. I always tried desperately to help—like a grown up—so I had taken four or five plates together to put on the table, but they were so heavy I dropped them and every one was broken. [Her voice suddenly sounded like that of a terrified six-year-old.]

JM: [After a relatively long silence, imagining that I myself had broken the plates, I spoke] And what did mother say?

MIA: Oh, she said, "Those who break plates pay for them"—and I paid for months and months out of my pocket money until every plate had been paid for.

JM: You said my husband was in the dream; was your father in the real scene on that occasion?

MIA: Oh, yes, he was! *Tiens!* Now I remember he came forward and said, "But she's only trying to help; she didn't mean to break the plates!" But my mother was adamant, and of course she was right! I'd done something quite unpardonable. [She makes a gesture toward my chair as though to convince me of the seriousness of her misdeed.]

JM: [Impulsively I wanted to say something like, "Why are you so hard on yourself," but I immediately recognized that this was my problem. Then I tried to feel the situation as the six-year-old had lived it.] As though you'd broken your mother into pieces?

MIA: Hmm . . . just the kind of fantasies I never want to admit to having. [Long pause] You know I still worry about her and whether I really looked after her properly all those years. I did everything I could to make her feel cared for. Did I smash her in my childish mind?

JM: [I thought back to former sessions in which Mia had come to feel that in a childlike megalomanic way she was responsible for the baby boy's death.] Well, you smashed her tummy when you got rid of that baby boy—and maybe you wanted to do it again when Sue was inside her?

MIA: Yeah . . . I know now that all my fears of dying when I was a kid are connected with such wishes. [Long pause] But those broken plates are still a searing memory. I felt so humiliated.

JM: Perhaps you, too, were the broken plate—the image of yourself as a helpful little girl was smashed.

MIA: In last night's dream, I was bringing the broken pieces to you in quite a happy frame of mind. And you and your husband seemed very loving and quite happy about everything, too.

JM: Could the happy couple also represent your own parents? And perhaps your feeling that the broken plate was not catastrophic may express a wish for your parents to be a loving sexual couple?

MIA: That's true! I always thought of them as disunited. Well, maybe that's what I wanted to believe. [Pause] Since it was you and your husband, does the dream relate to us also?

JM: I was wondering if you were also counting on me to mend the broken pieces of yourself, to give you a better image of yourself as the helpful and caring little girl you tried so hard to be . . . and it might suggest that you can envisage our separating one day without your feeling broken or abandoned?

MIA: Yes, I'm beginning to think that that's possible. You know, the most precious thing I've gained in these years of working with you is to have discovered my identity, not only my feminine identity but also who I am as a person. I no longer feel broken—and I want to thank you for that.

I communicated my feeling that I too sensed she no longer felt "broken" but at the same time themes of separation and loss had been predominant throughout our psychoanalytic relationship and I proposed that we might look more closely at those losses that had been traumatic for her before the break with Cristina.

MIA: Yes, indeed! I now understand that when people commit such treachery, they're making others suffer the pain to which they had to submit when they were children. [A long pause] I'm thinking back to how bad I felt every weekend when my father left town, leaving Mother alone. [Pause] And also how important it's been for me to discover that I was not the boy my parents wanted. I had to lose some illusions there, too! [Another long pause] But you showed me how I always fought to protect my feminine self and sexuality—and thanks to our work, I now feel I have a perfect right to my lesbian identity. I still remember your saying "that little girl of the past made a creative choice in a very painful situation." [Another very long pause] For some strange reason, I've never told you something my mother confided to me when I was an adolescent and which she never told my sisters: that she had been sexually abused by her own father. [I was taken aback by this revelation and also thought to myself that this gave a glimpse into special projections that the mother may have made onto this particular daughter.] Mum always used to say to me, "Don't ever depend on a man for support. Be sure to have your own career and keep your independence." [Another pause] All those adventures I had with different men up to my twenties were just a cover-up. I was trying to do what my mother proclaimed the world expected of me.

JM: [For a moment I felt somewhat confused—just as Mia might have felt in listening to her mother's implicit messages.] Were you try-

ing to do what your mother said was expected—get yourself a
man, while at the same time receiving a contrary message, "Trust
no man"?

MIA: [Laughing] Oh, yes! That was the main message! And I now understand in a new way, why, when I'm making love, in my mind I
always imagine I am bringing my woman lover what a man could
have brought her if that had been her sexual choice. To give my
lover pleasure has always been my greatest pleasure.

At this point I felt I understood more profoundly why the idea of
treachery had been so totally unimaginable to Mia. In her unconscious fantasy, she was repairing her mother not only for the abandonment by the father, but also for the abuse her mother had suffered
at the hands of her own father and—as with everybody's fantasy concerning the profound significance of their love relations—this had
become Mia's lifetime ideal.

At a later session Mia said, "I now realize that those who commit
such treachery are making others suffer the pain to which they have
had to submit, as though to prove their own power to annihilate another." She then went on to say that she had been trying to gather her
own history together and to detect the role of the different women
lovers in her life. Looking back on what she still referred to as
Cristina's "treason" or "treachery," she added that she now understood clearly what she should have known all along—namely the role
that she had played in Cristina's inner psychic world—and how it was
almost predestined that the relationship would end in catastrophe for
Mia. She also recognized that Mia's suffering would be incomprehensible to Cristina who, in spite of having endured much pain in her
own life history, would never accept that she was now wreaking ven-
geance on Mia for the pain of the past.

I would like to make a couple of remarks concerning patients
whose suffering stems mainly from the traumatic effect of the onslaught of either a primary caretaking or present-day love object.
When the analysand begins to understand that her suffering receives
added intensity from dramatic situations of the past, this acquisition
of meaning is a powerful factor in promoting psychic change. Thus,
when the analysand is able (and willing) to seek some understanding
of what may be taking place in the internal world of the hurtful other

that might give meaning to his or her behavior, the pain of the abandonment, cruelty, absence, or treachery frequently becomes more
bearable. For this reason I had encouraged Mia to try to imagine the
blind forces that might shed some light on Cristina's behavior.[3]

The second point I want to emphasize is that clinical experience
has led me to discover that when an analysand can make sense of the
other's hurtful behavior, particularly in the case of an internal parental figure experienced by the child within as a consistently trauma-
tizing object, this frequently releases creative potentialities that have
been paralyzed so that the psychic energy endlessly tied to the traumatic event can now be liberated toward other ends.

Although Mia suffered still from her moments of longing for the
lost paradise she had known, she began to analyze the factors in
Cristina's own life history that might account for her treachery.
Around this point in her analysis, she agreed to see Cristina once
again but resisted the latter's attempts to induce her to come back.
"Cristina says I talk about nothing but her treachery, and that this has
no meaning in a love relationship, that true love does not submit to
obligations . . . and so on." As Mia was to write later, "The love we
shared, which I believed was evidence of an enduring peace, was
nothing but an armistice."

The beneficial effect of Mia's attempt to understand Cristina's
hurtful or incomprehensible behavior inspired her to take extensive
notes on two major themes: one on the internal and contrasting family
dramas of the three sisters and their very different images of their
mother and ways of relating to her, and another dealing with her frac-
tured love relationship and what she claimed was a growing awareness of the frequency of this kind of drama among her lesbian friends.

At one session, while trying to probe further the factors in Cristina's inner psychic universe that would account for her infidelity, she
said:

> But what is less clear in my mind is what Cristina represented
> for me. Anyway, thanks to her treachery, I've had the experience
> of my analysis. In a sense, she could not have brought me a
> greater gift. [Long silence] I felt totally destroyed—it was much
> more than the loss of the person I loved and the person I thought
> loved me. You told me years ago when I first came to see you,

that it was as though I'd lost a vital part of myself, as though I'd left so much of myself with Cristina that it would take time to recover these lost parts. Yes, I felt broken in two. [Long pause] That makes me think again of my mother's death. You have sometimes interpreted that I had not been able to take from my mother all the secrets of her womanhood that I longed to receive. Was I looking to Cristina to give me something my mother withheld from me? [Another long pause] I don't know why, but I'm now thinking about the new novel I'm writing . . . or rather the novel is writing itself. I don't even know where it's taking me.

Thinking to myself that this new novel might lead us to what she was searching for in order to integrate more profoundly her feelings connected with the loss of Cristina, I asked her if she felt like talking about the new novel—a thing I would not usually do regarding creative work!

I'd love to tell you about it . . . as far as it's gone. Well for the moment it's called *Le Sosie*.[4] [Mia stopped suddenly, then continued.] Well, I don't know where it'll go from there. [Pause] Does this novel have something to do with my relationship with Cristina? She was in no way my double!

I found it interesting that Mia made no link with her earlier association to what I had told her six years ago: that in losing Cristina, she seemed to feel she had lost a vital part of herself. Her novel could well be taken to mean that the heroine was searching for her own lost (and sad, orphaned) self. I didn't mention this since I usually refrain from interpreting the underlying significance of a piece of creative work—unless of course the analysand has come to treatment because of a severe block around this particular work. Mia then suddenly recalled a dream she had earlier in the week.

I had gone to what was my mother's apartment but strangely enough I realize that my old lover, Cristina, is living there. I don't see her anywhere, but I see all the books, paintings, and furniture that belonged to my mother. I'm afraid Cristina may not know how to look after these things properly or not know how the household runs so I begin leaving her a number of written messages to explain what she must do.

The only associations Mia could find were that she avoided visiting the apartment because of her sadness over her mother's death.

JM: You were writing something.

MIA: Yes, the words . . . as if I were telling Cristina through my words what she needed to know. Has this something to do with my writing?

JM: It seems that Cristina was to take over in some way from your mother—and perhaps the "messages" were to tell her how to do this?

MIA: Oh yes! . . . as though she was to fulfill what my mother should have done. It suddenly occurs to me that what I wanted from Cristina was all that I was unable to take from my mother, as though I were trying to recover something I had lost. [Pause] I believe I'm trying to re-create, through my writing, some lost parts of myself.

That was the end of the session.

### The "Memory Spasm"

In the year that followed the publication of her first novel, Mia was invited to Nice to take part in a colloquium on the following theme: "The Novel Today." She had carefully prepared her contribution: a study of the history of the novel from its earliest origins in French literature. On her return to Paris, she recounted the drama that had occurred during the colloquium.

First she recalled how proud she had been to find that she had been seated next to the renowned French playwright, Félicien Marceau. Then followed the presentation to the public of all the participants on the panel. When the woman president came to present Mia, to her surprise and discontent, the president began by making reference to Mia's autobiographical novel, and this unexpected public announcement precipitated a sudden strange amnesia: Mia's first reaction was to ask herself where she was and why she was sitting at this table with people whom she no longer recognized. She then felt intense panic at the idea that perhaps she was expected to talk—but she also no longer knew what she was supposed to talk about. All that she could recall was that the president had said there would be a pause for coffee in the middle of the morning. She understood nothing of the first speaker's presentation and anxiously awaited the coffee break. Turning to the elderly gentleman seated next to her whom she did not recognize, she said she didn't feel well and that she wanted to go back to her hotel. At the coffee break two women offered to accompany her to her hotel and showed surprise when she said she did not know where she was lodged. The organizers supplied the name of the hotel but she no longer knew the number of her room. The women, very concerned, called a doctor who gave Mia something to help her sleep.

She woke up several hours later and then remembered everything as well as realizing that the time for giving her paper had gone by. There was a message from the organizers saying that they had rescheduled her presentation for the following morning. She telephoned her lover, explaining what had happened and saying that she was going to return immediately to Paris. Suzanne, however, insisted that Mia must stay and give her paper—which she did, apparently with considerable success.

The clinical examinations undertaken on her return showed no neurological perturbation and when Mia asked the neuropsychiatrist, "Can you please explain the cause of my amnesia?" After a brief hesitation he replied, "You have suffered a memory spasm!"

In the session that followed, I encouraged Mia to examine carefully all the surrounding circumstances that may have contributed to this episode of hysterical amnesia. First of all, she recalled looking at Félicien Marceau and thinking to herself, "He must be the age my father would have been were he still alive," and we came to understand that she had projected a kind of paternal transference onto the playwright. She then recalled thinking, "If my Dad were still alive, he'd be proud of me for presenting a learned paper on 'the history of the novel.'" But after the president's introduction and her mention of Mia's autobiographical novel, Mia suddenly realized that if her father had been there he would also have learned for the first time that his daughter was lesbian! She had never wished to reveal this to him because she thought he would not be able to tolerate this knowledge.

I then reminded her that when she returned from California, where, for the first time she had assumed her lesbian orientation, her father had died in her arms. I proposed a working hypothesis to the effect that her "memory spasm" might well have been an unconscious attempt on her part to protect her father from the fantasy that this revelation "might have killed him," which of course would have engendered intolerable feelings of guilt. Mia felt convinced that this hypothesis pointed to a profound inner truth.

At a subsequent session, Mia further recalled that it was in Nice that her mother had a love affair some years after the death of Mia's father—a detail of her family history that she had never once mentioned in our seven years of analytic work! Thus new heterosexual and homosexual Oedipal elements began to appear on the analytic stage. Mia then talked for the first time about her father's "distant and cold way of relating" and that, until she became more clearly aware of her lesbian orientation, she had chosen male lovers who, like her father, were cold and distant in their attitude to her. Discovering what she had experienced as the fierce passion of her first female lovers had been a powerful factor in leading her to assume her lesbian identity and to fully accept that this was her desire and her destiny.

We also came to understand that by admitting that her mother was able to love another man—someone whom Mia thought was a warmer and more passionate partner for her mother, she began to sense that her attempts "to keep father and mother separate" in her internal world had played an inhibitory role in her creativity. It seemed as though, through permitting the masculine and feminine elements within herself to come together in a new way, she was now flooded with ideas for further creative works.

In a later session Mia began fulminating in angry tones against "the prevailing misogynous attitudes of every country in Europe."

JM: We might recall that you yourself suffered, so to speak, from a misogynistic attitude from the time of your birth (if not before); to be a girl was unexpected, humiliating, wrong.

MIA: How right you are. This was imprinted on me before I was even born!

She further recalled that her mother had similar feelings of suffering from antagonistic and denegratory attitudes toward women. The socio-cultural factors to which Mia referred are of course quite accurate, but for Mia, these had acquired increased intensity in view of her personal past.

### Excerpts from the Novel

I shall now conclude by quoting the opening lines of Mia's autobiographical novel since they express, metaphorically, some of the contours of our analytic voyage: she claims she would never have permitted herself to write an authentic autobiography of this period of her life nor would she have known how to write it without the insights that her analysis has brought her. She added that she thought that the courage to do so came from "the feeling of being understood and totally accepted by you."

Before quoting from Mia's first novel, I should mention that she gave me permission to quote this fragment of her analytic adventure. After reading the above clinical vignettes she wrote back: "I would be happy for you to make use of these notes in any way you want. And by the way I wish you could be my translator if ever my book is accepted for an Anglo-Saxon edition!"

Her novel begins with these lines [I'm translating them as accurately as I can]:

> Paradise lost haunts the history of humankind. A thousand times Adam and Eve are banished from their protected space radiated with warmth and friendship, a place where time is immobile and the infinite arouses no anguish. I see them, gasping feverishly and filled with fear, seeking everywhere for the entry door which has become forbidden, certain that they will find it again and convinced that their creator could never have treated them so unjustly. They penetrate many a secret cave with the hope of discovering their lost vision of the absolute; they climb incredible mountains in the attempt to catch a mere glimpse of the Eden they once had known, with its streams, its little decorative gardens set about with statues, water basins, hidden hedges and sweetly scented plants. Often, in the midst of an arid desert, im-

pregnated with thirst and death, the mirage reappeared. When they had not the strength to continue, when hatred turned them one against the other and weariness banished their desire, suddenly they would believe that they had found it once again. But it was never more than an oasis, a tamed volcano, violet-hued water haunted by sharks. Ersatz.

In turn, I have followed in their footsteps. I had never suffered such treachery. At least that's what I believed . . . but the anxiety that had been with me ever since my childhood, my raging need to exist, and my terror of death were already the trace of some bygone, unknown treachery. When, years later, the same thing happened to me, leaving me from one day to the next in the black hole of nothingness, I refound my childhood anguish . . .

And the little girl who sleeps in my memory has taken the same pathway. No one had explained anything to her. Of course. Does one ever explain such things? Can one ever truly know what one is seeking?

## NOTES

1. As one of my colleagues expressed it, I could more aptly be criticized for not having pursued this line of research further! In fact, I have been more involved in the last thirty years in trying to understand the enigmas of the psychosoma, child psychosis, and primitive mental states as well as the questions posed by inhibitions in creativity.

2. Editor's note: For example, see Erica Schoenberg's Psychoanalytic theories of lesbian desire: A social constructionist critique. In *Disorienting Sexualities,* T. Domenici and R. Lesser (Eds.). New York: Routledge, pp. 65-82.

3. I will not go into the lover's childhood background and the extent to which it illuminated the totally unexpected "treachery," but our analytic work on this theme proved helpful in enabling Mia to continue with the work of mourning—and also freed her to meet her new partner some time after the rupture with Cristina. In all, this took two years of intensive therapeutic endeavor on Mia's part as well as mine.

4. In English this would translate as "The Double," but includes the idea of an exact or almost mirror image of oneself. The word is derived from the character Sosia in Molière's *Amphytryon*. In Mia's new novel, the heroine has heard that she has a *sosie* and she decides that she will try to find this person, get to know her, see whether they have something in common, and whether there may be some mysterious link between them. The heroine follows many divergent and dead-end clues but

eventually meets the other woman. To her astonishment the *sosie* is quite unlike the heroine in temperament in that she's a very sad woman; her life has been filled with tragedy of every kind, beginning with the dramatic loss of both her parents. The heroine decides she must try to help her *sosie* find some fulfillment in life.

# REFERENCES

McDougall, J. (1964), Homosexuality in women. In *Female Sexuality: New Psychoanalytic Views,* J. Chasseguet-Smirgel (Ed.) Ann Arbor, MI: Michigan University Press, 1970, pp. 171-212.

McDougall, J. (1978), *Plea for a Measure of Abnormality.* New York: International Universities Press.

# SECTION IV:
# TWO CASES OF PSYCHOTHERAPY
# WITH PEOPLE WITH HIV/AIDS

Chapter 13

# Psychoanalytic Treatment of an Asymptomatic HIV-Positive Gay Man

Ubaldo Leli

## *Introduction*

This paper describes the psychoanalytic treatment of an asymptomatic HIV-positive gay man. At present, the analysis is in its fifth year, and termination themes are apparent and central to the analysis, although a termination date has not yet been set.

This particular patient presented a formidable challenge to psychoanalytic treatment, independently of his serological status. A history of alcoholism, suicide attempts, depression requiring pharmacological maintenance, and his general proclivity to acting out, coupled with the restricted nature of his object relations, made the decision of whether to treat him with psychoanalysis versus psychoanalytic psychotherapy (Kernberg, 1999) a very difficult one.

## *Background*

Mr. H. was referred to treatment by one of the AIDS treatment programs in New York City. He was sent for analysis by his psychiatrist, who felt he could improve his quality of life from an in-depth exploration of his internal world. Mr. H. was in his early forties, gay, asymptomatic HIV-positive with a T-cell count in the 500s, and compliant with medical treatment. He was a recovering alcoholic in Alcoholics Anonymous, who had survived his lover E., who had died of AIDS four years earlier after a relationship of four years. The patient had accompanied E. through his illness and painful death, becoming HIV-positive himself in 1991. My impression of Mr. H. from his autobiography was of a man with a chaotic lifestyle, dangerous binge-drinking, difficulties with interpersonal relations and impulse-control, and a pronounced sense of grandiosity, expressing itself in a negative manner, much like a child seeking negative attention.

At age nineteen, when he was not accepted into medical school, Mr. H. tried to kill himself by overdosing on aspirin. A year later, he slashed his wrists after attending a piano concert, where he became overwhelmed by a sense of inadequacy. Although not even an amateur pianist, Mr. H. despaired that he would ever become a concert artist as successful as the performer he had just seen. At that time he was already depressed and discouraged because of his relationship with a lover who came from a wealthier background and made him feel inadequate and worthless. He attributed part of his feelings of inferiority to the ethnic backgrounds of his family, which at that time he considered very undesirable.

He first consulted a psychiatrist at age twenty-one, but with no follow up. His second suicide attempt occurred shortly thereafter. At this point he was admitted to an inpatient unit where he received five times per week face-to-face psychotherapy (no medication) for one and a half years. Mr. H. admits that he attempted to undermine the therapy by engaging the therapist in arguments, threatening suicide, manipulating the staff of the hospital with oppositional and histrionic behaviors, and systematically attempting to defeat all their rules. Eventually, when his family's financial situation deteriorated and his father was unable to pay the private hospital fees, Mr. H. was discharged. He still ruminates angrily regarding the therapist's refusal to see him outside the hospital after he was unable to pay.

Throughout his life, with the exception of seven years (between 1987 and 1994) during which he was sober, Mr. H. drank heavily and experimented with various drugs. He earned a liberal arts degree, his main interests being literature and visual arts. Upon finishing school he taught until he moved to New York following the death of his lover.

Mr. H.'s parents were wealthy. The patient grew up raised by nannies. He also had encopresis until age seven. He describes his father as the person he was closest to—a sweet, loving man who would spend time with him hunting and fishing, and who continued to provide for Mr. H. throughout his life. The patient's mother was a fun-loving woman, intelligent and urbane, but moody, able to switch when upset from being loving and supportive to being cold, distant, and withdrawn. The patient felt "treated like a doll," placed on the shelf after use. His relationship with his two sisters was difficult. The patient's older sister died in 1987 of cancer, and he describes her as very close to him. His younger sister is an alcoholic and has no contact with the patient. Mr. H. describes his family as chaotic and lacking cohesion.

The patient had sexual feelings for other boys from age four. At age eleven, he fell in love and had his first steady affair with the twelve-year-old brother of his brother-in-law. The affair lasted for about three years, until the patient left to attend boarding school where he experienced an idealized asexual relationship with a boy in his class.

At nineteen Mr. H. "came out" to his family and friends as a gay man. He met a man of higher social status and they became lovers. They lived together for one year, followed by two years of fights, abuse, and humiliation. The relationship ended after the patient was discharged from his one and one-half year hospitalization. After the end of this relationship he became involved with a rich woman, a heroin addict, with whom he had a nine-month relationship, involving sex. He was attracted by her large fortune and by superficially glamorous aspects of her lifestyle, but ultimately the relationship failed. This was followed by an eight-year relationship with a man, which degenerated as Mr. H. grew apart from his lover: his stopping drinking was soon followed by the end of their relationship.

Six months later the patient met E., his most recent lover, with whom he remained until E.'s death of AIDS. E., the "love of his life," was of a socially inferior class, came from a rural area, and was nearly illiterate, but he was warm, intense, and able to make Mr. H. feel loved and excited sexually. Their relationship had sexual and psychological sadomasochistic elements. He feels that his love for E. was something meaningful in his life.

### Diagnosis and Indications for Treatment

I saw this forty-one-year-old gay man with severe character pathology as having a borderline personality organization, characterized by impulsivity, self-destructive acting out, free floating anxiety, perversity, narcissistic features, and a sense of emptiness. His object relations appeared primarily part-object relations and tended to be bidimensional and dysfunctional. I expected that the analysis of his character traits and the interpretation of his part-object relations enacted in the transference in a classic analytic setting would produce a coalescence of his internal fragmented reality, ultimately leading to more realistic and mature self-representations and deeper object relations. In sum, I felt that only the intensity and depth of classic psychoanalysis had a chance of producing mutative change in this patient.

### Treatment Summary

Mr. H. was a handsome, graying white man, fashionably dressed, with chiseled, high cheekbones and a shy demeanor. During the initial interviews he was verbal, articulate, and showed intelligence, education, and good taste. A love for all things European was connected with his choice of profession. His wit, humor, and a certain blasé attitude toward the sad reality of his situation all made my interactions with this patient stimulating. Before we first met, I was faxed an autobiography, hand-written by the patient, which made it clear that he had difficulties in many areas of his life. The document had a provocative tone, and in the first enactment of countertransference, I interpreted it as an attempt on the part of Mr. H., in an initial resistance, to present himself as worse than he was in order to dissuade me from accepting him into treatment. Eventually, with chagrin, I realized that the contents of the document were more than accurate, and I had countertransferentially colluded with the patient to accept him into treatment by overlooking the high risks intrinsic in working in a classical analytic setting with a person prone to acting out self-destructively and with powerful narcissistic defenses.

When we first met, Mr. H. was planning a long trip to Europe. He had just earned an MA in oil painting, and would be without a job after the end of the current academic year. It seemed that his HIV status—a ticket to death—and his apparent galloping financial impoverishment were purposely kept out of the scope of our initial meetings, and of the twice weekly therapy that followed, in preparation for classic analysis. During these initial meetings, I had a glimpse of an important theme of the analysis. Mr. H. nurtured a conscious grandiose fantasy of dying as a hero after having moved to the city of his dreams—New York—and finally having concentrated on painting, which he always had considered his deep-seated, all-encompassing interest.

Just before our first meeting, Mr. H. hired a gym trainer by the name of Aldo to supervise his athletic workout. Aware that he had known my name for some time, I interpreted that his trainer's name was contained in mine (U-B-ALDO), and one could speculate—I added jokingly—that he wished me to be his trainer: "You be Aldo!" The overlapping of me with the trainer was confirmed by the associations following my interpretation and its nature became clearer . "Maybe he [Aldo] does not care about me . . . I am just another client . . . I am just another paying client for you too . . . I would like to tell him my feelings, how much I admire him." And then: "Aldo is never going to be more than a friend. Then I think I want to kill myself. I'd rather die if nobody loves me. [Pause] As long as I think about Aldo . . . it's safer. I wouldn't lose control." I commented on the fact that he was blushing.

A series of sexual fantasies about me followed. He wanted to know whether I was gay or not, if I had a lover, where I lived. He wondered how I or he would react if we met in a casual social setting, whether I would be sexually available, how much easier it would be for him if I were a friend or a lover rather than a cold, detached analyst. His initial transference, as expressed in this material, was a blend of idealization and strongly erotized features. He wished me to be his friend/lover—I suggested that, perhaps, he could thus control me better and prevent us from entering a deeper layer of his feelings: a terrifying proposition for him. After twenty-four sessions, we commenced analysis, using the couch four times a week.

Mr. H.'s first dream appeared during the first week on the couch and portrayed him visiting his deceased lover, E., in a shop that E. had borrowed from a friend. It was located in the back of an art gallery. He was surprised that he did not have sex with E. as usual; rather, he experienced a feeling of dread that he was back with all his old problems. At the time, I was using an office borrowed from a friend that had his name on the door, sharing the entrance with an art gallery located upstairs in the same building. Mr. H. had no trouble identifying my office and the condensation of his deceased lover with me. In the dream, E. was wearing a shirt similar to the one I was wearing the first time we met, he remembered. I realized that some of the basic fantasies of the treatment would center on reenacting in the transference the relationship with E., and based on what I knew of their relationship, I anticipated that sadomasochistic elements would eventually surface.

In the first months of his analysis, Mr. H. became more and more obsessed with my life and continued to develop a strongly erotized transference. Sadomasochistic features started coloring it. I became the dark figure under an umbrella—a Nazi officer with a yellow flower on his lapel, he said—surrounded by cut-up animal carcasses, in Francis Bacon's famous *Painting, 1946*. He felt I had control over his life and I was making him undergo the quasi-surgical procedure of psychoanalysis. The couch became a surgical bed, the consulting room a torture chamber where he went everyday with a mix of anticipation despite a nagging feeling of dread.

"I hate to lie on this couch. I wanted to bring in the Bacon painting to show you what I mean . . . I also paint monsters myself . . . maybe they are me . . . those hideous figures . . . [Pause] . . . I feel like jumping out of the window . . . I am sick of myself. I hate my life. I don't know why . . . [Pause] . . . I am getting to be middle aged and I have to accept being unhappy, unattractive, unfulfilled. [And then, after a long silence] I have only you. . . . Nobody else in my life. Most of my best friends have died of AIDS . . . [Pause] . . . I wonder about how you live. . . . Are you like me? . . . Will you disappear on me? . . . I worry that you will move back to Europe, or just not show up one day . . . maybe you are HIV-positive too and you'll die on me like all the others."

Mr. H.'s wish to control me and at the same time his wish to be controlled by me, in order to make sure I would not abandon him, surfaced in a major episode of acting-out—a severe assault against the treatment frame that occurred around the seventh month of analysis. Mr. H. had accumulated a large unpaid bill and had spent all his inheritance, endangering the continuation of treatment. An exploration of the fantasies underlying this crisis revealed a wish on the part of

Mr. H. to see whether I would treat him as a special patient whom I would continue to see for free. When I refused to gratify this transferential wish, but rather interpreted it by clarifying that we had agreed that he had to pay for his treatment, and specifying a payment deadline, he became very angry, but promptly came up with enough money to pay his bill in full. Mr. H.'s erotic and seductive transference abated somewhat following a series of interpretations of his acting-out as an attempt to destroy my function as his analyst by drawing me into a dyadic, maternal relationship—I should gratify his wish to be loved, and should take care of him unconditionally.

This was only the first of many enactments aimed at undermining the treatment. Mr. H. continued to unconsciously attempt to transform my willingness and capacity to help him into a murderous collusion with his self-destructive impulses in a spiraling series of sadomasochistic temptations. For example, in one of the sessions later in the first year of treatment he asked, "I forgot to take my antivirals this morning, and I forgot to bring my pills to work. I wanted to ask you if you think I should go home to take a dose as soon as possible and miss my AA meeting, which is right after this session, or go to the AA meeting and skip another dose of antivirals."

I demonstrated the perversity in the transference by saying, "I feel cornered. No matter what I recommend, I will contribute to your self-destructiveness. Either you'll risk drinking by missing your AA meeting, or you'll be overtaken by the deadly virus if you miss your pills. You are drawing out my best part, the one that wants to help you, and transforming it into murderous aggression."

The patient realized with surprise that this is his primary mode of interaction with others, especially when love is potentially offered. This was followed by a series of genetic associations:

"I think it comes from my mother. She was cruel. She taught us how to be cruel. [Pause] She would be spiteful if she had to do something that bothered her. Once some little boys came in asking for a glass of water. They lived across the street. She was furious—Don't they have water in their house? [Pause] She and my sister also put my father down all the time . . . I was so resentful . . . they hated all men . . . they would say of a man whom they did not respect that he had to sit to 'wet.' "

I thought that Mr. H.'s sadomasochistic way of relating to me in the transference, and to his lover E. in the past, came from his early relationship with his mother, which oscillated between placing him at the absolute center of her attention, and then arbitrarily and without warning ignoring him, devaluing his masculinity and humiliating him. All these aspects were still alive, and were reenacted in his relationship with me, in his attempts to relate to others in his current life, and in his past relationships.

"I am not in mourning with E., and I don't feel guilty about it. It was so bad . . . fights . . . I wanted him sexually, but he was . . . very independent—alternating this loving child way with being a great lover. I wanted to show everybody that I could have this lover who was clearly inferior to me in education and social class . . . I thought he was a hustler, the first night . . . all the leather paraphernalia . . . I had never even been in a leather bar. He thought I was a preppy queen. I wanted to conquer him . . . he was so needy . . . we became so intertwined with each other we couldn't live without one another . . ."

My countertransference at this time was colored by feelings of disgust and, sometimes, silent condemnation. I felt relentlessly confronted by primitive, raw aggression and, at times, it was difficult to regard my feelings from a more detached vantage point. However, I persisted in my efforts to maintain Mr. H.'s conscious awareness of the perversity of these feelings, doing so by quoting his recollections using his own words in my interpretations. This allowed a deeper layer of transference to emerge in the sessions. The patient became gradually aware that his wish to destroy, murder, subjugate, and fragment my good gifts and to shake my analytic stance by trying to develop a nonanalytic relationship with me was his defense against a deep envy of my capacity to help him. This awareness activated in him paranoid fears of damaging me, by shaking me from my analytic neutrality, which would eventually lead to his losing me.

"I am scared you are going to be like those psychiatrists I had in [my hometown]. One of them offered me a glass of bourbon in his office once. You know . . . I have a drinking problem . . . I worry that I am going to make you like one of them . . . [Pause] . . . Psychiatrists are the richest . . . I wish I lived with an MD. In Fire Island last weekend I met this plastic surgeon, they call him Doctor Cocaine. He is beautiful . . . rich . . . owns an apartment in the Upper West Side. . . . It would take care of my problems . . . and I can relate to the sensitivity of doctors . . . they are not like lawyers . . . they are so well educated . . ."

I said, "I wonder if you want me to be your plastic surgeon, cure you of it all, take away aging . . ."

He said, "I would like you to kill me, put a stick through my heart like Dracula . . . [Pause] . . . Obviously I could go into a whole sexual thing here . . . I could steal your heart and kill you . . . at least professionally . . . [Pause] . . . I wonder if listening to this all the time doesn't take a toll on you . . . [Pause] . . . What you do is interesting . . . and you are independent . . ."

This painful transference constellation was paralleled outside the hours by his selection of beautiful potential lovers to whom he felt invariably inferior, and with whom he was regularly sexually impotent, in striking contrast with anonymous encounters where he was fully sexually potent. The intensity of the negative transference became progressively clearer.

Early in the second year of analysis, Mr. H. stated, "I am so angry at you. I feel like bashing your office. I would like to smear it with feces . . . I wish I could sit up and converse with you, know you as a person, how you live, have coffee with you and not have a relationship like this—artificial. . . . I don't even see you . . ."

The continuing interpretation of his envy of my capacity to love and to help him led to emergence of more early memories. He recounted that when he was six years old he pushed a friend off a rooftop high enough to be life-threatening, causing his friend to break an arm. He recalled burning lizards alive, stealing toys from his friends, starving to death two ducks received as a gift, and mercilessly beating the neighbor's dog daily for many months. He said that at his eighth birthday party, he beat up a friend with the gift he had received from him (a pair of handcuffs); the boy went home crying. After this incident, he hid in a garbage pail for hours, causing his parents much distress searching for him. These memories emerged in a stream of associations, mingled with memories of cruel behavior on the part of his mother. He commented on how envious he felt of his mother's having all his father's love: "I have always been envious of my parents . . . that they had one another. And my father—damn him!—was always there for her. He always loved her, and she had priority over all of us children. . . ." A growing awareness of an immense sense of deprivation eventually set in. Mr. H. repeatedly said, in reference to his father and E., "Everyone I loved has died. You too may leave, abandon me anytime."

Starting from the first summer break and through the second year of his analysis, Mr. H.'s general functioning outside the hours seemed to be deteriorating. Partially in response to this situation and also in an attempt to reduce acting out, I agreed with the patient's request to increase the frequency to five times a week. At this time the patient was unable to find a teaching job despite numerous applications and interviews with various schools. It is unclear if he unconsciously sabotaged his chances in order to remain dependent on my help. He had difficulty using his free time constructively, either by painting, an important creative outlet for him, or by extending his freelance tutoring, which was his sole means of support at the time. He reported many episodes of binge drinking, frequently with unpleasant hangovers, and his life seemed thwarted by chaos and lack of structure. He sometimes slept until four in the afternoon and spent many nights at the baths, where he engaged in anonymous, promiscuous sex,[1] as if he were seeking a retreat from the responsibilities of his daily life in a timeless fantasy world populated by beautiful men with erect penises and statuesque bodies. Despite his conveying his feeling of loss of control and a sense of fragmentation in his existence, several positive developments were also occurring, which he seemed unable to appreciate. He filed for bankruptcy—a positive effort to assume financial responsibility—and experimented with various relationships with men whom he portrayed as having depth of character beyond surface attractiveness. However, he experienced enormous difficulties shifting away from a totally dependent maternal relationship with me in which he continually attempted to maintain a dyadic stance, threatening my capacity to analyze by forcing me to care for him concretely.

Around Christmas, Mr. H. accepted a job as a temporary sales clerk at an elegant Fifth Avenue store, and soon he was nursing unrealistic, grandiose fantasies of being rescued by "the man of my life." He would encounter "a very rich, very attractive man"—he explained, with a thick southern accent—who would marry him, and with whom he would live happily ever after, a la Auntie Mame, a movie character with whom he consciously identified. Mr. H. responded to my comment that his accent was much stronger than usual with the rationalization that these were his "roots": "Blanche Dubois and Scarlett O'Hara." Soon he succeeded in engaging me in an enactment by persuading me to change the times of four out of five analytic sessions, implying that if he did not accept this job he may not even be able to pay his rent. I granted his request, but found myself frustrated and begrudging the unusual times at which I had agreed to see him: very early in the morning or late at night. He then proceeded to miss most of his sessions. The grandiose fantasies surrounding his job did not abate until I interpreted the enactment as another attempt to force me into a non-analytic stance—caring for him concretely—a trap into which I had fallen. I had agreed to his impossible schedule, and colluded with him in substituting fantasy for reality, all in an unconscious attempt to contain the aggression and perversity of his effort to make me "the bad one" should I have denied him the schedule changes. More simply put, I was placed in the no-win situation—similar to the medication versus AA dilemma—of choosing between a possibly life-saving job and analysis. I made the mistake of making the choice rather than analyzing the challenge. My eventual interpretation of this scenario caused Mr. H. to become sad and experience a sense of failure, occasioning depressive affects.

My countertransference had oscillated between a desire to protect the patient from himself, and anger and disgust at his self-destructiveness. The work of maintaining neutrality in the hours was daunting. A major dynamic, until then poorly accessible, crystallizing around the patient's HIV status, and involving a partly unconscious desire to die of AIDS as part of a grandiose, heroic fantasy, in which he perceived himself a holocaust victim, became more open to the analytic work. The analysis would be his last rites, with me accompanying him through his death as he did with E. This fantasy had surfaced indirectly very early in the treatment but I had not overtly interpreted it at the time, awaiting a more solid footing in the patient's associations. Nevertheless, it had been clear to me. At this time the fantasy manifested itself through the associations, in the context of Mr. H.'s gradual recognition that his life was continuing despite HIV, and that he had many opportunities and talents, evidenced by several good job offers. Interpretation of this fantasy as a defense against a sense of worthlessness was acknowledged by Mr. H., who realized that its function was to protect him against his fear of surviving AIDS and having to face his human limitations: especially aging, and the inevitable loss of physical beauty, which implied, in his view, loneliness. "I will have to be carted to a nursing home. I will have problems peeing, like all old men do. I will be a lonely bitter queen, out of shape and disgusting . . ." By being questioned in the analytic discourse, his grandiose self was now threatened.

We examined more deeply Mr. H.'s fear of losing his idealized self-image, exploring his profound envy of others who "have it all." More than ever he desired a fulfilling life, an exciting profession and, projecting on me, he said that I had a lover—perhaps a hospital administrator—and a house in Westchester with white fences and a dog. The exploration of these transference fantasies triggered more depressive affects. Mr. H. described various suicidal plans, e.g., stabbing himself with a boning knife or jumping into the East River. His associations became constricted and focused on his sense of inadequacy, meanness, and general failure as a human being—"I am a phony! . . . one who has faked all his life." He expressed feelings of emptiness, hopelessness, and lack of motivation in his work and other daily activities. Adjustment of his antidepressant medications, which I had managed from the beginning of the treatment, decreased the suicidal feelings and allowed the analytic work to continue. The depressed affects, however, exacerbated when hints that analysis is not interminable surfaced around weekend breaks and vacations. I interpreted his reactions to my exit from his life at the end of the analysis as a resistance to relinquish his wish to be taken care of by me in a maternal fashion. In this phase of the analysis I felt that I sounded at times like a broken record with my interpretations, and I remember I was somewhat bored in the hours. However, a dream illustrates how deeply I was now present in the patient's internal world and how, as the object of the transference, I represented both a withholding, sadistic mother ready to abandon him, and at the same time an impediment to his successful enactment of fantasies of dependence.

"I had gone to medical school. The family hadn't come to my graduation. Someone—perhaps it was you—had delayed them until after the ceremony. I was angry at that person because he had deprived me of my family seeing me going on stage and getting my diploma. It's not dissimilar to what happened in reality for my college graduation, when my mother was leaving before the ceremony because she was convinced that I was not going to graduate that day."

I commented, "Yesterday we talked about your sense of deprivation, and in the dream you feel that I am in the way of your mother being at the graduation. I am the mother also, as your analyst and as the object of your desire that cannot be satisfied. You have fought in your analysis against this awareness with all your might. To analyze it rather than expect gratification of it is difficult."

He responded, "What if one can't?"

This exchange illustrates the sense of hopelessness that dominates this patient's feelings when the issue of not acting/gratifying his desire is denied in favor of analyzing it and, also, how intense a traditional transference neurosis had set in.

We continued to meet five times per week up to the end of the second year of analysis. Meanwhile, with the progressive working through of Mr. H.'s unfulfillable oral dependency wishes, which I continued to interpret as aimed at maintaining a dyadic maternal relationship with me, his attempts to obtain direct gratification decreased. At the same time, his grandiose fantasies about himself were seriously threatened by events occurring in his external life, that could now happen, I thought, because of his increased capacity to experience frustration and loss. Mr. H. accepted a job with a salary lower than he would have desired, and in a school less glamorous than most he had applied to. Oscillating between enthusiasm for this new-found security, and disappointment at having to settle for a job he considered beneath him, and which placed him daily in a position closer to that of an ordinary person, he continued to seek his ideal lover and to fill the emptiness of his life outside his job with his analysis. In September 1998, after pondering the benefits versus the potential complications that could come from a decrease in frequency, I agreed to see Mr. H. four times a week. I hoped that this would give a new thrust to the analysis by bringing themes of independence and termination more to the forefront.

An important shift in the transference occurred at this time, when the patient finally accepted my interpretation that his erotic attraction for me and that his wish to have me as a partner was purely defensive. After a series of sessions in which Mr. H. expressed sorrow and despair at my unavailability as a lover, I stated bluntly, "If you met me socially outside the office, in a bar and didn't know me, based on the type of men you are attracted to [his current infatuation was a blonde British actor far from my physical type], I suspect that you would not even talk to me."

The patient admitted that I was right, that I was not his type, but was extremely ashamed of it. He feared that I would be disappointed and angry at him, and that I would reject him and stop his analysis. I pointed out the paranoid features of his fears, and added that short of relating to somebody sexually, he would be at a loss because he could not imagine, and had no experience of, a relationship in which he had participated meaningfully without sexual involvement. We continued to discuss the meaning of his erotizing of relationships in his current life as well as in his past. His facial expressions walking to and from the couch changed: compared to the triumphant grin he used to have at the end of every session, since then Mr. H. has had a sad, shameful expression, at times one of visible concern.

With the working through of the erotized transference, gradually another layer of feelings came into focus. The thought of losing me and the analysis, precipitated by the decreased frequency of visits, became a terrifying prospect for Mr. H. He reacted with increased drinking to the overwhelming fear of being alone in the world, surviving AIDS, and having to live an ordinary existence.

At the beginning of his fourth year of analysis he said, "It's funny, I have been really thinking about drinking today. One of my kids in class said he doesn't like licorice. I thought I would like to have a few drinks."

I said, "Licorice sounds like liquor."

"Yes, like Pernod or Pastis."

I paused long enough for him to recognize the connection in the speech between liquor and licorice, then I asked, "How do you understand that you feel like drinking, which has had devastating consequences in the past for you, at this point when your life is improving?"

"It just seems that I am missing something. . . . I dreamed last night that I had to change apartments, to a cleaner one . . . it was dreadful, scary."

I commented on the fact that the dream suggested that he was scared of change in his life. I also linked these feelings of fear of change with our impending separation for a long weekend break. "You have always drunk when I am away, from the first summer in Fire Island," I said.

"I wish," he responded, "that you would say I should not drink. I am aware I drink at somebody—at you—I feel lonely. You have taken away my fantasies, destroyed my ideal. I want a friend. . . . I wonder how it would feel if I stopped analysis."

I said, "Our separation, in addition to the decrease in how often we meet brings up feelings that are intolerable for you." Before I could continue Mr. H had fallen sound asleep on the couch, snoring loudly. When he awoke a few minutes later, I commented, "We were talking of feelings that are so difficult for you to experience that you fell asleep."

Along with an increasing capacity to experience the perceived catastrophe of separation from me in the present, and loss of me in the future analytic termination, Mr. H. became more able to tolerate non-sexualized relatedness, and started experiencing the positive side of things occurring in his life.

In a Monday session he said, "Saturday and Sunday I went to the drawing studio. I have done the best drawings I have ever done. That makes it even more painful. In a lot of ways my life is really what I want. I am doing some things I am happy with, but when I am alone I feel so empty. Then I say—this is as good as it gets. I have to get satisfied with it."

His fear of surviving AIDS and having to live a lonely, ordinary life is still very intense. Coming to session after having had good news from his internist—950 T-cells and undetectable viral levels—he appeared angry and very distressed. I commented on the discrepancy between his mood and the news.

He said, "I feel I am condemned to a lonely existence in the context of continuing to decay. Intellectually, there is another side to it . . . many of my friends would be happy to have this news . . . many have died already." For the first time some hints of mourning his friends' loss appeared in the material. "All my best and closest friends have died. . . . It used to be so much fun. K. just died . . . in a pool of diarrhea and blood . . . relationships like those take a long time to grow . . . there is no one else."

In recent months Mr. H. has demonstrated an increased capacity to think of himself as a man, which he had always experienced as dangerous.

"When I started developing and grew a bulge between my legs I used to walk with my school bookcase in front of my groin . . . I was terrified that people would see it. My mother caught me once when I was fourteen, masturbating. I caught a glimpse of her white nightgown in the hallway outside my bedroom. The door was ajar . . . I was doing it . . . making noise . . . I froze."

I believe that because Mr. H. has become more capable of experiencing loss, and has developed a deeper connectedness with me in the transference after the working through of the erotization, his sense of self is coalescing; he is now more able to experience himself as a man.

"I realize I wish my students were my children . . . ," he said, speaking of a school trip to Italy. "I was the senior person with twenty teenagers and it felt good. I felt responsible and it went very well . . . like a big family."

Recently, the patient had a dream that—I believe—points at a real progress in the treatment.

"I had a very disturbing dream last night. I really felt pulled away from a deep sleep when I woke up at the end of it. I was stuck with my family. We had to go to Mr. B. (a man he tutors). I felt stuck and wanted to get away. I had this little purple Triumph convertible. I had it in real life—I told you. I drove away from them . . . maybe to Italy . . . but I remember backtracking. When I returned, I came to an intersection and I had to turn right or left. I had an inclination to turn right . . . and I woke up. I woke right up and kept thinking of my last attempt to reconcile with my sister in California for Christmas . . ."

I asked what came to mind. Then he associated to a very bad period of his life in his early twenties when he had to be rescued by his family many times after breaking down with his car out of carelessness, running out of gas, etc. "What about the turn?"

"I feel I may have to make a turn in my life . . . start cleaning my apartment . . . go back to the gym . . ."

I thought the dream indicated a growing awareness of change, a distancing and growing out of his past . . . taking the right turn.

At the beginning of his fourth year of analysis, Mr. H. was hired by a high-profile private school as a teacher. It took some clarifying to help him appreciate the realistically positive meanings of this development because Mr. H. continued to feel that the change was as if in a dream, and that he would be uncovered as a phony at any moment and be publicly humiliated and fired—it was only matter of time. At the same time, his realization that the analysis would have to come to an end at some point—brought about by the decrease in the frequency of his sessions from five to four times a week—continued to present formidable difficulties. He harbored an omnipotent fantasy that his fifth weekly session could be reinstated at any time if he asked me convincingly enough, and if he demonstrated that he was still very ill. I repeatedly pointed out how difficult it was for him to cope with this loss.

Around this time, Mr. H. found a new AA sponsor who became for a few months the center of his life. He was a successful painter with a long history of sobriety, and Mr. H. idealized him intensely. His complaints about the reduction in treatment frequency faded. I thought that he was displacing his dependent, maternal transference onto his new sponsor where it would be more likely gratified. My direct interpretations of this state of affairs did not produce any appreciable progress. After about six months, however, Mr. H.'s relationship with his AA sponsor deteriorated. A final separation was brought about by a profound disagreement between them, about "working the steps" of the AA program. The sponsor demanded that the steps be worked literally, with strong behavioral emphasis, while Mr. H. was after a deeper meaning. He had worked the steps literally so many times in this life, he said, and had systematically failed to maintain sobriety. He hated the "cult" aspect of AA, and he was now resolved to do it his own way. The sponsor had interpreted this as a resistance to recovery, and had dropped him. I suspect that their relationship was also overburdened by the displacement of Mr. H.'s dependent transference onto his sponsor. I interpreted along these lines, and Mr. H. accepted this insight. After a few weeks of grieving, he repaired his relationship with his ex-sponsor, and now they are friends. At this point Mr. H. had not been drinking for about one year. When he stopped attending AA meetings altogether, however, I worried that he was out to destroy his life and his treatment in reaction to perceived rejection and abandonment. Encouragingly, Mr. H. has not been drinking significantly since then. He drinks socially, but not self-destructively. I am carefully monitoring his behavior, to intervene if it becomes necessary, but that time has not yet come. This remains an open issue in the analysis.

The issue of the future loss of the analyst at the end of the analysis has dominated the recent hours. Mr. H. has also been working through the grieving that followed the loss of his current job. He found out a couple of months ago that his contract would not be renewed. In this context, despite much pain about the loss of his "best ever" job, he recognized that even a couple of years before he would have reacted to his contract not being renewed with the conviction that it was his fault. "I would have felt like a loser—a phony. Like they finally found out who I really am: not good enough." I commented on his newly acquired capacity to grieve and move on.

In the sessions, Mr. H. is now finally grieving the various losses he has endured. Lately, he has been talking much about his lover's death, and of how after E. died he shut off all his feelings and acquired a profound, unspoken conviction that he would never meet anybody else again.

I sit through these sessions, sometimes holding back my own tears, in a position of concordant identification (Racker, 1957) with my patient, who is bringing up memories of my own losses. I recognize the termination phase proceeding successfully, and I believe the analysis has been helping Mr. H. to coalesce his fragmented internal world. Although I am aware that the patient may still act out violently during this phase, and I anticipate at least some reappearance of symptoms, especially in regard to drinking, I have not found it necessary to institute any parameter as of today.

We continue to meet four times a week in a traditional analytic setting.

## NOTE

1. The patient was practicing safe sex. The issue of potentially infecting others had been discussed in the very early phase of his preparatory psychotherapy, and he never gave the impression that he lost control in this area.

## REFERENCES

Kernberg, O. (1999), Psychoanalysis, psychoanalytic psychotherapy and supportive psychotherapy: Contemporary controversies. *International Journal of Psychoanalysis,* 80(6):1075-1091.

Racker, H. (1957), The meaning and uses of countertransference. *Psychoanalytic Quarterly,* 26:303-357.

# Chapter 14

# On Love, AIDS, and Emotional Contact in Psychotherapy

## Robert S. Weinstein

Over thirteen years have gone by since I wrote the paper which I titled "Should Analysts Love Their Patients?" (1987). There I quoted Ferenczi (1926) who remarked that it is the analyst's love which ultimately heals the patient. I wrote about the positive countertransference, that is, the good feelings analysts have about their patients, and how these feelings can be used therapeutically to explore and resolve certain difficult resistances to getting well. I encouraged therapists to allow themselves to feel as strongly as possible, using their feelings in the service of the patient. However, I was not prepared for the intensity of emotions I myself would experience, and the need to move, for a time, beyond the bounds of traditional psychotherapy, when first confronted with a special patient of mine discovering he had AIDS.

I am referring to a man whom I will call Bruce, now in his early forties. I had previously treated him for more than seven years, in what we both agreed to be a successful analysis. He had come to terms with being gay, and was now living happily with a man who had relocated from another country to be together with my patient, and who had become a physician practicing in the New York area. Both had made remarkable professional achievements, and my patient felt he had found a good life for himself, working and loving in very satisfying ways. I had worked hard with him and felt a special pride. Indeed, I had seen this patient through some very difficult periods of alienation, depression, anxiety, and promiscuity. We both agreed that, although we could go on talking forever, it might be time for him to leave. We parted with an embrace and a farewell. I heard from him every few months with good news.

More than a year had passed when Bruce called and asked if he could come in for a checkup, as he termed it. I responded that if he felt he needed to, I would be happy to see him. When he returned, he spoke about feeling anxious: some good friends had fallen ill with AIDS. He began mentioning some of his own symptoms, i.e., sore throat, swollen lymph nodes, night sweats. I suggested that he get checked. Why not know for certain what we were dealing with? This was at a time when AIDS testing was controversial and many advocacy groups and physicians were not in favor of it, for political and other reasons which seem foolish in the light of today's knowledge of the disease. Bruce decided to go and be tested, and to our mutual shock, found he was positive for the HIV virus, as was his partner, who was tested subsequently.

My reaction to this, in recollection, was extreme. How? Why? Bruce himself was in despair, wondering when he would die, denying the possibility that there was anything he could do to prolong his life. I began to feel every one of the forces of darkness that may overcome one's therapeutic love and ambition—despair, fury, hopelessness, helplessness. I felt that if I were a better analyst, I would have kept him from becoming ill; I would have foreseen this coming and prevented it. I thought that Bruce must be feeling, although he was not verbalizing it, some of what I was experiencing but was afraid to hurt me with accusations. When I explored this with him, he confirmed it, angrily letting me know that I didn't warn him early enough in treatment and stop him from having promiscuous sex; I didn't caution him to use condoms; I didn't make him straight, and so on. It took a lot for him to summon his anger toward me, but once his fury was expressed, he could go on beginning to take care of himself, to like himself once again. I suggested to him, after visits to doctors who contradicted each other, that it is he who must begin to take charge of his illness, and not deny the lethal consequences of the virus.

Bruce began a course of treatment, combining AZT with aerosol pentamidine to prevent pneumonia. We began working on how he might relieve as much emotional and physical stress as possible. The distinctions between psychoanalysis, case management, and crisis intervention became blurred. We began talking about death but more about love and loving. This brings me to the following crisis which expanded my previous notions about the role of love in psychotherapy.

Bruce is still alive and symptom-free twelve years after his diagnosis, but about nine years ago a crisis occurred—his blood count dropped precipitously, was still falling despite transfusions, and no physician was able to say why, nor did they know how to remedy the situation. We spoke on the phone. He wanted me to visit. Declining, I told him to get well and come back to the office. Although I had been practicing for over twenty-five years, never once, since my days as a hospital intern, have I ever visited a patient in the hospital. In the back of my mind there were always voices saying that real analysts only see patients in their offices, and there have always been theoretical reasons as to why one should not gratify patients in this respect. Fortunately, for both my patient and the therapy, my analytic posture could not stand up to his determination. When he said that I may not see him again, even in my office, so drastic was his condition at the time, I decided to go, and soon.

I go. I meet his partner in the elevator who tells me he'll wait in the lounge while I speak to Bruce, who looks jaundiced and very ill when I see him. He has blood is in his urine, his fever is high, and his condition is serious. Despite numerous consultations, the physicians do not understand what is going on. I give him a bottle of cologne I bought for him and he asks me if I thought a lot about the gift before I bought it, schooled as he is in analytic psychotherapy. I say, "No," and he says, "Well, I really can use this since I need a shower badly." He then begins to speak about his unfinished business with people he knows and then begins speaking about us. "What is our unfinished business?" he asks and says, "I've never told you how much you mean to me, how much our work together meant to me. I never wanted to be too vulnerable to you. Why?" I ask if I am here to help him to live or to die. Weeping, he says, "You are part of the ongoing circle of life, you help me to live, to be a part of all of life. Because of you I can feel connected to others." We speak of his past, of his friendships and family, and whatever remnants of guilt he may have in regard to them. It is an intense, loving interchange. As I leave to go, feeling closer to him in this moment than ever before, he holds me and cries into my shirt, "I don't want to die, I don't want to die." I stroke his hair and say, "Get better, let's continue our work together." When I look back at him before I leave the room, his face is transformed. His color is okay, and I feel right then that he will get better, which he does within a few days.

This incident, which touched me deeply, convinced me of the therapeutic power of love as never before. I am, of course, not suggesting that love cures AIDS. With the advent of the new drug combinations, it is the medication that is now keeping AIDS patients alive. I am saying, however, that love is a healing force that keeps us all connected to life and to health, and this is the critical ingredient of all successful therapy, whether the patient is gay or straight.

Shortly after this incident, when Bruce returned to therapy, he reported the following dream:

> There's a wrestling match between a very tall, weighty man and a much smaller guy, and it is clear that the smaller guy is very aggressive, kicking at the bigger guy, and I have the feeling he might just do it, i.e., win, since he has a plan of attack. The big guy seems to be stunned for a second.
>
> Then, at some point, the big guy throws the little guy out of the ring. At any moment he could just destroy him. The big guy was just playing with the little guy. At this point, I go out of the ring, realize the clock is ticking and in a few seconds the bout will be over. A draw would be a great victory for the little guy. Is my watch right? I can get into trouble if I am not absolutely certain. The match ends in a draw. The big guy didn't realize that time was running out. He forgot about the clock. I had rung the bell from outside the ring.

I, as his analyst, had also gone outside the ring, the frame of our sessions, and the bout with death had been a draw. Bruce wondered, that session when he reported the dream, if he would be able to stick around long enough for a cure to come, and I told him we would work hard together on his doing so.

I am reminded here of Michael Balint, who stated in his book, *The Basic Fault* (1979),

The analyst's role in certain periods of new beginnings resembles . . . that of the primary substances or objects. He must be there; he must be flexible to a very high degree; he must not offer much resistance; he certainly must be indestructible, and he must allow his patient to live with him in a sort of harmonious interpenetrating mix up. (p. 136)

In the years following these events, Bruce continued to thrive, working in therapy to find satisfaction and fulfillment in his life as well as freedom from excessive stress. Subsequently, another bout with illness (leading to fevers, night sweats, and fatigue), led him to have the following dream, similar in kind to the one I just described; again, a test of strength and endurance, and also a reflection of the importance of the therapeutic relationship:

I was a college wrestler and there was a bout. The match had not yet begun. There were barbells on the mat and the referee told me to move them off. I didn't feel that it was my responsibility—someone else had placed them there. The clock was ticking. If I didn't move the barbells off the mat, I was going to lose the match for disobeying the referee.

This dream depicts another serious struggle with AIDS, fortunately dreamt before a more serious crisis developed. Perhaps Bruce and I wouldn't have to go outside the ring to decide this match.

Though Bruce's associations to this dream, his sense of helplessness and rage emerged. He was upset about the injustice of the situation—why should he have to move the barbells; why should he become sick again and face such obstacles. If he didn't move them, however, he would be in default. I understood and interpreted this dream to him as his unconscious letting him know that this turn of events required him to do what was necessary to win this new struggle, despite his feelings about it. He could not allow his fury and despair to lead him to inaction and default. With this said, Bruce responded with sadness and spoke of his feelings of helplessness, but with a new sense of resolve about again taking charge of his life. The next week he reported feeling better; he had seen two physicians for consultation and obtained additional opinions to better understand what was happening with his medical condition. With the working through of the dream, Bruce became better connected with the unconscious forces at work that could have led to defeat but instead brought him again to a renewed fight for his life, a life which happily is still going on, after many years of hard work, and with no major illnesses.

This analytic experience with Bruce has been of great personal and professional importance in my life, part of my spiritual growth. It taught me something more than I had known about loving, and it taught me how as analysts we need a sensitive and caring flexibility with our patients. Inside or outside the ring of psychotherapy, sometimes we serve as referees, other times as contenders. However our function, when this is done with love and compassion, we promote the health and integration of body and spirit, establishing the kind of contact with our patients which enable them to connect to life and to hope.

## REFERENCES

Balint, M. (1979), *The Basic Fault*. New York: Brunner/Mazel.

Ferenczi, S. (1926), To Sigmund Freud on his seventieth birthday. In *Final Contributions to the Problems and Methods of Psycho-Analysis*. New York: Brunner/Mazel, 1980, pp. 11-17.

Weinstein, R. S. (1987), Should analysts love their patients? In *Love: Psychoanalytic Perspectives* J. Lasky and H. Silverman (Eds.). New York: New York University Press, pp. 104-109.

# Chapter 15

# Two Cases of Psychoanalytic Psychotherapy with People with HIV/AIDS: Commentary on Papers by Leli and Weinstein

## Gilbert W. Cole

As a therapist who has become interested in discussing his own HIV-positive status publicly, one of the questions that has been on my mind is how HIV and AIDS present unique problems to the psychotherapist, not only clinically, but also as we think about writing about our work. Writing about work that involves something as laden with meaning as HIV/AIDS might lead the therapist to feel as if she or he is risking exposing more of herself or himself than in writing about less anxiety-provoking subjects. In some discussions in the psychoanalytic literature, for example, HIV/AIDS seem pushed into their metaphoric meanings rather quickly, as if it might be difficult for both analyst and patient to stay with the meanings particular to HIV/AIDS for too long. Hoffman (1998) suggests that a general taboo haunts the psychoanalytic community, inhibiting our capacity to think or write about mortality in any great detail, and the analyst's mortality least of all. I wonder whether conditions like HIV/AIDS, so loaded with stigma, mystery, and fears, not to mention their construction as the nexus between sex and death, make them themes that are particularly difficult for psychotherapists to write about. Ubaldo Leli's and Robert Weinstein's contributions to the clinical literature pertaining to HIV/AIDS are important for many reasons, not least because they demonstrate, in very different ways, how questions of mortality that have been so inextricably bound up with HIV/AIDS figure into the therapist's daily work.

In terms of narrative, the papers present widely divergent stories. Leli writes about his struggle to maintain the treatment frame, withstanding the pressure applied by an extremely difficult, seductive, and manipulative patient. Weinstein traces for us his struggle to allow his own boundaries and the treatment frame to become more flexible, withstanding the internal pressures from a "psychoanalytic superego." Clearly, these two patients are very different in their strengths and vulnerabilities. The clinical decisions each therapist made, so different with regard to matters of the frame, gratification, and expressiveness, were attuned to their patient's differing psychic and "daily life" situations.

With regard to what it is about these cases that pertains specifically to HIV/AIDS, Weinstein's work with his patient's dreams offers one theme that stands out. His interpretations of the dreams stay very close to the patient's situation of having AIDS, rather than moving too quickly to transference interpretations where AIDS might be construed as a metaphor of some kind. I tend to think that this shows his fortitude in staying with this specific content, regardless of its difficulty. It seems entirely possible that another, more classically oriented psychoanalyst, might interpret such dream material for its transference meanings because, among other reasons, staying with the HIV/AIDS content could be too anxiety provoking for the analyst.

The dream motif of the wrestler proves to be especially resonant, both for his patient and for Weinstein. His willingness to let his readers know how much he wrestled with an "analytic superego" with regard to whether he ought to visit his patient, and that he brought him a gift, is a generous invitation to know more about the therapist's own process. Sometimes we learn more from cases where we fight against what has come to be known as "standard technique," than from those where things seem to go more smoothly. When any method of practice becomes a source of inhibition, rather than that which allows us to do the work of therapy, work that includes some expression of love, that method deserves to be reexamined.

Leli's paper seems to me a particularly good example of how maintaining the frame and adherence to standard technique are precisely what helps a patient, and so are an expression of the love that is part of an effective treatment. In addition to all the tools his patient had in his relational arsenal, Leli mentions the strain of confronting the terrors associated with HIV/AIDS. In such a situation, as Leli describes, the therapist may encounter her or his own fantasies in response to the anxiety of assessing whether the patient is putting himself and others at risk in sexual relations. Leli's work enabled his patient to feel sufficiently held so that Leli, too, could feel more certain about how his patient was conducting his sexual behavior. But Leli's patient's medical condition places the concerns that specifically entail HIV/AIDS on a different point in the unfolding story of HIV/AIDS than Weinstein's patient.

The "protease moment" (Rofes, 1998) challenges psychotherapists in particular ways. We must now confront the paradoxical task of helping the patient to mourn the loss of such fantasies as Leli's patient reported: dying a romantic, tragic death as a hero, nipping in the bud his career as a painter. Such a fantasy is heavily layered with potential meaning, and may have performed important organizing functions for the patient facing a terrifying potential, even while remaining asymptomatic.

A patient with whom I've worked since before the introduction of the protease inhibitors, but who has remained asymptomatic throughout our work together, had to come to grips with the loss of a similar fantasy as his medical condition improved. In his case, dying before his time was a way of unconsciously paying for his (imagined) sins, mostly associated with being in a fury. Such examples of the psychic ramifications of the "Lazarus Syndrome" indicate the challenges to psychotherapeutic work brought about by the progress in treating HIV. Our seropositive patients now have new opportunities to mourn narcissistic losses in the context of approaching the future as a person who has time to build a life, as opposed to preparing for death.

Leli's patient, however, had a way of using his HIV seropositivity to avoid the painful process of mourning the terrible losses he'd experienced. Leli describes how the patient would force him into impossible positions, in an attempt to destroy him as a source of progressive work and goodness. At such a moment, HIV/AIDS function to increase the dramatic intensity of the patient's pressure. The effectiveness of the patient's strategy depends on Leli's fears that missing a dose of medicine would in fact be risky. Whether missing a single dose of a "drug cocktail" would in fact place an individual at risk for developing full-blown AIDS is not the point here. That Leli was able to shift the emphasis to the patient's determination to transform goodness into malevolent aggression is the salient issue. Leli's conviction that maintaining a more psychoanalytic posture was the best option in such a moment is justified in how the treatment unfolded: the patient was able to remain involved in the psychotherapeutic work. For the psychotherapist, withstanding this kind of pressure for an extended period of time involves the willingness to know about one's hate for the patient, a willingness that is also an expression of love.

Weinstein tells us of the despair, fury, hopelessness, and helplessness he felt at the time of his patient's medical crisis, generously relating his fantasies, as well as those of his patient, that he ought to have been able to prevent his former patient from becoming ill. Here we note (to me) a familiar expectation that as psychotherapists we ought to assume a responsibility that is unreasonable. It is a narcissistic affront to us as therapists that there are limits to our capacities, both to know whether and how to intervene about such matters as sexual behaviors, and that we are helpless in the face of such phenomena as HIV/AIDS.

Although there are aspects of both of these cases that pertain specifically to HIV/AIDS, these papers are also about challenges that are not limited to our work with people living with the virus. Leli's paper is a particularly effective description of a successful psychoanalytic treatment of a patient whom many would assess as not appropriate for a "classical" analysis. In a very substantial way, the patient's HIV-positive status is incidental. And I do believe that, whatever illness his patient was suffering from, Weinstein would have made that hospital visit, because it was the appropriate, human, thing to do, not because his patient had AIDS.

But as to the question of what specific role HIV/AIDS might play in the treatments that are so movingly described, I find myself wondering about what might be missing, that is, the range of the therapist's own feelings about HIV/AIDS. Leli comments at one point about Mr. H.'s tendency to keep HIV out of the treatment relationship. Certainly we can understand Mr. H. having a variety of reasons to do so, and I think we can understand that a therapist working with a patient as challenging as Mr. H. would have reasons to avoid the feelings aroused within himself or herself about HIV/AIDS as well.

The theme seems a bit confusing and confused. For example, we don't know for sure whether Mr. H. was exposed to HIV by his late partner. If so, then the possibility of closeness with another person, already fraught with chaotic feelings, is invested with an objectively life-threatening potential, including a threat to the unfolding transference relationship Leli describes. Perhaps the most striking moment when an avoidance of such material might be revealed is in the paragraph where Leli tells us of his countertransference. Several sentences into this paragraph he takes up the subject of his patient's HIV seropositivity, then describes Mr. H.'s fantasies about this, omitting his own feelings about HIV in general, and Mr. H.'s seropositivity in particular. Since this happens in a paragraph that begins with a description of the therapist's countertransference, a potential omission or avoidance of difficult feelings seems possible. One association I had at this moment was to Mr. H.'s worries that he might make Leli into one of the psychiatrists he'd consulted back home; that his infectious potential is too dangerous to be contained. The fantasy of being dangerously infectious to others is a theme I've noticed both within myself and in my patients. Mr. H.'s fears of his destructive impulses and behaviors are convincingly conveyed, and Leli's capacity to withstand the attacks on himself and the treatment is remarkable. I wonder, though, if there is something about the confrontation with HIV in the interplay of transference and countertransference that can be teased out more explicitly?

Weinstein invokes Balint (1979) on the necessity for the therapist to be indestructible. Is there a tradition, repeated in Balint's statement, for therapists to focus on their capacities to withstand anything, to the exclusion of admitting into conscious awareness their own fears and anxieties about illness and death? Dewald (1990, p. 88), speculates that therapists "harbor a fantasy that their own personal analysis has 'immunized' them against some of the diseases that afflict others." Once again, it seems understandable that we need to emphasize our robustness, rather than our vulnerability, particularly when working with challenging patients.

I cannot help wondering whether, in work with our patients who are HIV positive, we encounter an opportunity to address in detail our feelings about our own mortality and illness, a theme that has been identified as a gap in our literature. The daily work of psychoanalytically oriented psychotherapy resonates with the scarily infectious capacity of HIV in that therapists regularly must become aware of and begin to understand their own fantasies in response to their patients' material. We must stay open to becoming "infected" with our patients' psychic processes, and an HIV-positive patient's serostatus is sure to evoke the analyst's fantasies about the virus. As Pizer (2000) has commented, therapists are coming out "from behind the wizard's curtain" (p. 197) and are detailing far more about their own subjectivity than ever before. I suggest that the risks involved with detailing more of our responses to HIV/AIDS will yield benefits for our field, both with regard to the specific issue of HIV, and to more general concerns of those who are not at risk for infection.

At the same time, however, these papers make a significant contribution to a growing literature on the neglected topic of HIV/AIDS in psychoanalytically oriented psychotherapy. As a field, psychoanalysis' public response to HIV/AIDS has, until the late 1990s, been rather reticent. Schaffner (1996) tells us that when he revealed to colleagues that he was treating people who were ill with AIDS, they asked him why. "What is the use of treating such a patient? You can't cure him anyway!" (p. 63 in Blechner, 1997a). Schaffner does not speculate as to whether his colleague was referring to the patient's certain eventual death, or to the personality problems that might have been assumed to be present in someone who would be likely to have AIDS.

Of course, many psychoanalytically oriented therapists have been working with those affected by the syndrome throughout the last twenty years. Nonetheless, the psychoanalytic literature on working with people with HIV/AIDS has been a relatively sparse body of work, considering the magnitude of the crisis during its first twenty years. It is the exceptions that emphasize this general reticence. Goldman's (1989) contribution emphasizes the strains of "bearing the unbearable," not only on those affected by the illness directly, but also on those psychotherapists and physicians who work with them. Goldman's article is notable in that he includes remarks of a psychologist who is himself diagnosed with AIDS, clearly stating that those called upon to care for those affected by HIV/AIDS are themselves, sometimes, AIDS patients. Goldman also movingly describes the funeral of one of his own patients, who had requested an informal memorial at which friends and family would speak. Noting the difficulty the group had in beginning, Goldman relates how he spoke first, "sharing knowledge that a psychotherapist is almost never justified in doing during the usual practice of our profession; these are not usual times" (pp. 273-274). The readiness of the psychotherapist to adapt to challenges, at times being willing to forego the comforts of "standard technique" is a crucial point that Goldman addresses.

The appearance of Blechner's *Hope and Mortality: Psychodynamic Approaches to AIDS and HIV* (1997a) marked the first major psychoanalytic contribution explicitly on HIV/AIDS. In his introduction, Blechner describes the stigma attached not only to the disease, but that also tended to accrue to those who worked with people with the disease at the beginning of the AIDS epidemic. He considers this to stem from psychoanalysis' historical difficulties addressing the problems of the poor or the socially marginalized, as well as the field's attitudes to gay men (p. xix). Another important early contributor is Isay, who in his 1989 and 1996 books included important chapters on HIV/AIDS.

Looking for a moment at the literature prior to Blechner and Isay, in a survey of psychoanalytic journals through 1997, the direst period of the epidemic, one finds sixteen articles that directly confronted questions of working with people living with HIV/AIDS (Aronson, 1996; Bauknight and Appelbaum, 1997; Blechner, 1993, 1997b; Cohen and Abramowitz, 1990; Grosz, 1993; Hildebrand, 1992; Kappraff, 1995; Kobayashi, 1997; Mayers and Svartberg, 1996; Olsson, 1997; Rosenbaum, 1994; Sadowy, 1991; Schaffner, 1994, 1996; and Stevens and Muskin, 1987). This literature explores such questions as whether HIV/AIDS presents difficulties different from other chronic or catastrophic diseases, and, if so, how might we tease out what is specific to HIV/AIDS in the treatment relationship. In addition, there are passing references to HIV/AIDS in a handful of other articles, often pointing to the syndrome as an example of a situation requiring the analyst to rethink the analytic frame in the context of the connections between love and death (e.g., Leary, 1994), or as an example of an unusually difficult case to take on (Mayer, 1994).

As Drescher (1998) has demonstrated, theory matters a great deal in clinical work with gay men. Blechner (1997a), describing the modifications in technique that he advises in the work with HIV patients, situates his theoretical point of view in the interpersonal tradition of Harry Stack Sullivan, one of the major influences on the contemporary American relational school (see Aron, 1996). In that theoretical context, classical psychoanalytic ideals of objectivity and anonymity are not seen as attainable, let alone pertinent. Those theoretical and technical concepts that guide Blechner's recommendations include "the fundamental question . . . 'what is the patient trying to do?' We need to formulate this question with the patient and then determine whether we can and should help him or her to do it, and if so, how" (Blechner, 1997a, p. 13).

The question of what the patient wishes to do in a therapy and what the analyst may think would amount to a "cure" are two different things. The clash that could ensue when this difference is not given sufficient respect shows up in Grosz (1993), a description of a psychoanalytic treatment with a man with AIDS. This article is also an example of how the therapist's theories may determine the meanings that emerge from the therapeutic work. In this case, the analyst seemed to become preoccupied with the question of the origin of his patient's homosexuality, rather than with the patient's experience of having AIDS (on psychoanalysis' preoccupation with the origins of homosexuality, and the deleterious clinical effects of this, see Drescher, 1998). Written from a theoretical point of view best described as the object relations school of Melanie Klein, the author notes his frustration that his patient's homosexuality could not be "cured." Grosz's contribution details the analysis of an unconscious fantasy regarding HIV infection that is elaborated and expressed in a patient's actions and affective life, and it is a valuable one. But it is filtered through a theoretical orientation in which the therapist's contempt (for the patient, his homosexuality, or his HIV infection), is thinly veiled by a purported "scientific" objectivity. For example, his recounting of his patient's history strongly implies that Grosz believes homosexuality is "caused" by the familiar recipe of an absent father and over-involvement with mother. As if to confirm this understanding, Grosz's patient does describes himself as "a mama's boy" (p. 965). Grosz imputes his theoretical concern to his patient, interpreting that "at a critical level, Mr. A's phantasy of infection is not so much concerned with the origin of his HIV infection, as with the origin of his homosexuality" (p. 971). He understands his patient as unconsciously seeing his HIV seropositivity "as a result of having been 'poisoned' by his maternal object: that 'poison' is nothing but his *need* for his maternal object" (p. 973). Because homosexuality is thought by Grosz to be a compromise formation defending against unconscious rage at the "maternal object," there is a linkage between needs, poison, and mothers. But it is not at all clear, given Grosz's consistent, perhaps *insistent,* interpretations, beginning in the initial consultation, that the person Mr. A has come to for help is a maternal figure, and that the helplessness Mr. A feels refers more to his early history than to a diagnosis of HIV seropositivity.

It is striking both that what Grosz discloses to his readers is that he is married and has two children, as if to more clearly separate himself from his patient, and that he seems unable to imagine his patient as wishing for a paternal object that could help him. This point of view is consistent with a traditional psychoanalytic conviction that homosexuality represents either a compromised, defensive relationship with a phallic mother, or an identification with mother such that the homosexual man psychically regards himself as a woman. There is no room in psychoanalytic theories of this kind for desire that is actually same sexed. Health is equated with a privileging of difference and desire for sameness is regressive. Further, sameness and desire are exclusively *genital* sameness and difference (see Frommer, 2000).

I do not wish to argue that Grosz's patient's linkage of his HIV seropositivity with his homosexuality may not have been apparent in the material. I do wish to suggest that there are a variety of ways of handling this sort of linkage in the clinical situation. Grosz's admission of his regret that his patient's homosexuality could not be cured suggests to me that his patient may not have been helped to work through the terrible conflicts over his being gay. Such a working through might have helped this patient move toward relieving him of the self-punishment apparent in his fantasy that his seropositivity was *caused* by his being gay.

The question as to the influence of the analyst's theoretical point of view on how matters concerning HIV/AIDS are handled is often a difficult one to tease out. I argue that a homophobic attitude, supported by one strand of traditional psychoanalytic theorizing, may have been a potential determinant in how the material was handled in the case presented by Grosz. Nonetheless, homophobic and heterosexist attitudes need not be an inherent part of any theory guiding psychotherapeutic practice. My own classically oriented analyst, at the time that I tested positive for HIV, interpreted an oblique but resonantly resentful remark from me as an expression of anger that she hadn't been able to keep me from sero-converting, an event that occurred some years before my analysis had begun. (I had changed my sexual behavior several years before confirming my serostatus by getting tested, by which time I had begun my analysis.) I do believe that this was a helpful interpretation; it quickly assumed a metaphoric function, extending back in time to include all the ways that I'd felt unprotected and unwarned about the dangers that the world presents. This interpretation, referring to the transference relationship, was made in a classically psychoanalytic context but without a concern for the origins of my sexual orientation, which could have figured in some additional comment on resentment toward my analyst as a woman, for example.

Isay (1989, 1996), a classically oriented analyst, also describes psychoanalytic psychotherapy with gay men at various stages of the HIV/AIDS illness. He describes the meanings of HIV seropositivity that patients elaborate, particularly the confluence of shame over wishes that are considered "feminine," such as the wish to be penetrated by a man. That anal intercourse is one of the most risky sexual behaviors for exposure to HIV compounds the difficulty of working through feelings of shame over this desire. Here Isay points to the value of staying with HIV/AIDS long enough to work on the meanings specific to the syndrome, rather than moving to metaphoric elaborations that move away from the feelings and meanings more immediately linked to HIV/AIDS.

In his 1996 book, Isay includes a description of his own fears of having been infected with HIV. He considers how this fear may have affected his need to give advice to his patients. Isay's willingness to describe his own fears of infection stand out in the literature, an exception that points up the lack of attention in the literature to the role of the analyst's fantasies evoked by HIV/AIDS in such treatments.

Isay also describes the request of a patient who has been hospitalized that his analyst come to the hospital in order to continue his analysis there. Isay tells us that his patient instructed him to move the hospital bed away from the wall so that he can place a chair there, to assume his customary position, behind the patient (p. 61). Though Isay regards this man's wish as indicative of a denial of the strong possibility of his death, it was also clear that the patient was committed to an analytic, exploratory treatment. Isay tells us that the treatment was useful in addressing the issues of AIDS and death, as well as the characterological problems that led this patient to psychoanalysis.

Leli's and Weinstein's sensitive and enlightened papers, one written from a more classical point of view, the other written from a contemporary object relations point of view, are excellent contributions to a growing psychotherapeutic literature on HIV/AIDS that is free of subtle, or not so subtle, homophobic interpretations. Weinstein goes on to make the compelling argument that it is love that keeps us connected to life and health, and it is crucial to successful therapies. HIV/AIDS has tested the limits of our culture's capacity to love, and will continue to do so as the epidemic ravages the developing world. Necessarily focusing on our work as psychotherapists, we note that expressions of love can assume many forms. My own analyst's interpretation of my wish that she'd been able to prevent me from seroconverting was such an expression, and so is Leli's steadfast attention to providing the adequate frame so as to enable his patient to organize the chaotic inner world that had prevented him from living with more freedom and creativity.

Now that we in the developed West have entered the "protease moment," perhaps HIV/AIDS is beginning to become part of the background for some gay men and their therapists, rather than the emergency it was prior to 1996. It is tempting to claim that AIDS is an emblematic post-modern affliction. A protean *syndrome,* rather than a single disease, it has changed the way many think about illness because it is not one entity, but rather a process of sometimes dizzying variety. AIDS in women has been notoriously underdiagnosed because it manifests so differently than in gay men, in IV drug users, and in children. Even in the body, the virus thought to be associated with AIDS can hide, or be obscured when the host's immune system is so robust that it continues to produce millions of T cells despite the damage that HIV exacts. In the history of the medical response to HIV/AIDS, there have been so many divergent narratives of the course of the illness that compiling a database to guide clinical decisions has been nearly an impossible task. Before the medications that seem to have changed HIV/AIDS into a chronic condition for some, the course of the illness could be strikingly different from case to case, but with the same terrible ending.

Background or foreground, now that the course of the syndrome has, for many, been changed, we more often have the luxury of considering the meanings associated with HIV/AIDS in a different context where it is possible to consider life continuing rather than impending death. In these two contributions to the growing psychoanalytic literature on work with people living with HIV, to be differentiated from work with people dying of AIDS, we can trace this transition: from work in a mode of crisis to work that can include mourning the terrible losses associated with HIV/AIDS, as well as the more nearly expectable insults of "normal" life.

## REFERENCES

Aron, L. (1996), *A Meeting of Minds: Mutuality in Psychoanalysis.* Hillsdale, NJ: The Analytic Press.

Aronson, S. (1996), The bereavement process in children of parents with AIDS. *Psychoanalytic Study of the Child,* 51:422-435.

Balint, M. (1979), *The Basic Fault.* New York: Brunner/Mazel.

Bauknight, R. and Appelbaum, R. (1997), AIDS, death, and the analytic frame. *Free Associations,* 41:81-100.

Blechner, M. J. (1993), Psychoanalysis and HIV disease. *Contemporary Psychoanalysis,* 29:61-80.

Blechner, M. J., Ed. (1997a), *Hope and Mortality: Psychodynamic Approaches to AIDS and HIV.* Hillsdale, NJ: The Analytic Press.

Blechner, M. J. (1997b), Psychological aspects of the AIDS epidemic: A fifteen-year perspective. *Contemporary Psychoanalysis,* 33:89-107.

Cohen, J. and Abramowitz, S. (1990), AIDS attacks the self: A self-psychological exploration of the psychodynamic consequences of HIV. *Progress in Self Psychology,* 6:157-172.

Dewald, P. (1990), Serious illness in the analyst: Transference, countertransference, and reality responses—and further reflections. In *Illness in the Analyst,* H. Schwartz and A.-L. Silver (Eds.). Madison, CT: International Universities Press, pp. 75-98.

Drescher, J. (1998), *Psychoanalytic Therapy and the Gay Man.* Hillsdale, NJ: The Analytic Press.

Frommer, M. S. (2000), Offending gender: Being and wanting in male same-sex desire. *Studies in Gender and Sexuality,* 1:191-206.

Goldman, S. (1989), Bearing the unbearable: The psychological impact of AIDS. In *Gender in Transition.* J. Offerman-Zuckerberg (Ed.). New York: Plenum, pp. 263-274.

Grosz, S. (1993), A phantasy of infection. *International Journal of Psycholanysis,* 74:965-974.

Hildebrand, H. P. (1992), A patient dying with AIDS. *International Review of Psychoanalysis,* 19:457-469.

Hoffman, I. (1998), *Ritual and Spontaneity in the Psychoanalytic Process.* Hillsdale, NJ: The Analytic Press.

Isay, R. (1989), *Being Homosexual: Gay Men and Their Development.* New York: Farrar, Straus, and Giroux.

Isay, R. (1996), *Becoming Gay: The Journey to Self-Acceptance.* New York: Pantheon.

Kappraff, A. (1995), Boundaries of time and space in the treatment of an HIV-positive man in mid-life. *Bulletin of the Menninger Clinic,* 59:69-78.

Kobayashi, J. S. (1997), The evolution of adjustment issues in HIV/AIDS. Bulletin of the Menninger Clinic, 61:146-188.

Leary, K. (1994), Psychoanalytic "problems" and postmodern "solutions." *Psychoanalytic Quarterly,* 63:433-465.

Mayer, E. L. (1994), Some implications for psychoanalytic technique drawn from the analysis of a dying patient. *Psychoanalytic Quarterly,* 63:1-19.

Mayers, A. M. and Svartberg, M. (1996), The manifestation and management of countertransference on a pediatric AIDS team. *Bulletin of the Menninger Clinic,* 60:206-218.

Olsson, P. A. (1997), Time compressed: Psychoanalysis in the days of HIV and AIDS. *Journal of the American Academy of Psychoanalysis,* 25:277-293.

Pizer, B. (2000), The therapist's routine consultations: A necessary window in the treatment frame. *Psychoanalytic Dialogues,* 10:197-208.

Rofes, E. (1998), *Dry Bones Breathe: Gay Men Creating Post-AIDS Identities.* Binghamton, NY: Harrington Park Press.

Rosenbaum, M. (1994), Similarities of psychiatric disorders of AIDS and syphilis: History repeats itself. *Bulletin of the Menninger Clinic,* 58:375-382.

Sadowy, D. (1991), Is there a role for the psychoanalytic psychotherapist with a patient dying? *Psychoanalytic Review,* 78:199-207.

Schaffner, B. (1994), The crucial and difficult role of the psychotherapist in the treatment of the HIV-positive patient. *Journal of the American Academy of Psychoanalysis,* 22:505-518.

Schaffner, B. (1996), Modifying psychoanalytic methods when treating HIV-positive patients. *Journal of the American Academy of Psychoanalysis,* 25(1):123-

141. Reprinted in *Hope and Mortality: Psychodynamic Approaches to AIDS and HIV,* M. Blechner (Ed.). Hillsdale, NJ: The Analytic Press, 1997, pp. 63-79.

Stevens, I. A. and Muskin, P. R. (1987), Techniques for reversing the failure of empathy toward AIDS patients. *Journal of the American Academy of Psychoanalysis,* 15:539-552.

# Chapter 16

# Working Outside the Frame: A Discussion of Papers by Robert Weinstein and Ubaldo Leli

Adrienne Harris

These two papers, though markedly different in tone and stance and theoretical backing, can be approached as an ensemble. Both papers are serious, engaged attempts to work outside the frame of conventional approaches to analysis and analytic understanding. Both are attempts to integrate new ideas about body/mind, about sexuality and character, about analyzability and about the revisioning of homosexuality as a category of experience to which psychiatry and psychoanalysis have paid hitherto quite toxic attention. Both also take on the question of the serological status of a patient in analysis.

I think, however, that each essay also demonstrates the difficulties of our current situation in which paradigms are changing but clearly are also still in transition. One feels the burden in Leli's presentation of an older diagnostic language impinging upon his clinical acumen and attunement and one feels the limits of the explanatory models Weinstein is deploying in his exploration of the transformative aspects of care.

I must confess that I am not in sympathy with the theoretical language (I actually experienced it more as baggage and carapace than frame) with which Leli surrounds his essay and the treatment discussion. I felt his conceptual language distances him from his patient and from his audience. Early in the paper, he delivers a diagnostic summary that functions like a kind of fire wall between us and the patient. The judgment of "severe character pathology" is anchored by terms like "impulsivity, self destructive acting out . . . perversity" with no elucidation of the mixture of descriptive and moralizing aspects to these terms. The danger, I think, in the grafting of an experience-distance, symptom-driven descriptive language of character pathology and perversion onto new forms of understanding nonnormative sexuality is that homophobia (along with other judgments more moral than clinical) simply migrate into the language of character. Although I often felt alienated and dissatisfied with Leli's theorizing about his patient, I immediately felt his clinical attention to the patient and the complexity of his experience of the patient which seemed quite separate from the theoretical framing.

I might begin with Leli's consideration of the analytic suitability of a patient. I question a rehashing of analyzability as a condition either solely of the analysand's character or behavior. I would suggest that it is useful to rehearse Green's (1986) idea that a wide range of people, often with powerful disturbances in experience and relatedness and self understanding now come for analysis, including candidates in training. Green's useful corrective is to ask us to ask the question "is this person analyzable by me?" If you make that quite simple turn, you must then work out the questions of whether you offer analysis to a patient on the basis of transference phenomena and potentials but particularly on the basis of your own countertransference dynamics. You are then, I believe, in a more two-person system of understanding.

I found Leli's presentation of the patient's background and dynamics a mixture of complex appreciation and experience-distant diagnosing. Often the juxtaposition of analytic understanding and descriptive judgment coexist in the same paragraph. In his account of the first experience in the analysis, where conflicts over the fee and the patient's feelings about control and care emerged, Leli speaks to the patient thoughtfully and openly reveals his conflict and feelings of being "cornered," yet speaks to us about "perversity in the transference." I felt sometimes that I was reading about two different treatments, or at least two distinct understandings of a treatment. We hear of the patient's losses and then of his chaotic "lifestyle" without hearing how the analyst sees these in relation to each other. Grandiosity seems more a moral charge than a descriptive rendering that allows us to come close to the patient's experience.

It was a relief to me when Leli acknowledged the dimensions of his negative countertransference, although I would have appreciated knowing more about how he thought it tempered or shaped the analytic experience. I actually found his interventions and interpretations both firm and attentive (I would actually say fond and affirming). When Leli spoke to his patient, I felt he did so with a consciousness of the patient's aggression, desperation, and longing, but in his judgment-laden descriptions of the patient's character, the analyst seemed to this reader to be feeling contemptuous and disgusted by the patient.

The problem of a value and morality-laden technical language in psychoanalysis is not, of course, unique to Leli. It takes both work and psychic openness to stay close to one's phenomenological experience. Subtle shifts in terminology in the field: the shift from "acting out" to enactment; Schafer's (1983) transformation of "resistance" into its inevitable shaping of transference, are useful because they pull out more of the analyst's subjective involvement in the clinical process. We need shorthand, generally comprehensible language to speak to colleagues, but it seems particularly important to me that the *Journal of Gay and Lesbian Psychotherapy* take a leadership role in focusing attention on the hidden costs of many kinds of terminology. Foucault's (1977) analysis of the gatekeeping and constitutive functions of knowledge bases like psychoanalysis is useful because he speaks to the seamless, almost undecipherable way that social norms stain into theory and practice.

The interesting paradox, as I thought about it some more, is that it is from Kernberg's (1975, 1984) powerful theoretical accounts of the aggression and destructiveness in certain patients that we have the tools to work analytically, yet the moralizing and judgmental tone of Kernbergian diagnostic categories alienates this reader. Leli's deployment of Kernberg makes me think that when the theoretical understanding of character pathology is bound in techniques that hierarchialize certain patients as unfit for analysis, the theory becomes a weapon, not a tool. In fact, Leli concludes, despite enactments, collusions, and countertransference disturbance, that analysis is the only suitable approach and undertakes analytic work. Again, the split in the writing of this paper between theory and clinical intervention is really quite striking.

Whether you include the analyst's subjectivity in your technical intervention or not is obviously quite a personal matter, but believing that your subjectivity is part of any enmeshed action is now pretty well accepted across many theoretical fronts (Aron, 1996; Bromberg, 1998; Cooper, 1998; Hoffman, 1992; Jacobs, 1991; Mitchell, 1998; Renik, 1995). So, in the threatening enactment around money, one is entitled to wonder what was the analyst's contribution to the large unpaid bill. Isn't a large unpaid bill both something unpaid and also unremarked? Only at the end of the paper does the analyst tell us of the experience of identification and shared affect with the patient. And only in a somewhat abstract way do we hear of the contempt and disgust in the countertransference. I could well believe that work with this patient was demanding and frightening. I would certainly have found the attacks on the analysis and the life crises extremely difficult. The analyst holds the frame. When he talks to us about it, he seems harsh and disaffected and punitive. When he speaks to the patient, he sounds robust and steady. What is this difference?

Dr. Weinstein's essay opens up a fascinating and provocative area for discussion, one that pushes the envelope of our thinking about the effects of love upon the body, bodily health, and psyche. His essay is brief, having almost the force of a short story, a dramatic fiction with surprise, catharsis, and transformation. His report takes his patient and the reader across a long history of our understanding and work with AIDS. One reaction I had to the paper was to see how much shifting and dramatic history there is in the experiences and interpretive understanding and framing of AIDS and its management for patients and doctors. It is an accelerated but also emotionally complex history where the equation of sex and death, the catastrophe of diagnosis and the meaning of shame and stigmatization has given way to a great variety of strategies for management. Yet, as the experiences of Weinstein's patient Bruce attest, the course of disease, the enigmatic process of maintenance and chronicity, the emotional plunge into fear and danger is never far from the surface for everyone.

It seems to me that a fuller understanding or exploration of the therapeutic impact both of love and of breaking the frame needs both a more demanding and self-demanding discussion and a wider framing. Because of the sparseness of the presentation, I was left wishing Dr. Weinstein had written about the experience in a much more multifaceted way. We have the dreams and their interpretation by the analyst. What was the patient's understanding of what had occurred? What kind of exploration into the relation of bodily health and psyche, and relational processes and attachment, would illuminate the experience Weinstein is charting. He is modest and clear in his claim—not that love cures but that loving experiences are crucial elements in health. It would be a great service to the mental health community to have this process explored and speculated about in much greater detail. What is the vision of body/mind integration that underwrites Weinstein's ideas? How is the body theorized? What of the specifics of this patient's experience—of connection, of hopelessness, of being loved, of being loved by his analyst might have felt mutative? There is a need to expand the repertoire of what we talk about and how we explain phenomena. Just as the work goes outside the frame, I think we need a writing format that also moves beyond the simple description of an experience.

Another difficult issue is raised by this paper. When is it loving to let someone go and when is love the link to life? There is an importance to connecting body mind processes in the progress and fate of disease and Weinstein makes a case for this. But these same arguments can make diseases, diagnosis, or prognosis seem to be under psychic control and victim blaming is a clear danger. The question of will and of unconscious intention in people who are ill and in those that care for them is complex but deserves much more play in this paper than Weinstein gives.

I also found myself puzzled as to why there was such personal and internal resistance to the hospital visit. I would want to know much more about the analytic and professional culture in which Weinstein positions himself and what the meaning of being out of frame is. Is the problem of the frame more acute when either the patient or his situation is related to sexuality and to nonnormative sexuality? In the clinic environment at the William Alanson White Institute, for example, where psychoanalytic therapy was offered to HIV-positive people many variations in treatment modalities were utilized, certainly often including hospital visits.

These two papers are different in scope, in tone, in agenda, and in orientation to theory and to practice. What connects them in my mind is that they each raise for me the question of how one conveys the problems, pressures, and values of working outside the frame. Treating gay or lesbian patients requires an attunement to pathologizing aspects of our theories even where the sphere of sexuality or gender identity is less clearly involved. It is important to cleanse our conceptual language of its moralizing tone while maintaining clarity when experience is destructive and/or self-destructive. A psychoanalytic exploration should be disinclined to stop with descriptive terms—such as promiscuity, perversity, anonymous encounters—and pursue the subjective as well as objective meaning for the patient (and for the analyst). An analytic investigation seeks out the richest account of personal meaning and subjectivity that is available and works hermeneutically with that.

Writing about work that is mutative and powerful but unconventionally so (cures by love that seem to effect physical stability in the context of loving attachments) needs a distinct and rich exploration both of processes and meanings. We need to widen the epistemological frame and the aesthetic frame in our case write-ups and our essays if work outside the frame is to really take hold of our imaginations.

## REFERENCES

Aron, L. (1996), *A Meeting of Minds: Mutuality in Psychoanalysis*. Hillsdale, NJ: The Analytic Press.

Bromberg, P. (1998), *Standing in the Spaces: Essays on Clinical Process, Trauma, and Dissociation*. Hillsdale, NJ: The Analytic Press.

Cooper, S. H. (1998), Analytic subjectivity, analytic disclosure and the aims of psychoanalysis. *Psychoanalytic Quarterly,* 67:379-406.

Foucault, M. (1977), *Discipline and Punish: The Birth of the Prison*. New York: Vintage Books.

Green, A. (1986), The analyst, symbolization and absence in the analytic setting. In *On Private Madness*. London: Hogarth Press, pp. 30-59.

Hoffman, I. (1992), Some practical implications of the social constructivist view of the psychoanalytic situation. *Psychoanalytic. Dialogues,* 2:287-304.

Jacobs, T. (1991), *The Use of the Self*. Madison, CT: International Universities Press.

Kernberg, O. (1975), *Borderline Conditions and Pathological Narcissism*. New York: Jason Aronson.

Kernberg, O. (1984), *Severe Personality Disorder*. New Haven, CT: Yale University Press.

Mitchell, S. (1998), The analyst's knowledge and the analyst's authority. *Psychoanalytic Quarterly,* 69:1-31.

Renik, O. (1995), The ideal of the anonymous analyst and the problem of self-disclosure. *Psychoanalytic Quarterly,* 64: 466-495.

Schafer, R. (1983), *The Analytic Attitude*. New York: Basic Books.

Chapter 17

# Questioning Some Traditional "Rules" in Psychotherapy

Bertram Schaffner

When I was invited to write a discussion based on the clinical cases reported by Ubaldo Leli and Robert S. Weinstein, I felt I had been given a fine opportunity to share some insights into psychotherapy that I have learned over the years. What I have to say may not all fit under the rubric of "psychoanalytic," but I hope it will be relevant to the process of "psychotherapy," the work to which our professional lives have been dedicated. I very much appreciate the fact that both authors were willing to explain in such detail the history of their work with patients and the ways in which they tried to help them.

These two cases illustrate some of the conflicts and dilemmas confronting today's therapists when they are faced with decisions about how to conduct treatment. I am referring to such issues as frequency of visits, use of the couch, degree of self-disclosure in response to personal questions, and willingness to step outside a traditional therapeutic "frame," as for instance, in deciding whether to visit a hospitalized patient, or meet with a patient's lover or relatives. At times, unseasoned, and even relatively experienced, therapists tend to fall back on treatment guidelines derived from their didactic training, guidelines which they have not yet had time to question or to test in practice. Sometimes those rules of thumb are helpful; sometimes they work badly, and can shake our confidence in "rules" and in our own abilities. Gradually, most of us develop private opinions about whether to follow traditional guidelines, gaining a sense of confidence in our own capacity to judge when a tried-and-true standard should or, perhaps more important, should *not* be applied.

I had been in practice less than six months when a patient brought me a gift at Christmas time. During psychoanalytic training, I learned that gifts can represent a bribe, or be a manifestation of resistance, and therefore analysts should refuse them. My patient, whom I will call "Ellen," drew the gift out of a bag she had brought with her and handed it to me at the end of the hour as she was leaving. I was unprepared, but said "Thank you," and, flustered, I blurted out, "I'm sorry, I cannot accept your gift, as this is against the rules in psychiatry." Ellen looked crestfallen, took the gift back, and left. Although she returned for a few more sessions, I knew deep down that I had badly damaged our chances for a working relationship. I tried, rather awkwardly, to revive the subject and repair the damage, to no avail.

I tried to make sense of what had happened. Ellen was the wife of a well-known man, and I hoped that succeeding with her might help me build a practice. She had been urged by her family to undergo therapy because of her listlessness, lack of spontaneity or interest in life. She seemed quite unaccustomed to expressing feelings of any kind. Looking back, in my reflexive response to her offer of a present, I completely ignored what the giving of a gift might mean to Ellen, as well as the significance to her of my refusing it. Clearly, I caused her to feel that something about her feelings, even in her relationship to me, was out of order. I made her feel that her impulse to generosity, whether spontaneous or conventional, was subject to disapproval. Little did I realize how much this had paralleled her experience in growing up in her own family. I had unwittingly lowered Ellen's already battered self-esteem, and doubtless increased her tendency to withdraw and inhibit herself.

This incident affected me very painfully, and gave me doubts about my future. On one level, I was embarrassed to fail "publicly" with such an important patient. Even now, as I write this, I still cringe at the thought of my naiveté then, and remind myself to be forgiving, as I do with my patients and supervisees. Unfortunately, on another level, I worried whether I could ever be adequate professionally. After all, I had failed to gauge or predict my patient's potential responses. I had also failed to grasp the meanings to myself: I had coped poorly with a "simple," unexpected clinical situation. I was troubled for a long time, until finally I was able to assess where I had failed, and what I might have done instead. What I learned from this incident has made it one of the more helpful experiences I have had.

I had given no thought to how my "obedient" response to Ellen's gift might affect her view of me, both as a person and as a therapist, or whether it would help or damage the therapeutic relationship. I am fairly sure that she experienced me as rude, unappreciative, or unfeeling. She would have been entirely correct in thinking me out of touch with her, but it seems, in retrospect, unlikely that she would have allowed herself to make such a judgment. She probably felt ashamed and hurt, but was unable to say so, and not just because of the lack of time remaining in the session. She may have emerged from the session feeling powerless and confused. Quite understandably, she probably felt at that point that she was a hopeless case. At any rate, shortly afterward Ellen gave up therapy with me.

Gradually, I came to recognize and admit more of what I had actually felt in the moment when Ellen offered me the gift. I was indeed pleased with her gift, and felt that it was an indication on her part of good feeling about what we had accomplished so far. I really meant it when I said "Thank you" to her, but then felt that I would be regarded as "improper" to accept her gift should my peers learn of it. In my effort to avoid such potential criticism, I became tongue-tied, and unwittingly ended up refusing her offer in a way that implied that there was indeed something wrong with *her* for wanting to give me a present. In my preoccupation with trying to ward off being criticized, I failed to think of what I was communicating to Ellen.

With that in mind, I would like to turn my attention to the two case reports. They raise many interesting "technical" issues which I would like to comment on, but I will restrict myself to just two of them: (1) How should treatment be delivered? (2) How long should treatment go on?

Both Dr. Leli and Dr. Weinstein seem to have been concerned with these questions. For example, Dr. Leli pondered whether to treat his patient "with psychoanalysis versus psychoanalytic psychotherapy." He also brought up the matter of frequency of appointments, and the length of time that the treatment was taking. Dr. Weinstein described his struggle over whether to see his patient in the hospital instead of in his office, and described his surprise (as well as his pleasure) at discovering the effectiveness of demonstrating real feeling on the part of the analyst, in helping a patient to recover from serious illness.

The issue as to whether a given patient should be treated with "psychoanalysis" or psychoanalytic psychotherapy has been a much-debated question in some psychoanalytic institutes. As I understand it, the principal technical differences between psychoanalysis and psychoanalytic psychotherapy have been the issues of whether the patient lies on the couch during therapy, and attends sessions more than once or twice a week. Since I am a graduate of the William Alanson White Psychoanalytic Institute, I am understandably less deeply involved in that debate, as my Institute does not share in the belief that the use of the couch is absolutely essential for psychoanalysis. Because of that departure from orthodoxy, the American Psychoanalytic Association, for a time, refused to admit W. A. White graduates as members, although eventually that policy was rescinded. Nevertheless, in spite of the differences in our backgrounds and training, I respect and understand Dr. Leli's concern with the question, which I believe is of clinical and/or political importance at his own Columbia Institute. I wish that he had been more explicit about the details of his concern, and had explained how he reached the decision to use "psychoanalysis" with this particular patient.

It is my impression that "psychoanalysis" has customarily been restricted to patients who can ordinarily symbolize experience in verbal terms, and who are able to refrain from the more serious forms of "acting out." Dr. Leli recognizes that his patient's history of alcoholism, serious depression requiring medication, several suicide attempts, and "general proclivity to acting out" presented formidable challenges to treatment. The patient's HIV-positive serological status only added to the problems that Dr. Leli had to address. Perhaps it was these aspects of his patient's presenting problem which led him to debate about whether or not psychoanalysis was the treatment of choice for this patient.

In trying to understand why the formal aspects of treatment took on such importance, I have reminded myself that Freud's preferred method, i.e., psychoanalysis, evolved from his belief that he was essentially conducting an investigation into how the human mind works. He wanted to obtain the maximum information with the minimum distraction for the patient. Therefore he was concerned with having sessions frequently, and avoiding interfering factors by eliminating the distracting sight of the analyst's facial expressions and bodily movements (Freud, 1912). In contrast, since the W. A. White Institute followed Harry Stack Sullivan's (1953) conception that human beings only develop and are understandable in terms of *interpersonal* relationships, it has been my usual practice to treat a patient face to face, and to encourage the patient to verbalize his reactions to seeing me, using them therapeutically to understand himself and his relations to other people.

I am not implying that I have never made use of the couch in my work with patients. On the contrary, at times when a patient requests it, saying that he feels too embarrassed to face me while revealing certain, shame-ridden, material, I have encouraged it. This has turned out to be a useful method for getting around a patient's resistance, and all the more effective when it was suggested by the patient himself or herself. Such use of the couch has usually not been prolonged, and after the initial revelations, patients were often comfortable enough to continue their discussions of the material which had been brought to light on a face to face basis.

Early in my career, during the 1950s, the word "psychoanalysis" was so tied up with the couch that the majority of patients initially wanted to be able to lie down, and I never refused. However, to my pleasant surprise, many later asked to be allowed to sit up, usually with the explanation "I need to see your face and your reactions, and I need you to talk more with me." I recall one telling moment, when a patient said to me, "I can't lie down. I can't even sit. I am just too agitated inside. Would you mind if I pace around the room while I am talking to you?" I replied, "Please do whatever puts you most at ease. The most important thing is that you are able to express yourself and that I am able to listen to you."

Dr. Weinstein seems to have reached a similar conclusion regarding what is important in deciding about the "technical" aspects of psychotherapy, in his case, the issue of visiting his patient in the hospital. He writes that when the patient became ill and requested the therapist to come to the hospital, the therapist initially balked. He had been trained to believe that real analysts only see patients in their offices, and there have always been theoretical reasons as to why one should not gratify patients in this respect. Fortunately, for the patient and the therapy, the therapist's analytic posture could not stand up to the patient's determination to be visited by his therapist. Dr. Weinstein describes his happiness at having been able to respond to his patient's insistence, and their consequent success in restoring the patient's will to fight and get well.

As a physician, I am always distressed when a psychiatrist feels that he should not respond to a patient's expressed need for a hospital consultation. I have always felt that this was part of a physician's duty, and cannot understand why this should not apply to lay analysts as well. Therefore, I had a hard time conceiving of the dialogue between Dr. Weinstein and his patient as a struggle of wills in which Bruce's "determination," as Dr. Weinstein phrased it, won out. I saw the patient's request, rather, as a desperate appeal for help, feeling that he needed his therapist's actual presence. Dr. Weinstein questioned whether he would be "gratifying" Bruce by acceding to his wishes. The use of the concept of gratification has always troubled me, since "gratifying" has frequently connoted the idea of meeting a spoiled child's needs when the parent really does not approve of the need and does not wish to meet it. In my own mind, I have attributed this way of thinking as deriving from the Calvinistic *weltanschauung* which approves of struggling against one's needs, rather than accepting them. This attitude seems to me to have permeated the early history of psychoanalysis.

Dr. Weinstein's resistance to "gratifying" his patient's expressed need for him to come to the hospital may partly explain why the patient dreamed of a wrestling match. Bruce may have experienced with Dr. Weinstein an impression that authorities do not wish to meet one's needs, and have to be influenced or coerced to do so. It would be interesting to ascertain whether the patient had also experienced his relationship with his parents as a struggle to get his needs met.

I am not forgetting the historic background for discouraging a psychoanalyst from consenting to visit a hospitalized patient. There was great fear that such a visit would disrupt or even destroy the patient's transference by introducing more "reality" into the therapeutic relationship than it could stand. This consideration provided the rationale for an inflexible view of the analytic frame, i.e., the idea that a transference could flourish only under austere conditions, in which a therapist assumes the role of a "blank screen." Fortunately, time and experience have demonstrated that transferences are not that fragile, and can be recognized under a range of conditions.

I see Dr. Weinstein's conflict as parallel to my difficulty in dealing with my patient's Christmas present. I attribute my behavior to prior training, and fear of exposing my actions to the scrutiny of my peers. I believe Dr. Weinstein uses the words "analytic posture" to indicate a professional convention deemed necessary to bring about therapeutic results, but which is primarily concerned with the therapist's "authority."

I have always felt that the way a therapist becomes an authority is by understanding what a patient says and responding well, thereby demonstrating his or her professional abilities. A patient is more likely to respect a therapist who takes into account what occurs between the two of them, as well as the physical and psychological realities of the patient's life outside the consulting room. In showing willingness to adjust to real circumstances, the therapist is not lowering his or her authority in the eyes of the patient, but is actually establishing it, leading to greater respect and trust, not to mention a sense of the therapist being a truly caring individual. From this point of view, a therapist's refusal to visit a patient in the hospital could be harmful, both to the patient's welfare, and to the treatment. The patient's capacity to make use of therapy depends on a genuine trust in the therapist's legitimate authority, which is rooted in a humane response to a patient's total circumstances.

Now, I would like to take up the topic of the length of treatment. Dr. Leli's case report indicated concern with the length of time the analysis had taken. It seemed clear that termination of the treatment, that is, a successful outcome, was important both to him and to his patient. I was sympathetic to Dr. Leli's dilemma. I recognize that termination is also a much debated question in some psychoanalytic institutes, but I have often been puzzled about the reasons for that. From my point of view, termination occurs when a patient has come to feel that his problems are greatly relieved, that he understands them well enough in order to cope with them, and that he feels competent, and able to function independently, although always with the proviso that he may return to the analyst at a future time, if need arises. I feel that the analyst has the privilege and the duty to tell the patient whether he agrees or disagrees, but my point is that termination of a successful treatment should be initiated by the patient.

Dr. Weinstein, with his twenty-five years of experience, appears to regard the issue similarly, as he writes of his initial termination with Bruce: "We both agreed that, although we could go on talking forever, it might be time for him to leave." For psychoanalysts at the beginning of their careers, who may be confused by the controversies surrounding "termination" to which they were exposed during their analytic training, this may be difficult to recognize.

In order for me to follow the progress of a treatment, my habit is to formulate a brief outline of the patient's central problems. I use these formulations in order to have a yardstick to judge where the patient is improving and where he or she is stuck. In the course of the therapy, as the patient becomes freer to reveal more about himself or herself, I usually find myself modifying my conceptions. These formulations, however primitive, have helped me gauge whether the patient is making progress or not.

In Dr. Leli's case, as I saw it, Mr. H. was accustomed to regular, albeit superficial, gratification of his needs from his father. He was untrained to adjust to refusals, and equally untrained to fulfill his needs through his own efforts. His mother had been an undependable and unsatisfactory source of interest and caring. I believe that he did not learn how to tolerate feelings of disappointment and frustration sufficiently. Instead, he retained grandiose expectations that his needs should always be met. When they were not, he reacted by (1) the use of comforting drugs; (2) attempts to "prove" his worthiness (pursuit of idealized male lovers, etc.); or (3) hateful actions which made him feel extremely ashamed, all of which eventually led to self-destructive behavior. As I see him, Mr. H. has not yet established a stable sense of identity and has little tolerance for painful affect. The patient must deal with feelings of inadequacy and fears of separation and loss. I feel it only natural to assume that therapy with a patient like Mr. H. would be long and arduous.

It is my opinion that Dr. Leli underestimated the amount of time it would take to bring treatment of Mr. H. to a successful conclusion, in terms of the parameters for deciding on termination that I outlined above. Although Dr. Leli mentions "termination themes" as a central feature of the analysis, it is not clear from his report just what features he has in mind. I think it likely that he may be mistaking the patient's reference to separating from his analyst, as demonstrating an achieved readiness to terminate, rather than recognizing it as another instance of Mr. H.'s fundamental difficulties with separation and loss. At any rate, it is my impression that as Dr. Leli describes him at the end of the fifth year of analysis, Mr. H. is nowhere near ready for termination. However, I do agree with Dr. Leli's feeling that the patient has made some real progress. I feel that Dr. Leli's genuine interest in his patient, in distinct contrast to the patient's experience of having been "played with" by his mother, and superficially attended to by his father, has had a profound healing effect.

Before concluding, I would like to add a few thoughts based upon my own experience working with patients who are HIV positive (Schaffner, 1994, 1997). It is my impression that a subtle and dangerous change has taken place to the meaning therapists assign to a patient's being seropositive. From the beginning of the epidemic, an AIDS diagnosis was regarded as terrifying, ultimately fatal, and always accompanied by a soul-searing stigma. It was automatically assumed that anyone infected would be preoccupied with fears of impending death, and a profoundly disturbing sense of unworthiness, epitomized by the phrase "diseased pariah," which was often applied in discussions of societal attitudes toward AIDS patients. Naturally, a large part of psychotherapy with HIV patients had to be directed to these issues since they were of primary importance in causing their ubiquitous profound depression.

This outlook continued, despite the beginning of discernible improvement in the medical fight against AIDS with the advent of AZT. Patients and therapists still regarded HIV disease as a death sentence, and inseparable from the patient's basic psychology. However, when protease inhibitors became available, and HIV patients showed dramatic improvements, basic assumptions about the course of the disease underwent a equally dramatic shift. HIV patients and their therapists began to visualize potentially long lives ahead, even if a "permanent" cure was not yet on the horizon. In the 1980s the idea of "living with AIDS" had been mostly a defiant attempt to cheer AIDS patients, to relieve their gloom, and to muster their courage to hold out until a medical breakthrough was achieved. By the mid-1990s, that medical miracle seemed to have arrived, and "living with AIDS" took on a different meaning. It now came to imply that HIV disease was no longer necessarily fatal, providing the HIV patient would adhere to the incredibly arduous medical regimen required.

Very unfortunately, many individuals, both patients and therapists, began to underestimate the gravity of HIV infection, much as has occurred in past epidemics such as tuberculosis, syphilis, and gonorrhea when effective treatments were made available. Such a human reaction to genuinely hopeful news is understandable, but essentially represents a defensive form of over-elation. I believe it has had a regrettable effect on therapist's conceptions of the psychological impact of the disease on an HIV patient. In spite of a superficially more optimistic outlook, my experience in clinical practice with HIV patients is that they still harbor deep-seated fears that they will die of the disease. These patients also fear that medical treatments will ultimately prove to be ineffective, and they dread unforeseen adverse consequences of the new medicines, such as those that occurred with earlier treatments. Now that many HIV patients are maintaining their health quite well, therapists may be misled by their excessive hopefulness, and overlook the continuing underlying terror.

Therapists now tend to underestimate the importance of HIV as a primary factor in their patients' psychopathology. They may come to regard a patient's HIV disease and his or her depression as two separate things. For example, in Dr. Leli's case report, the fact that his patient is HIV positive seems not to have influenced his decisions concerning treatment. Perhaps the fact that his patient was asymptomatic contributed to his lack of emphasis on this factor. He states, "This patient presented a formidable challenge to psychoanalytic treatment, *independently of his serological status* [my italics]," and then lists a number of symptoms, e.g., alcoholism, suicidality, depression. Dr. Leli's list could, in part, be understood as the patient's expectable reactions to his HIV positive status, and therefore not intrinsically independent of it.

Similarly, Dr. Weinstein's initial reaction to his patient's request to see him in the hospital seems to reflect the idea that being hospitalized was a fact about his patient which he could think of as distinct from the patient's other treatment issues. While the rule that analysts ought not conduct treatment outside of their offices might be reasonable (although some would question this) for patients who *happen* to be hospitalized, for therapists working with HIV patients, hospitalization usually implies a serious turn in the illness, and most HIV patients experience it as fraught with danger to life. In his case report, Dr. Weinstein provides evidence that he was aware of the potential lethality of Bruce's HIV diagnosis, and encouraged his patient to realize and deal with this aspect of his condition, but may himself have been denying his patient's fear of dying. It is my impression that Dr. Weinstein may have had an unconscious selective inattention to his patient's fear of dying, which caused him to want to resist Bruce's plea for a hospital visit. He states that Bruce's "determination" made him willing to act in his patient's best interest in spite of his reservations about relaxing his analytic posture. Dr. Weinstein succeeded in understanding his patient's sense of a potentially fatal emergency unfolding. Bruce's subsequent discussion of his gratitude and appreciation for Dr. Weinstein were typical of a dying person's "last words" to a loved one he might never see again, and confirm my impression that Bruce insisted because he felt he was in danger of dying.

The rest of Dr. Weinstein's report indicates that he had come to fully appreciate his patient's positive HIV status as an intrinsic aspect of their therapeutic work together. Dr. Weinstein suggests that Bruce's recovery following his loving encounter with his therapist shows the importance an analyst can have in supporting his HIV patient's fight for life. His interpretation of his patient's dream as a wrestling match with death, is followed by a comment in which he reassures Bruce of his ongoing commitment to playing a role in maintaining his patient's health "until a cure is found." Dr. Weinstein's describes his "function" in the following words, employing "a sensitive and caring flexibility," "with love and compassion we promote the health and integration of body and spirit . . . establishing the kind of contact with our patients which enable them to contact to life and to hope."

*Ars longa, vita brevis!* Becoming a therapist is a life-long task, and a complicated one. Teaching the art of psychotherapy is also very difficult and complicated. It is inevitable that the best students will come away from the best teaching with narrower conceptions than their teachers intended. No teaching can cover every contingency. Unfortunately, the do's and don'ts of psychotherapeutic technique become embedded in our minds, and we often fall back upon them unconsciously in clinical situations. This tendency can interfere with our ability to discern the patient's real needs, and to respond to them appropriately and humanely. The two cases reviewed provide fine examples of clinical dilemmas that resist ready solution by the automatic application of traditional guidelines. Isn't the old saying true, that "rules are made to be broken"?

## REFERENCES

Freud, S. (1912), Recommendations to physicians practicing psycho-analysis. *Standard Edition,* 12:109-120. London: Hogarth Press, 1958.

Schaffner, B. H. (1994), The crucial and difficult role of the psychotherapist in the treatment of the HIV-positive patient. *Journal of the American Academy of Psychoanalysis,* 22(3):505-518.

Schaffner, B. H. (1997), Modifying psychoanalytic methods when treating the HIV-positive patient. *Journal of the American Academy of Psychoanalysis,* 25(1):123-141.

Sullivan, H. S. (1953), *The Interpersonal Theory of Psychiatry.* New York: W.W. Norton and Company.

# Index

# PSYCHOTHERAPY WITH GAY MEN AND LESBIANS
## Contemporary Dynamic Approaches

_____ in hardbound at $37.46 (regularly $49.95) (ISBN: 1-56023-397-4)

_____ in softbound at $18.71 (regularly $24.95) (ISBN:1-56023-398-2)

Or order online and use Code HEC25 in the shopping cart.